Rethinking Security in Nigeria

RETHINKING SECURITY IN NIGERIA

Conceptual Issues in the Quest
for Social Order and National Integration

Edited by
Dapo Adelugba & Philip Ogo Ujomu

CODESRIA

Council for the Development of Social Science Research in Africa

ISBN: 2-86978-211-X
ISBN 13: 9782869782112

Typeset by Daouda Thiam

Cover image designed by Ibrahima Fofana

Printed in Senegal by Imprimerie Graphiplus, Dakar, Senegal

Distributed in Africa by CODESRIA

Distributed elsewhere by
African Books Collective, Oxford,
Web site: www.africanbookscollective.com

The Council for the Development of Social Science Research in Africa (CODESRIA) is an independent organisation whose principal objectives are facilitating research, promoting research-based publishing and creating multiple forums geared towards the exchange of views and information among African researchers. It challenges the fragmentation of research through the creation of thematic research networks that cut across linguistic and regional boundaries.

CODESRIA publishes a quarterly journal, *Africa Development*, the longest standing Africa-based social science journal; *Afrika Zamani*, a journal of history; the *African Sociological Review; African Journal of International Affairs* (AJIA); *Africa Review of Books;* and the *Journal of Higher Education in Africa.* It copublishes the *Africa Media Review* and *Identity, Culture and Politics: An Afro-Asian Dialogue.* Research results and other activities of the institution are disseminated through 'Working Papers', 'Monograph Series', 'CODESRIA Book Series', and the *CODESRIA Bulletin.*

CODESRIA would like to express its gratitude to the Swedish International Development Cooperation Agency (SIDA/SAREC), the International Development Research Centre (IDRC), Ford Foundation, MacArthur Foundation, Carnegie Corporation, NORAD, the Danish Agency for International Development (DANIDA), the French Ministry of Cooperation, the United Nations Development Programme (UNDP), the Netherlands Ministry of Foreign Affairs, Rockefeller Foundation, FINIDA, CIDA, IIEP/ADEA, OECD, OXFAM America, UNICEF and the Government of Senegal for supporting its research, training and publication programmes.

Contents

Acknowledgements

Since the NWG investigations on security commenced in 2003, we have become increasingly and extensively indebted to different people and institutions. We shall mention a few of them. The NWG researchers are most grateful to the coordinators at CODESRIA, Dakar, Senegal, for providing the National Working Group research grant used to pursue this investigation. We thank them for their trust and encouragement. Some of the NWG researchers have had the privilege and opportunity to visit CODESRIA on different occasions for capacity building and to participate in the success story of African research. We commend the good work CODESRIA is doing all over Africa, and in the world at large.

We are also grateful to the various individuals and organisations that participated in testing some of the ideas, methodologies and arguments employed during the different stages of the research. We are most grateful for their diverse and valuable contributions to the research. Specifically, we thank the following members of staff of the University of Ibadan for their participation and contributions to the NWG seminars and investigations: Professor Egbokhare of the Linguistics Department; Dr Oshitelu, Dr Ayantayo, Dr Akintunde, Dr Aiyegboyin, and Dr Labeodan all of Religious Studies; Dr Oladosu of the Arabic and Islamic Studies Department; Dr Onayemi Dr Odebowale, and Dr Olasope, all of the Classics Department; Dr Raji Oyelade, Dr Odumosu, Dr Olorunyomi, all of the English Department; Dr Ajayi of the History Department; Dr Awosamni of the Theatre Arts Department; Dr Alla Fawole, Dr Ayeleru, Dr Babalobi, Dr Omotade, all of the European Studies Department; Dr Omole of the Communication and Language Arts Department; Dr Aderinto of the Sociology Department; and Dr Nwolise of the Political Science Department, among others.

We received valuable information and support from a number of organisations and institutions. For reasons of confidentiality we may not be able to mention some of these organisations here. We nonetheless thank them for sharing with us and giving us the opportunities to test some of our ideas, positions and arguments. Let us however appreciate the following institutions. We thank Olawale and others at the Academic Staff Union of Nigerian Universities' National Secretariat, and at the University of Ibadan, Nigeria; Iwuala; Courson of Environmental Rights Action (ERA), Port Harcourt, Nigeria; correspondents of the

Guardian Newspapers from Lagos and Ibadan; correspondents of the *Comet* Newspapers; Balogun, Saseyi, and other staff at Galaxy television, Ibadan and Lagos; Afonja, Orimolade and other staff of the BCOS, Broadcasting Corporation of Oyo State Ibadan; Nwachukwu of Hilary Sydenham Nig Ltd., Ibadan; and Agbo-Areo of the Philosophy Department, U.I., who kindly facilitated access to data on some authors and titles in the popular Pacesetters Series. We are very grateful to you all.

We appreciate the academic contributions of some undergraduate and postgraduate students of the following departments at the University of Ibadan who participated in the various seminars and round tables on the thematic concerns: Philosophy, History, Zoology, Theatre Arts, English, Law, Psychology, Biochemistry, Communication and Language Arts, Institute of African Studies, Library Studies, Kinetics and Human Education, Peace and Conflict Studies, among others. Thank you.

Contributors

Irene Omolola Adadevoh was appointed Lecturer in the Department of Philosophy, University of Ibadan, Nigeria, in 1998. Since then she has written a number of articles on feminism, gender and ideology, and has participated in a number of local and international seminars and conferences on feminism and gender with reference to the African experience. Her doctorate research was on gender philosophy and myths.

Aduke G. Adebayo is a Chair and Professor in the Department of Modern European Studies, University of Ibadan, Nigeria. She recently completed a tenure as the Dean of the Faculty of Arts in the same university. She has made contributions to French Studies especially aspects of Francophone African Literature and Comparative Literature.

Dapo Adelugba is a former Chair and Professor in the Department of Theatre Arts, University of Ibadan, Nigeria. He has been a visiting professor at various universities in and outside Nigeria. At the moment he is at the Ahmadu Bello University, Zaria, Nigeria. He is a leading authority on Theatre Practice and Development especially Theatre History, Theory and Criticism of the Arts and Approaches to the Theatre Arts. Also he has pioneered some of the efforts to interface Philosophy, Aesthetics and the Theatre in Nigeria.

Felix Amanor-Boadu was a Lecturer in the Department of Modern European Studies, University of Ibadan, Nigeria. He is currently based in Ghana. He has done some work in the area of German Studies especially German Language and Literature and the cross-cultural implications of these for African social experience.

Olusegun Oladiran holds a postgraduate degree in African Studies from the University of Ibadan, Nigeria. He is currently in the United Kingdom for further studies in the areas of culture and belief systems. He is keenly interested in security matters.

Philip Ogo Ujomu, PhD is a Lecturer in the Department of Philosophy, University of Ibadan, Nigeria. He is interested in social philosophy, African philosophy, ethics, security issues and aspects of public policy. He has published some works in these areas.

1

Introduction: A Preface to the Understanding of the Aesthetic and Ethical Imperatives for Viable National Security in the Post-colonial African State

Dapo Adelugba

This study emerges on the intellectual landscape and gains its significance because it has become imperative for us as scholars to re-examine the intellectual, moral and social foundations of our lives, especially with regard to the idea of security. We can achieve this re-examination by recognising the human ability (and not necessarily the desire) to consider new possibilities, and to deepen the understanding of things. This rethinking of national security in Nigeria has compelled the aggregation of a number of intellectuals from a multi-disciplinary background in the humanities. The investigators seek to offer a national spread both in terms of geographical location and in terms of disciplinary focus. The aim is to achieve a more systematic and broad-based research for national development. This group comprises researchers having the requisite knowledge and experience in their core disciplinary concerns and they will bring this epistemology to bear on the quest for security. The researchers are from a wide variety of fields such as Theatre Arts, European Studies, Philosophy, African Studies, etc. They share the courage to escape from restrictive and received doctrinal engagements as these affect security. Given this new template of discourse, the scholars retain the capability to enhance the theoretical viability and consistency of the vision and mission of the project on rethinking national security.

This project, as it exists, is geared towards fostering national security and, ultimately, national development. Indeed, it opens the opportunity for a more creative interlinking of disciplinary methodologies. It recognises the need to develop certain aspects of our traditional ways or ideas on security, and, more significantly, it insists on the need to blend such traditional concerns with the realities and security needs of our modern society. In this sense, the study is a project on the conditions or machineries for the emancipation and transformation of the discourse on security, especially in post-colonial Nigeria. This study, which focuses strongly on the empirical, conceptual and historical approaches to the idea of security, combines rigorous comprehensive rhetoric with a realistic analysis of the wider social and political processes that define the contexts of the security problematic. These approaches, therefore, pave the way for a more systematic analysis of the problematic.

The study of the problem of national security in Nigeria is compelling because of the hitherto restrictive analysis of the nature of national security and the unexplored character of the critical conceptual and empirical interfaces between the ethical and aesthetic dimensions as key contributors to national survival and integration. The important point must be made that to a large extent the aesthetic value relies on ethical values. In most cases, we become aware of the aesthetic value by means of a recognition and consciousness of immanent ethical values. More than anything else, this project is a search for new strategies of research and action-based interventions that are capable of defining and establishing a new kind of public policy. The idea of policy that we are interested in is one that takes the interest of the people or the majority into consideration. Such a principle will depend on the redefinition of the meaning of the value of life, among other core notions. We seek a strategy by which people's perception will blend with government action in order to create a new system of social re-engineering. This study examines the ways by which we can facilitate the urgent imperative of establishing viable and rational patterns of socio-political action. It is a contribution to the quest for defining the vital socio-cultural norms and doctrinal imperatives needed for responsible cooperative human action. It examines the roles of dominant works of philosophy, literature, plays and performances in the creation of a philosophical basis for political stability and social reconciliation in the society. It extends the boundaries of previous aesthetic studies. In short, it redefines the roles of ethics and aesthetics as crucial contributors to security, human development and world civilisation.

At the heart of the entire project is a re-conceptualisation of the ideas of security and political community. This study places the failure of existing approaches to national security within the real context of the spectral insecurity that has continually plagued the Nigerian state. We insist that a restrictive militaristic conception of security cannot lead to the desired form or level of social and economic advancement required by a country confronted by diverse post-colonial socio-cultural challenges. This policy is not only limited in its scope and method, but is prone to perversion. The point is that even the military approach to security that has become a feature of Nigerian national security and state policy has not been attained due to the lack of a viable ethical and aesthetic foundation. This is a significant point and the reason is simple. Over the ages, virtually every arm of the military has played a role in the political tyranny and corruption of past military regimes. This has led to endemic social violence and national decay. At the professional level, the internal contradictions occasioned by ethnic politicisation, the generational gap and ideological tensions have led to the vitiation of the military's integrity, and its capability to attain operational efficiency. At the social level, the pervasive pattern of employing the military to act aggressively, extort and oppress the citizens is unassailable evidence of a certain entrenchment of institutional disorder and anomie. The diminishing stature and capacity of the military model for the maintenance of personal and collective security is a reflection of the failure of the state to assure conditions for safe and peaceful human life. This has diminished the opportunities for individuals to seek their well-being. The lack of faithful implementation of the favoured security model is not only the outcome of its inherent deficiencies, but also due to the institutional failure in the promotion of complementary models of educational and technological growth as the critical drivers of social and ethical transformation and security.

The current situation is that the state and its agencies have not been able to manage such a virulent fluidity, and the malignant contradictions arising from these have led to spiralling insecurity. This is seen in the inability of the government and society to establish social values such as trust, dialogue and tolerance. There has also been a deficit in the state's potential to provide the basic amenities of life, infrastructures, etc. At another level, there has been the problem of antinomies and the real context of the repudiation of political obligation, as seen in the regress in people's disposition to obey laws made for ensuring that human life is interesting, rewarding and manageable.

Central to this tragedy is the post-colonial situation that Nigeria confronts. It has been suggested that over the years insecurity has prevailed because different governments, individuals and institutions have systematically entrenched a culture of marginalisation within the social order. This has led to the reproduction of widespread violence, arbitrary hierarchies and avoidable deprivation. This situation has often led to the perpetuation of poverty, widened material inequalities, sustained militarism, fragmented communities, subordinated groups, and fervid intolerance. The prevailing injustice and exploitation have created a regime of marginal peoples, whose defining feature is their structural irrelevance. Structural irrelevance is highlighted and engendered by the realities and consequences of the notions of difference and dichotomies, dependence, disorder and discriminatory power, contestation, tension and genocidal oppression.

From the above, we must agree that this study contains the potential for ensuring liberation and transformation, to the extent that it insists on the need to conceive viable ideas of security. It is the view of the researchers that a new security theorising can be nurtured by the interlinking of the ethical and aesthetic approaches that examine the wider context of the security imperative and show the value and need for viable alternative theorising that acknowledges the roles of epistemological spaces and multi-disciplinary discourses. Therefore, aesthetic and ethical imperatives for national security in Nigeria require the establishment of vital normative foundations that interlink the ideas of action, vision, purpose, responsibility and justice, as well as their impact on the security problem.

Conclusion

Finally, the significance of this study lies in its power to facilitate better insight into national security and political morality by appropriating the creative inputs of ethical and aesthetic analysis as a new theoretical basis for the understanding of the national security problem. It can have the potential for translating the concrete conceptual reconstruction into empirical and practical solutions to the problem. The combination of aesthetics, ethics and anthropological accounts can go a long way in enhancing the quest for more imaginative ways of fostering positive human values and social reconciliation. The study can contribute significantly to national development by redefining the multi-disciplinary basis of a genuine search for a resolution of the problem of security. It provides the potential for generating new conceptual and methodological trajectories in tackling the issues of national security. More importantly, such a detailed study of the national security imperative and the role of ethical citizenship in the attainment of a just and harmonious society will go a long way to restore public confidence in the capacity of the government and society to attain national development and national survival. This project will help to foster intellectual analysis and reconstruction of the basis of national survival and peace and progress for those in society. It will mitigate the potential for socio-political and economic crises besetting the country and lead to an appreciation in the quality of human life, greater public trust and a collective adherence to the rule of law.

2

The Bounds of Security Theorising: Envisioning Discursive Inputs for the Rectification of a Post-colonial Situation

Philip Ogo Ujomu

In Place of an Introduction: Of Epigraphs and Transitions to Discourse

> There can be no security in traditions that failed us, there is no black market in truth. (Nelson Goodman 1972)

> The United States spends $30 billion a year gathering intelligence. But the inability of the government to even guess that nineteen suicidal terrorists might turn four jetliners into guided missiles aimed at national icons was more than a failure of intelligence. It was a failure of imagination. (*Newsweek International Magazine*, 1 October 2001)

> Yield to Nothing. (Motto of the School of Infantry, Jaji, Nigeria)

> This is a critical moment in the history of African peoples. If I had to suggest one word to characterize their current status, it would be 'insecurity'. (Richard Joseph 2002)

I cannot but use this occasion to draw upon some lessons from the epigraphs and the fact that there is a need to rethink some of them. This is significant insofar as we must struggle to understand the fundamental nature of security and the need to exploit all resources for its comprehension and application in the personal and social realms of life. The philosopher Anthony Quinton (1993: 102) has put it that 'security is the fundamental consideration without which the other things that it provides are barely worth having' (Quinton 1993: 102). Still on epigraphs: in my opinion, one of the most fascinating epigraphs (not included above) configured in the form of a motto has always been that of the Boy Scouts; it states categorically 'Be Prepared'. It has such a demanding perhaps ominous tone of appeal, warning or finality, depending on the circumstance or condition in which you find yourself. But how or in what way can we be prepared in order to be secure? How many means of preparation are imaginable and how many are realisable within the limits of human history, knowledge, culture and biology? Another question is: what should one be prepared for?

With respect to security we must be prepared to see things in a new light and to work assiduously towards change in human, personal and social life. This change is now needed more than at any other time with reference to the issue of security. To start with, the first epitaph, 'there can be no security in traditions that have failed us, there is no black market in truth', is an important assertion suggesting that we are in need of a courageous and concerted attitude towards changing those very ways and ideas that have guided us wrongly. Yet we have the mission to move humanity forward. It is a statement encouraging self-criticism and systematic interrogation of our principles and visions as created or inherited by us. It is a call to transit from old to newer or better values. It is a call for humanity to take fuller control of its own situation and to come to a realisation of the dialectics of auto-interrogation and auto-rectification.

The second epigraph, 'The United States spends $30 billion a year gathering intelligence. But the inability of the government even to guess ... was a failure of imagination', is indeed the clearest possible testimony to the fact that it is ideas and imagination that rule the world. It is ideas and imagination that give security. This failure of imagination is further underscored by Zehfuss (2003: 513, 516) who says that 'September 11 has been etched on our memories, the superpower caught off-guard, humiliated, devastated; people's basic trust in security within the state is severely threatened'. The philosopher, as one of the professionals better placed to generate and appropriate ideas, must work in combination with other professionals desiring the same mission and the means of attaining it. Such cooperation will ensure that the opportunities for the expansion of the horizons of theory and practice become brighter.

The last one, 'Yield to nothing', compels us to raise some issues: is this a statement of rigid deterministic doggedness that smacks of militaristic demagogy, nationalistic isolationism or febrile fanatical fervour? Or is the statement merely an attempt to bring to light the imperative of a requisite moral and physical courage considered as a necessary and sufficient condition for the vocation in question? Does 'yield to nothing' mean that one should not yield to superior ideas, arguments, strategy, tactics or fighting capability? Does the statement represent the termination of all knowledge or endeavour? This point is significant because it goes to the very root of the problem of traditionalism and realism in security theorising which has perhaps put greater emphasis on brawn, demagogy, ideology and force and thus less emphasis on the fruits of profound intellects.

The epigraphs are inevitably a perpetual reminder of the fact that we are faced with the multifarious struggles between a rigid, hegemonic and restrictive mono-perspective view of things and the expedient and unyielding demand for the recognition and toleration of alternatives at the levels of theory and practice. In the quest for security and the development of humanity there can be no monopoly of knowledge or of methodology. I refuse to throw away the opportunity to inform ourselves about the visible difficulties that militarism can encounter in the face of a wider internal and external conspiracy or ignorance. The reality of collusion, ineptitude, inefficiency and ignorance places a certification on the crisis confronting Nigeria's security agencies in the quest for true national and human security in Nigeria. Thus we can understand the statement of the citizen's forum for constitutional reform (C.F.C.R.2001: 3) that 'the transitions to democracy have presented African countries with the challenge of establishing effective and accountable security agencies'. Let us move to the opportunities for continuous and further discussions offered by the above quotations.

Reinventing the Humanities in the Modern Quest for Security

The American philosopher John Dewey instructively tells us that 'insecurity generates the quest for certainty' (Dewey 1977: 153). How can the humanities contribute to the quest for certainty in social, cultural and economic life in a post-colonial society? Are we certain about concepts, methods, values or practices that impact on security? What are the things that we must be certain about in the search for security? To engage the linkages between the arts and security we must once again fall back onto the question of roles, social order and social responsibility. For example, Plato in his *Republic* insists that the supreme craft of security is the art of the legislator and educator. He emphasises the power and role of the guardian class and the value of education for the security of the ideal state. Security comes from better enlightenment, training and lawmaking. This is then the project of security through human formation. A humanities or an arts focus on security essentially provides us with the aesthetic tools of critical thinking and evaluation (within a disciplinary framework) that remain the indisputable prerequisites for creative new solutions. It prides itself on the ability to think outside the traditional parameters. The arts focus on the investigation of fundamental issues around human involvement in the community, the appreciation of culture, active citizenship and the desire to better it by providing innovative strategies for meeting future challenges in the economic, ethical, cultural and social realms. The truth is that 'we are faced with great decisions about what future we want. What do we prefer? For what reasons do we prefer it?' (Bell 1994: 17). These are obviously matters of ethical and aesthetic choice and the phenomenological bases of values, which any substantial examination of security must confront. Thus, in the search for security the humanities vocation is concerned about human relations and conduct. There is a central concern with humanity, what it does, the way in which it does it, and so forth. How do these things impact on other realms of existence? The central concern of the humanities is to build a society in which people can live according to higher principles.

One of the main concerns of the humanities or arts is to focus on the cultural life of the people. The education and control of the citizens are attempts to strike at the heart of the security problem. These efforts provide some conceptions of 'order and security within which men can turn their attention more and more to the positive enrichment of life' (Lamont 1945: 57-58). This view of security stresses that the role of human agents is to perform social actions. Thus, the concern of the arts is to guarantee the indispensable and proper character formation of humans. The emphasis on character and institutional practices for virtuous conduct inevitably underscores the need for morality and humane attitudes that define a secure environment. Thus, philosophical and aesthetic security seeks to build a conception of social responsibility, which makes all concerned groups act in ways that are conducive to the common good. Thus, the quest for the common good and total structural integrity and efficiency of things is the irrefutable province of security.

Typological Configurations of the Idea and Scope of Security: A Conceptual Clarification

The idea of security suggests so many different things to different people. Every meaning carries its own deeper connotations. According to Makinda (1998: 282), 'security is generally regarded as a "contested concept" because it does not have a clinical definition'. It is not solely this but also the idea that security is fundamental to human existence and is a carrier of value, culture and prestige. It is a battlefield of ideological contention. According to Sandlers (1997: 5), given that 'modern threats to security are complex and assume myriad forms: thus, the notion of security needs to be rethought'. As such, there is a sense of complexity and controversy underlying the idea of security. However, despite this flexibility in the definition of the idea, Ochoche (1998: 105) maintains that 'security for all entities, organizations and especially nations is a first-order concern'.

It is thus beneficial to sort out these meanings on a more consistent and systematic basis in order to escape from the preliminary conceptual muddle that can arise from the problem of the contested character of the idea of security and the theoretical and methodological equivocations and ambiguity embedded in this situation. This typological account we seek to embark on also has the significant advantage of illuminating the concrete trajectories of the discourse and hence sets the template for the distinctive contribution of this essay.

The classical idea of security

Security can be seen from a classical viewpoint. The classical idea of security is linked to the Latin word 'securitas'. This refers to 'tranquillity and freedom from care or the absence of anxiety upon which the fulfilled life depends' (Liotta 2002: 477). This suggests a lack of hindrance or restriction and a sense of harmony and a stable undisturbed sense of purpose and attainments.

The realist or state-centric realist perspective

The state-centric view of security is explained by Ayoob (1984: 41) as follows: 'the term security has traditionally been defined to mean immunity (to varying degrees) of a state or nation to threats emanating from outside its boundaries. A nation is secure to the extent to which it is not in danger of having to sacrifice core values. By security we mean the protection and preservation of the minimum core values of any nation: political independence and territorial integrity'. This is the most common and prevalent view of security. However, Hoogensen and Rottem (2004: 158) have offered the clearest possible reason why we must move away from the realist view of security. They observe that 'state security is essential but does not necessarily ensure the safety of individuals and communities'. We have to look elsewhere for further inspiration and clarification of the concept of security.

The international security approach or system oriented perspective to security

International security is a concern for the security of the world insofar as it is immanently conducted on the basis of states. Hence, Ayoob (1984: 41) observes that a broader view of the idea of security depends on the recognition of the state, or better still, states, as the objects of security. Thus, 'if there is an international society, then there is an order of some kind to be maintained. The security of the parts of the system is inextricably intertwined with that of the whole'.

The idea of a security dilemma

This is a form of security that depends on the consequential fluidity of the power balance among competing and contending states in the international arena. To put it more clearly Messari (2002: 416-417) describes a security dilemma as that process by which 'as a consequence of this condition of international anarchy, states are permanently arming themselves in order to protect their borders. Through this process, states aim at self-protection. However, the unintended consequence of pursuing such a policy is to create a feeling of insecurity among one's neighbours. Thus, one state's effort to ensure its own security becomes a source of insecurity for other states'. The security dilemma is a complicated dialectical process that can lead to convolution and instability in international affairs. According to Roe (2001: 103), 'the security dilemma has the capacity to say something important about the responsibility of those actors involved'. Therefore, Roe (2001: 104) proposes a qualifying classification, namely, 'a categorization of the security dilemma into three types: "tight", "regular" and "loose"'. This is as far as we require for this essay.

The idea of a security community

The idea of a security community can be understood analytically or politically. However, the essential feature of a security community is, according to Moller (2003: 317), 'the belief in and the expectation of a peaceful resolution of conflicts among populations and policy makers, as well as the renunciation not only of the resort to large scale physical force but also of significant preparations for it. Within a security community, individuals in a group believe that common social problems must and can be resolved by processes of peaceful exchange'.

The idea of non-traditional security

Non-traditional security is a concern for both human and environmental security. This concern stands in antithesis to the traditional (realist) security. According to Liotta (2002: 475), 'security is about more than protecting a country from external threats; security may well include critical infrastructure protection, economic security, social security, environmental security, and human security'.

The idea of human security

Human security seems to be a new concept. According to Bellamy and McDonald (2002: 373), 'human security marks a much needed departure from the statist and militarist approach to security that dominated the field of international relations. The approach should prioritize the security of the individual and that security is achieved only when basic material needs are met and meaningful participation in the life of the community and human dignity are realized'. In the view of Hoogensen and Rottem (2004: 157) 'human security embodies a positive image of security'. This image of human security is embodied in what Suhrke (1999: 269) refers to as 'part of a vision for a "people-oriented" economic development'. Human security means 'safety for people from both violent and non-violent threats'. This seems to be the more recently embraced paradigm of security analysis and planning in some parts of the world. In our view, the forms of ontological security and aesthetic security are included herein.

The idea of transnational human security

Transnational human security as an idea supports the guiding tenets of human security but adds a major qualifier to it. When trying to understand the problem of human security Thomas and Tow (2002: 179-180) insist that 'the problem of threat is not necessarily constrained within the confines of state conflict. Specialized basis of measurement tends to omit critical referents of transnational human security - such as political prisoners, refugees and victims of environmental and pandemic tragedies - that transcend individual sovereign boundaries and agendas'. In the case of Nigeria, the human and geopolitical contexts of the Niger Delta crisis seem to fall into this category.

The idea of societal security
The idea of societal security is also placed in contradistinction to the notion of state security. Hoogensen and Rottem (2004: 162) hold that 'societal security is about identity, the self conception of communities, and those individuals who identify themselves as members of a particular community. Societal security is recognized as a security sector independent of state security but important to the dynamic of state legitimacy'.

The idea of comprehensive security
Comprehensive security is more specific in its claims. This idea, according to Biscop (2003: 185), is 'a broad and integrated approach that will address all dimensions of security: not just military, but also political, socio-economic, demographic, cultural, ecological, etc. Security is the sum of several interrelated factors and therefore requires an approach that encompasses more than just traditional "hard" security'. For Liotta (2002: 477), 'comprehensive security demands a multifaceted recognition of multiple levels of interaction'.

The idea of cooperative security
For its part, the notion of cooperative security is different from the crude state-centric view in other significant ways. According to Knudsen (2001: 357) the concept of cooperative security 'essentially represents the policy, demonstrated in practice, of dealing peacefully with conflicts, not merely by abstention from violence or threats, but by active engagement in negotiation and a search for practical solutions, and by a commitment to preventive measures'.

The idea of securitisation
The Copenhagen school uses the idea of 'securitisation' to represent a wider range of visions in relation to security analysis. Central to its concern is what Knudsen (2001: 357) refers to as the stress on the broad security concept. Specifically, 'the concept of securitization was in part a move along the path of the wideners. But its innovative value was to shift the attention away from a mere widening of the security concept to spotlighting of the way in which issues do or do not end up on the political agenda. Securitization gave a name to the process of raising security issues above politics and making them something one would never question. In securitization, the focus was on how some problems come to be considered as security matters while others are not'.

The idea of women's security

The idea of women's security has been identified as a distinct area of security investigation. Caprioli (2004: 412) holds that 'feminist theory in which security can only be fully understood by examining gendered structures of inequality facilitates an analysis of security differences by sex'. So in a way we can talk about women's security as a domain of security theorising.

The idea of gender identity and security

The idea of identity is crucial if we are to have a viable comprehension of security. For Hoogensen and Rottem (2004: 156), 'recognizing gender as a significant dimension of identity and security opens the door to the non-state based views of security and aptly illustrates how identity shapes individual and collective security needs. Gender analyses reveal the structures that neutralize identity through assumptions of the Universal Man'. This trend seems to confront the security problem as an index of gender with all that it connotes.

Mythical and symbolic representations of security

Security can be viewed as a myth or symbol. Thus security is taken in this context to represent an idea that receives its connotations and certification through the instrumentality of language. The idea of security carries little or no force outside the trappings of the linguistic couching of its possibilities, limitations and emotive appeal. In the words of Edelman (1975: 14), 'political language can evoke a set of mythic beliefs in subtle and powerful ways. Security is very likely the primal political symbol. National security, Social security and similar terms are therefore potent symbols'. The reason for the above is simple. Edelman (1975: 14) insists that 'given the setting of anxiety and ambiguity characteristic of the dilemmas in which people look to government for protection, susceptibility to social cues is strong. The cues come largely from language emanating from sources that people want to believe are authoritative and competent enough to cope with threats'. Thus, security and all it entails is tied to the problem of language and meanings.

The idea of security as production and provision

This view holds that we cannot understand the notion of security except when it is interpreted in terms of the concepts of production and provision. According to Kolderie (1987: 47), 'providing is a distinct function involving policy making, deciding, buying, requiring, regulating, franchising, or subsidizing. Producing implies operation, delivering, doing, selling, or administering. The production of service can be divided into direct service and support service. Provision of a service is more complicated'. Kolderie (1987: 47) further suggests that 'a service can be publicly, socially or privately provided'. It is obvious here that the concepts of provision and production elicit numerous and intricate conceptual matters with respect to security analysis, which are best left for another time.

The Third World perspective on security

There is a third world perspective on security. This view of security, as Ayoob (1984) has rightly observed, can be summarised in the statement that 'Despite the rhetoric of many Third World leaders, the sense of insecurity from which these states suffer, emanates, to a substantial extent, from within their boundaries'. Since it is these regimes, and their bureaucratic and intellectual hangers-on, who define the threats to the security of their respective states, it is no wonder that they define it primarily in terms of regime security rather than the security of the society as a whole' (Ayoob 1984: 42, 46).

The philosophical idea of security

Philosophy offers to security analysis a critical examination of the central funda-mental concepts of life and existence that are inextricably tied to security. These include the notions of vision, values, imagination, human nature, inner states of consciousness, justice, etc. An analysis of the relevant ideas offers a valuable in-sight into the fundamental workings of the worldview and beliefs underlying human life. The function of philosophy is, and remains, to examine the intellec-tual foundations of our life, in order to facilitate our understanding of the nature of man and social order. Philosophical ability, as evidenced in the powers of imagination and extrapolation, constitute the hallmark of human existence as a future-oriented venture. Thus, philosophy focuses on the question of security as basically a concern about the possibility of life and the guarantee of the future.

Repudiating Methodological Conservatism and Disciplinary Ethnocentricism

We cannot but agree with Eggerman (1975: 211) that 'the proper task of the philosopher is precisely to transcend the particular by uncovering principles or models by which to make sense intellectually of the domain in question'. This essay seeks to contribute to theorising on security from a philosophical perspec-tive. It employs some valuable philosophical, conceptual and historical approaches, and then sets the trajectory for the concrete interrogation of national security. It seeks to identify the potential of current theorising for liberation and transforma-tion in Africa. This study thus aims to facilitate better insight into security analysis, and to provide a new theoretical basis for the understanding of the security problem. The study can make a significant contribution to national development by redefining the multi-disciplinary basis of a genuine search for security. Its po-tential is to generate new conceptual and methodological trajectories in tackling the issues arising from the subject. The method of this work is mainly philo-sophical, analytical and conceptual. It must be stated that recalcitrant conserva-tism, in any form that it appears on the intellectual and socio-political landscape, must be repudiated because it cannot be allowed to block the development of new knowledge, creative theorising and the alternative futures that it might encourage.

Any discourse that tends to view security in a predominantly military or defence light will pose a problem for the proper definition and conceptualisation of security. We need to jettison the view that national security dictates a discourse which is mystified in a cult of technical expertise and public information characterised by selective disclosure. The clarification of the issue of values is important in the question of security. The maintenance of security implies the protection and preservation of certain values. It is the assurance against threats to core values as they affect the lives of persons and groups. It is our view that the reconsideration of key ethical values guiding the entire gamut of personal, social and national life can make the much-desired difference in the area of security. The focus in the quest for security can either be the narrow concern for survival or the wider focus on the attainment of peace and progress of individuals, groups and society. It is possible for a person to be capable of surviving, but this will not indicate that the person enjoys peace or progress. It seems reasonable to suggest that the quest for peace and progress will contribute to the happiness of people. Yet the philosophical statement by Cuffel (1966: 323),that 'no man can be accounted happy until death has given him security from the perils of life', is striking here. This is to the extent that it underscores the futility of man's search for security while alive. Despite the metaphysical strength of Cuffel's view, we cannot refuse but to try our best.

Hence, there is a need for a more thorough analysis of security that does not merely discuss broader issues of security, but also engages in a conceptual analysis of the issues involved. With reference to Nigeria, the problem of national security is seen mainly in the inability of the various governments and state agencies to consistently and institutionally guarantee the adequate protection, peace and well-being of the citizens. It is seen in the serious tendency towards fear, chaos and conflict as these arise from situations of violence and instability. This study is a response to the hitherto restrictive analysis of the nature of national security and it places the failure of existing approaches to national security within the real context of the spectral insecurity that has continually plagued the Nigerian state and other societies. Let us engage the main conceptual and theoretical issues.

The Mythological Allure of Realism and the Elusiveness of Liberalism

The mythical allure of security theorising, which has been compellingly, yet dubiously, certified by heightened feelings of professional possessiveness and expertise has been perforated. The real contexts of the failure of conceited realism and elusive liberalism have paved the way for an alternative theorising on the security problematic. Our quest for a political philosophy is understood as the need for a new basis of secure human social life and the quest for a new set of strategies that can ensure the liberation, redemption, emancipation and transformation of the order of things. Thus, it is true that there can be no security in traditions that have failed us, whether these are intellectual, cultural or socio-historical. There can be no security if there is a closure of space, whether conceptual or theoretical. Experience regarding security dilemmas all over the world, and all through human history, shows that mere militaristic or economic strength, though vital, will never be, and has never been, enough as a long-term guarantee of viable security.

Merely appropriating the traditional or liberal accounts of security will never stop the potency of vulnerabilities, threats or actual attacks. The reality of the shortfall of the realist approach has been glaringly obvious in the situation of many states and societies all over the world. No amount of military power, intelligence-gathering ability or even economic strength will be sufficient to maintain security where basic ideas such as appropriate imagination and ethical character are lacking. The appeal of the liberal approach has been to widen the scope of issues that can be discussed under the umbrellas of security to include gender, environment, social, medical and allied ideas. But also, this approach is not enough, due to the problem of articulation of the historical, cultural specificity of the problematic. More so, where the liberal position has been taken into account, the specific contexts of the interventions have revealed a more surreptitious deficit in the power, critically and imaginatively, to conceptualise and apply notions which, if well appropriated, are foundational to security. Both realism and liberalism have omitted an analysis of the core ideas of imagination, ethics, vision and action among others. This, then, serves as the reason for asserting that a philosophical intervention can be a linchpin in security theorising that can promote liberation and transformation.

From the above analysis, we share the idea of Dandeker (2001: 16) that 'changed perceptions of risks and threats have encouraged new conceptions of national security'. In fact, we may say that these changes will continue to yield new ideas for the management of human and national security problems and dilemmas. As things stand, our study can take the form of either an analytical, conceptual or historical perspective, or a combination of these. We can defend our approach by agreeing with Bush (Bush 1997: 12-13) that 'we will confront the hard issues - threats to our national security - before the challenges of our time become crisis for our children'. In other words, we are engaged in the struggle for the future as we know or imagine it. This futuristic pursuit assumes a comprehending and preemptive stance in respect of negotiating and navigating the security challenges in a post-colonial setting.

The Value of Philosophy and the Quest for an Ethical and Aesthetic Perspective on Security

What, if anything, does philosophy have to offer to security theorising? Philosophy is essentially a critical examination of fundamental problems of life and existence such as security, justice, truth, God, man, etc. Thus, the philosopher is capable of discussing security but then how must he discuss this idea? In relation to security analysis, Hare (1973: 71), one of the leading lights of contemporary philosophy, has insisted that 'the nature of the philosopher's contribution and interest will become clear if we consider the main forces in the world which endanger peace ... these forces are ideas'. Ideas can be good or bad even as ideas. But they begin to be dangerous or beneficial when individuals or groups begin to modify and apply them to other persons or objects. Ideas in themselves are the things that philosophy engages. Philosophy is an intellectual enquiry or search for truth through rational inquiry and analysis. It is a critical reflection on the world views and beliefs underlying human life. The quest for the development of new knowledge, creative theorising and the options for the future that this might encourage, particularly when far-reaching questions of human and planetary security are at stake, is all the more significant when we realise that there have been, and always will be, threats to security. The challenge is whether human beings will always be able to meet with these threats and the present and future consequences that they will impose. According to Clinton (USIA document 1997: 12), 'many of these new threats are as old as civilization itself. They are the struggles between the forces of order and disorder, freedom and tyranny, tolerance and repression, hope and fear. They threaten not just peoples and nations but values and ideas'. It is not surprising that ideas can threaten ideas and values can threaten values. One way out of this conflict is to examine the ultimate ends of some of these things.

The function of philosophy is, and remains, to examine the intellectual foundations of our life so as to facilitate our understanding of the nature of man, justice, social order, security and freedom. Human beings cannot live without philosophy because it leads us to consider new possibilities, deepens our understanding of things and exercises our intellectual and investigative abilities. There is a need for a new philosophy for Africa, which must be aimed at clarifying and consolidating the ideas of justice, truth, security and positive modernity. This philosophy must be critical, reconstructive and capable of making a difference in human personal and social life. The powers of imagination and extrapolation deriving from philosophy, which constitute the hallmark of its normative character, are important for human existence as a future-oriented enterprise. Human beings cannot adequately make sense of life if they do not consider the future. This point illustrates the importance of the philosophers' input into security that deals with individuals' or society's chances of survival, peace and progress. Thus, the question of security is basically about the possibility of life and the guarantee of the future. The significance of philosophy is best seen in its generation of new ideas and discourses through the process of internal criticism, responding to changes in the existing social and intellectual environment, and above all by encouraging the independent exploration of novel possibilities of thought. This point is all the more important because, despite the meticulous efforts of men to plan, control and predict certain realities, things are not certain and there is always the possibility of error, mutation, deviation or change. Let us examine some philosophical and conceptual interventions in security issues.

Jeremy Bentham's Philosophical Analysis of the Idea of Security: A Conceptual Point of Entry

The ideas of the English philosopher Jeremy Bentham most aptly picture the character and trajectory of a philosophical interest in security. Bentham's theory of security seeks to make a connection between property and security by weaving a theory around the concepts of community, law, punishment and evil. The primary concern of Bentham was to 'establish a code of laws - a social system - which would automatically make men virtuous' (Russell 1995: 741). But this concern was situated against the backdrop of a thorough devotion to intellectually benefiting humanity by introducing 'into morals and politics, habits of thought and modes of investigation, essential to the idea of science. Bentham's method may be shortly described as the method of detail, hence his interminable classifications, his elaborate demonstrations of the most acknowledged truths' (Mill 1974: 85).

In his security theorising, Bentham is clear on the following presuppositions. Security can only come from the principle of utility, which serves to promote the interest of the community. The interest of the community can also be understood in terms of the principle of ascetism. Thus, for Bentham, utility and ascetism taken together 'may be considered as having been a measure of security' (Bentham 1971: 264). The task of security is the more important when juxtaposed with the overwhelming role of law to obstruct the stocking of the 'body politic with the breed of highway men, housebreakers, or incendiaries, swarms of idle pensioners, useless placemen, robbery' (Bentham 1971: 264, 270). Thus, Bentham insists that security can be maintained if those concerned know and play their parts effectively. As such, 'the business of government is to promote the happiness of the society, by punishing and rewarding' (Bentham 1971: 267).

For Bentham a security problem can be encountered knowingly or unknowingly. Hence, 'when a man suffers, it is not always that he knows what he suffers by' (Bentham 1971: 266). But Bentham makes it clear that an act violating security can be a mischief. This can be classified as primary, where it affects specific or assignable individuals, or secondary, where its outcomes extend to the community. At the secondary level, a mischief can be construed as a pain, where people worry about the insecurity they may face or a danger, and the actual risks open to those that are most vulnerable to the threat (Bentham 1971: 268-269). Thus Bentham came to the strong conclusion that insecurity can be said to be an evil that has both immediate and remote consequences. There are different kinds of evil. We have 'evil of the offence and evil of the law; every law is evil for every law is an infraction of liberty. An evil seldom comes alone. A portion of evil can hardly fall upon an individual, without spreading on every side, as from a centre' (Bentham 1972: 204-205).

Thus Bentham insists that insecurity was to be seen as an evil that had the strong potential for dispersal and projection. Insecurity of the first order impacts on assignable persons. Primitive insecurity impacts directly on the victim. Derivative insecurity impacts on the well wishers and beneficiaries of the victim. Divided insecurity is defined by a loss that is not exclusively the victim's burden, but rather a shared liability. Consequential insecurity can be the further losses incurred by a victim after the primary loss. Insecurity can be permanent where the loss incurred by the victim is final or irreparable. Insecurity can also be evanescent where it is capable of being forgotten by restoration or obliteration. Insecurity of the second order permeates the entire society. Second order insecurity can be based on alarm or the fear and anxiety of falling victim. At another level, second order insecurity can be based on danger or the fear that such threats will proliferate and mutate into other sundry evils. Furthermore, insecurity of the second order can be extended where it embraces a large class of affected persons (Bentham 1972: 206-207).

Bentham therefore insists that the law has a key part to play in the provision and maintenance of security. In his view, 'the general object which all laws have, or ought to have, in common, is to augment the total happiness of the community; and therefore, in the first place, to exclude, as far as may be, everything that tends to subtract from that happiness' (Bentham 1971: 270). Put more directly, Bentham was of the view that 'civil law should have four aims: subsistence, abundance, security, and equality' (Russell 1995: 742). According to Bentham, security is a dominant end of civil law, thus 'acts injurious to security, branded by prohibition of law, receive the quality of offences' (Bentham 1978: 42). Therefore security is an object of law insofar as it necessarily embraces the future. Insecurity is capable of overturning social order. Without security, nothing is attainable, that is why the law must engage security matters. Thus 'in legislation, the most important object is security, laws are directly made for security' (Bentham 1978: 43).

Bentham emphasises the powers of laws as guarantors of subsistence; understood as existing, remaining alive or surviving, either as individuals or groups. He argues that laws are effective to the extent that they 'provide for subsistence indirectly, by protecting men while they labour, and by making them sure of the fruits of their labour' (Bentham 1978: 44). The connection between laws and security is profound and valuable when we realise that existence and survival can be threatened by variable factors such as 'bad seasons, wars, and accidents of all kinds' (Bentham 1978: 45). It is for these reasons that laws are also made so as to serve as buffers for periods of vulnerability and insecurity. Therefore the work of law is to enhance the prospects of man, not only 'to secure him from actual loss, but also to guarantee him, as far as possible, against future loss' (Bentham 1978: 50). It becomes clear that the law is central to security for the reason that everything that is of value centres on man and his possessions. A human-centred conception of security must be conceived in combination with other vital notions such as values, vision, human nature, cosmology and genealogy.

Security remains an imperative of humanity and is a good, insofar as insecurity is seen as an evil. Bentham further holds that poverty, exploitation and stupefaction are signs of insecurity. Therefore, non-possession or the loss of a good, knowingly or otherwise, is insecurity. If my possessions are part of my expectations, then insecurity comes from either dispossession or the pain of losing my possessions. Also, where dispossession is so strong as to vitiate existing supplies of materials, then the results can be that 'the fear of losing prevents us from enjoying what we already possess, besides, I am unwilling to give myself cares which will only be profitable to my enemies' (Bentham 1978: 54). Thus it is security that has turned 'frightful solitude, impenetrable forests, or sterile plains, stagnant waters and impure vapours' (Bentham 1978: 56) into cultivated fields, pastures, habitations, rising cites, roads, harbours, and other abundances of human imaginative ability. Thus from the above analysis, Bentham is right to say that man has a definite picture of the progress of security and it is necessary to prolong his idea of security 'through all the perspectives which his imagination is capable of measuring. This presentiment is called expectation, the power of forming a general plan of conduct' (Bentham 1978: 50-51).

Imagination and the Quest for Security

The discussion of the possibility of an original security theorising or conceptual discourse cannot be separated from a review of the concept of imagination. According to Thatcher (1997: 51), 'the power of reason and imagination is undeniable. By man's ability to think, science is possible; by the sheer power of the creative mind, men have travelled to the moon and released the enormous power of the atom'. By man's ability to think and rethink some level of security is possible. On the issue of imagination, Russow (1978: 57) states that 'imagination is part of the mental life of most people, and, as such deserves to be considered as a legitimate topic in philosophy of mind'. We also insist that imagination is a legitimate topic in the discussion of security. In confronting this problem we cannot avoid some level of theorising such as is available within metaphysics and modality, as well as philosophy of mind, etc. That thing or being which is necessary for conceiving a viable idea of security is the power of imagination.

Given that there are basic data or impressions of the world around us, and the nature of such data is varied, then every one may not have the same capability for processing these data in the same way, at the same time, and even with the same level of imagination. In discussing the idea of imagination and its linkage to security, we can appeal to Ryle (1973: 117-119) who holds that imagining is linked to the concept of 'seeing' or picturing. People are capable of 'picturing' or 'visualising' things. The operations of imagining are exercises of mental powers. However, Ryle's view raises the problem of whether there is only one univocal idea of picturing or visualising. Shorter (1973: 155-156) holds that the notion of 'imagining' can be clarified by distinguishing visualising or picturing from the sort of imagining that a drunkard engages in. A perfectly healthy woman, who casts her mind back to some experience, is engaged in an experience that is different from that of a person suffering from 'delirium tremens' or hallucinations occasioned by high fever. Although Shorter (1973: 157, 163) holds that to visualise is to do something, he notes that a man's excellence at visualising may not count at all in favour of saying that he is imaginative. Indeed, the fact that a person can visualise complicated diagrams, solve problems in her head or have a good visual memory does not mean that one is imaginative. Rather, the notion of imagination is close to that of originality.

In discussing the idea of imagination and its linkages with the futuristic realms of real and possible worlds, we can still appeal mildly to the view that imagining is linked to the concept of 'seeing' or 'picturing'. What do we see? What can we picture? A range of things can be pictured; simple or complex ideas, mental or physical images, logical or factual possibilities, fictional or actual existents, spiritual or abstract categories, micro- or macro-life forms, ontological or cosmological entities. Given whatever it is that we see, Rabb (1975: 76) has insisted that 'this imaging or imagining consciousness is necessarily intentional. That is, it must be a consciousness of something'. This point is shared by Russow (1978: 57) who says that 'when we imagine we always imagine something, but the object imagined is usually not present, and may not really exist at all'. People are capable of 'picturing' or 'visualizing' things. The operations of imagining are exercises of mental powers.

However, there is the problem of whether there is only one univocal idea, procedure or result of picturing or visualising. Rabb (1975: 77) has observed that 'there is a distinction between visualizing and imagining in the sense between thinking in images and imageless thought'. To escape from this conceptual confusion there is a need to disaggregate the idea of imagination from imagination-induced forms of consciousness such as hallucination, delirium, neurosis, psychosis, delusions of persecution, delusion of grandeur, illusion, phobia, monomania, and megalomania. Hence, we cannot depend solely on imagination for security because 'imagination alone cannot be trusted. Unaided imagination cannot differentiate fact from fancy. Indeed, it can breed illusions and delusions' (Perlman 1995: 17).

To escape from some of these problems we may hold that imagination must include a cocktail of experience among which are: the power to visualise, to extrapolate, to configure original or novel ideas, to solve real and anticipated problems, and generally to exhibit a methodical, meticulous and holistic perspective on things. The ultimate aim of imagination is, in the words of McLean (2000: 73), to 'enable one to take into account ever greater dimensions of reality and creativity and to imagine responses which are more rich in purpose, more adapted to present circumstances and more creative in promise for the future'. Imagination makes sense only if it effectively and efficiently ties action with vision, which together then tilt towards strategies for the good of humanity. Palma (1983: 31) makes it clear that there is some connection between imagination and action. For Palma, 'one's imagination can of course be guided by reason. But one's imagination, as a source of action is not necessarily governed by reason. In this context, by "imagination" I do not mean the wherewithal by which we postulate possibilities (sometimes fantasies). I mean the ability to seize and act upon a certain course of behaviour'. Imagination, if it is to enhance or guarantee security, must link up with action, values and visions.

Vision, Action and the Security Imperative

Security depends on imagination, and both are inevitably linked to the ideas of vision and action. The point must be made that without imagination, vision and action, no amount of information, prowess and resources can make a difference in the determination of things. The question of human action is significant when we note that the philosopher is interested in, and makes his or her contributions through ideas. The philosopher must seek to understand ideas and how they come to exert so much influence on the lives of humans. Ideas make more sense when they are defined as visions. And visions are attainable if they can be translated into action. This is why the analysis of the interface between vision and action is significant.

To escape from the quagmire of defective and purposeless action such as is inimical to security we are definitely in need of rethinking the value of vision for action. According to Locke (1991: 49), the idea of vision can be referred to as an 'overarching goal, mission, agenda, central purpose; an ideal and unique image of the future'. A vision is an instrument or a means by which an individual or group integrates and guides his or her efforts. Without a vision, other qualities such as motives, knowledge, traits, skills and abilities will not amount to much. They cannot be appropriated, channelled or diverted in an innovative and systematic way for security-inclined designs and goals. More than that, a vision is valuable since it is an idea and unique image of the future as elicited from a combination of current facts, dreams, dangers and opportunities.

A vision retains ethical propensities that impute into it some normative and prescriptive value. In this way, a vision is a mental image of a possible and desirable future state of affairs. In the course of establishing a vision, there is a corresponding sharpening of the power of choice, and the discernment of alternate forms and a trajectory or direction. There can be no security without action and vision. This point is reinforced by Alaya (1977: 262) who says that vision could be contained within the simple principle that 'bad external circumstances inhibit human development, and good ones foster it'. Hence, there is a need for a clear, distinct and positive vision if we are to have security. Furthermore, security can be a vision that an individual or a group possesses. It may be an outcome of the possession of certain gifts, talents, resources and abilities. Such a vision may be a positive or negative one and it will have the consequence of promoting the survival or annihilation of a person or a group at any level (cultural, physical, social, political, etc).

But then vision without action is vacuous creative instinct. What do we mean by action especially in relation to the notion and operation of security? Grimm (1980: 235) holds that 'actions are purposive, every action is performed by an agent with some purpose'. Grimm argues that if every action has a purpose then every action is performed by an agent with a purpose, it is performed in order to achieve some goals, either the performance of another action, the bringing about of some state of affairs, event or condition or the obtaining of some thing or some experience. There is another dimension, which suggests that an action may have no purpose or that an action is its own goal. Some actions can be performed for their own sakes. Doing something for its own sake is doing it just because one wants to. It is doing that thing for a reason and not doing it for a purpose. Thus, the issues of intention, intentionality, purpose, reasons, results, consequences, causes, performance, and so on are key concepts necessary for the clarification of the meaning of security. However, we must transit to a discussion of the idea of values.

Axiological Imperatives in the Quest for Security

For vision and action to make sense and yield results, we must retain values that define the basis of our actions. The maintenance of security implies the protection and preservation of certain values. The significance of values for security can be drawn from the analysis of Appadurai (2002: 97) who says that in the context of terrorism, 'the attack on the World Trade Towers was not merely an effort to kill civilians. It was an effort to end the idea of civilians. And surely values are part of the carnage of the battles that have taken place since then'. However, we can understand the nature of values better when we realise that every society sets for itself 'an ideal form of life or an image which it seeks to attain and to which it constantly refers in the process of going through life' (Sogolo 1993: 119). These ideal forms of life refer to the standards that guide the society. These standards are known as the values of that society.

Given the variation existing in human social systems and its effect on the diverse values people uphold, it has been argued that 'the issue of the nature of value is one of the central and most persistent problems of human existence'

(Titus 1970: 331). It is clear from the above that the existence of values is a generally admitted fact and, more importantly, values form the basis of all cultural life. They are in fact the 'foundation of all cognition and they constitute the category structure of the human consciousness' (Brunner and Raemers 1937: 87-88). To capture the essence of the notion of value, Perry affirms that a thing or anything has value when it is the object of an interest, which is a train of events determined by an expectation of its outcome (Perry 1968: 336). Thus Titus (1970: 331) affirms that when people make value judgements regarding the function of their values, their efforts are to be seen as an appraisal of the worth of objects. And so he suggests that value can be found in terms of the positive property of having worth or being valuable.

Singer adds an extra dimension to the conceptual analysis of values when he suggests that a 'person's values are what the person regards as or thinks important' (Singer 1989: 145). The same is applicable to the society insofar as a society's values are what it considers important. According to Ackermann (1981: 451), 'values must, then, be considered in intimate connection with what could be called the collective interests of the very social groups that hold them'. By way of analysis, if value is that which is desirable, important or interesting, then something can be desirable but not necessarily important. Something can be interesting but not important. Something can be important but neither desirable nor interesting. Something can be both important and desirable but not interesting. We have utility value, instrumental value, intrinsic value, ethical value and aesthetic value among others. Kupperman (1972: 259) has made the important point that 'the aesthetic value depends on ethical values, and we become aware of the aesthetic value by means of awareness of ethical value'. For these reasons, we must analyse our ideas of value and security further. A value is a belief about what is good or what ought to be. The link between values and security has been captured by Nietzsche (1986: 104) who wrote, 'A society in which the members continually work hard will have more security'. This suggests that the value of hard work or diligence and commitment can enhance security for a person or a group. But then the truth is that not every society or person shares the same values with others, especially when these affect the conceptualisation of security. For instance, in most post-colonial African societies there cannot be security because of inefficiency, carelessness, lawlessness, ineptitude, laxity and levity on the part of the leaders and followers.

This is why we can agree with a passage in the work of the popular novelist Clancy (1994: 542) that says, 'Don't forget, that their culture is fundamentally different from ours. Their religion is different. Their view of man's place in nature is different. The value they place on human life is different'. In short, when the lines are drawn, we are forced to reconcile security with ways of life which are most visibly seen in pre-existing values. We can examine the character of existing values as opposed to how they ought to be. If the individual accepts a value for himself, then it becomes a goal for him. Many of the attitudes of the individual reflect his values or his conception of what is 'good' or desirable. Shared values express our preferences for goods or things that are considered worth striving for. We are supposed to be interested in those values that can make life in society more peaceful, secure and progressive. We need to distinguish between individual values and shared values. We face the challenge of reconciling our values with the demands of modern change. We seek new values that can effectively provide identity and security for the individual and the group.

The study of values is an inescapable imperative for rational and meaningful security theorising, human edification and national development. But our vision, actions and values are clouded by human nature, especially its negative manifestation, which, though a central part of life, is yet a major cause of the deliberate and accidental man-made problems facing humanity. What has human nature got to do with security? Before we answer that question, we need to establish a nexus between security, the value of human life and consciousness as a prelude to appreciating human nature.

Security and Consciousness

Why is security difficult to conceive and achieve? Why do men all over the world persistently fail in the most vital task of defining and assuring security? It seems that part of this problem lies also with consciousness (just as well as human nature). Security requires the development of a consciousness related to it. Consciousness at the human level connotes a kind of awareness of phenomena. According to Holme (1972: 723), 'consciousness is the totality of a person's mental experiences; the self; that part of the self that is aware of its own ideas, acts or surrounding'. Also Scott (1972: 626-627) adds that 'there are external conditions of consciousness such as the things of which I am aware. There are general physical conditions of human consciousness as well as general cultural conditions'. However, how many people or even societies are aware of the full import and value of security and then consciously aspire to this? Or what level and quality of awareness do people have as individuals or as a group, which can lead to the conscious quest for security? What, if any, is the level of commitment of the people to security either at the individual or national levels? We talk about security consciousness in the sense that it is recognised cognitively as knowledge, or rather, a state of natural and reflexive consciousness.

In this context, the human consciousness is aware of the security dimensions of the self, the family, community, society and the nation. Security consciousness is the awareness of those qualities that make up the different stages or strata of the national consciousness or socio-polity. The constituting elements of national consciousness include a nation's history, language(s), cultural values, political system, geographical territory, religion, economy, etc. All of these have a lot to do with the search for security. Why is this so? From the above, it is clear that national consciousness has implications for national security. The concern for the security of a nation receives greater significance in the light of questions of national cohesion and social integration. National security cannot come about unless there is, in the society, some degree of consciousness of shared features. The various aspects of human, personal and social consciousness such as the economy, science, geography, education, etc., all form critical factors in the security equation which retains a fluidity or volatility. Thence arises the difficulty of estimating or maintaining security.

Security and Human Nature

Traditional security, which places so much emphasis on militaristic structures – tactical weapons platforms, elaborate war-game strategies as well as the cutting edge products of advanced science and technology – cannot not meet some core security challenges. The reason is simple. It overlooks a critical aspect of human existence in the security factor; human nature. But the reason in this case is not supernaturalistic. It is linked to the problem of the person and society in philosophy. We must share the view of Berry (1986: xiii) who insists that 'social and political organization has to accommodate itself to the human nature and not vice versa'. In other words, human nature is a primal symbol in the quest for security in human existence. The question that is crucial here then is what is human nature? This is a conceptual question, which has far-reaching empirical consequences. According to Dewey (1974), human nature can be defined by the innate needs of human beings. Dewey (1974: 116) says that 'I do not think it can be shown that the innate needs of men have changed since man became man or that there is any evidence that they will change as long as man is on the earth. Needs for food and drink and for moving about, need for bringing one's power to bear upon surrounding conditions, the need for some sort of aesthetic expression and satisfaction, are so much part of our being'.

Furthermore, Dewey (1974: 118) points out that 'pugnacity and fear are native elements of human nature. But so are pity and sympathy'. The quest for security and the context of human nature is tied to what Mill (1962) refers to as the natural sentiment of justice, which is defined by the interplay of the ideas of punishment, self-defence and sympathy. What is this idea and how does it connect with the conceptual clarification of security? Mill (1962: 306) states that 'two essential ingredients in the sentiment of justice are the desire to punish a person who has done harm, and the knowledge or belief that there is some definite individual or individuals to whom harm has been done. The desire to punish ... is a spontaneous outgrowth from two sentiments, both in the highest degree natural, and which either are or resemble instincts; the impulse of self-defence, and the feeling of sympathy'. Mill (1962: 307) further argues that a 'human being is capable of apprehending a community of interest between himself and the human society of which he forms a part such that any conduct which threatens the security of the society generally is threatening to his own and calls forth his instinct of self-defence'.

From the above analysis, there is a natural dimension of security as embodied in human nature and its operations. These natural feelings and instincts of humanity are themselves again constrained by other natural factors. According to McShea (1979: 389), 'men need what other animals do not, a method for the restoration of the functionality of feelings. Their freedom to imagine all possible things cannot, consistently with survival, entail enslavement to the necessity of action on the basis of an emotional reaction to each imagination'. The analysis of human nature takes a different dimension when Bacon (1972) sets the pedestals of the operations of human nature at two distinct but important levels. This he does through the theory of idols.

According to Bacon (1972: 92), human nature is captured by the idols. 'The idols of the Tribe have their foundation in human nature itself, and in the tribe or race of men. The idols of the Cave are the idols of the individual man. For everyone (besides the errors common to human nature in general) has a cave or den of his own, which refracts or discolours the light of nature; owing to his own proper and peculiar nature'. Human nature and its significance for security make further sense only in the context of the social nature of man. According to Mackenzie (1963: 35), 'human association, societies are first formed for the sake of life; though it is for the sake of good life that they are subsequently maintained. The care of the young, the preservation of food and drink, the provision of adequate shelter and protection would suffice to account for the existence of human societies'.

This implies that society is necessary for some level of security for the human being. But we also know from history that human associations have been the core sources of security crises or problems. For example, there is the crisis of women's security as seen in the operations of the family. There is the problem of tyranny and man's inhumanity to man, as seen in the internal operations of human actions in a society. There is the wider social insecurity generated by human inter-cultural conflict among human associations. We can connect the human factor in cosmological security by illuminating what Grayling (2003: 131) says is the 'murderous grip of humanity's various immemorial belief systems, intolerance, bigotry, zealotry and hatred'. All of these forms of security problems can be predicated upon the workings of human nature and human actions as clearly motivated by psychological, cultural or economic factors among others. Another implication of the above analysis is that we confront the general problem of human nature as seen in the problems of our finitude and limitations described by philosophers as our ethical, human and metaphysical imperfections. We also confront the restrictive limitations of our peculiar human natures as individual men. All of these taken together pose a stumbling block to our search for perfect security. As an example, the truly uncommon human inability to foresee the future of things is a hindrance to personal and social security on a long-term basis.

Behaviourism and the Defeat of Morality and Security

Traditional security also suffers a shortfall by failing to take into adequate consideration the issue of human nature especially as it further relates to mentalist and non-observable aspects of human conduct, such as intentions, motives, and levels of moral judgment in the determination of how far anyone or set of persons could go in making a point using terrorist action. In short, there is the problem of inner states of consciousness and other minds. Ayer (1973: 346-347) has captured this problem of other minds in the statement that 'the only ground that I can have for believing that other people have experiences, and that some at least of their experiences are of the same character as my own is that their overt behaviour is similar to mine'. But the problem with this kind of position is an irreconcilable binarism that has been aptly put by Malcolm (1973: 373), when he writes that 'when I say "I am in pain", by "pain" I mean a certain inward state. When I say, "He is in pain", I mean behaviour. I cannot attribute pain to others in the same sense that I attribute it to myself'.

The particular problem of finding out whether we can know things concerning the self in the same way we can know things concerning the other is significant in itself. It is also significant for the determination of those features that truly make up the human agent or human being. The person is generally perceived to be made up of two parts, the physical and mental dimensions. These parts do interact. But the problem arises because the way by which I can know myself as a self, subject or I, is different from the way that I can know other persons or others. I seem to know my experience directly without any intermediary. I know myself because I have inner states that essentially constitute my being or myself or my nature. These inner states that I have are exclusive to me. No two inner states are the same. And no other person has access to my inner states except by my consent and through my disclosure. This is one of the essential defining features of a human being; the almost intrinsic inaccessibility of the inner states.

The ability of other persons to know my inner states depends significantly on whether I reveal certain experiences that define myself. Thus, the details of my consciousness, experiences, plans, inclinations, desires and thoughts are virtually hidden from others. This is the reason why criminals, looters of state treasuries, tyrants, terrorists, and so on, succeed. Sometimes, even aspects of the inner states of a person can be inaccessible or incomprehensible to oneself. We can appreciate this point by recalling the examples of actions tied to amnesia, hypnosis, subconscious streams of experiences, beliefs, dream states, trances, dual personality, psychosis, mysterious experiences, hallucinations, etc. And these unknown factors or qualities can be called up and utilised for specific ends. This can explain the emphasis on the psychological aspect of man in the attainment of projects.

There is a more serious problem of knowing the inner states of other persons whose experiences are not directly available or accessible to us. To escape from this contradiction, the theory of behaviourism emerges as the idea that we can know the other by watching his or her behaviour or overt activities. But the pitfall of behaviorism has been that there is a logical possibility of error. I can pretend or deceive others, if the only thing people use to know that I am human is my overt behaviour. I can appear to be what I am not; I can hide my inner feelings or situation. This is one of the key features of humans that poses a grave problem for security. We can therefore understand the ways by which individuals, groups and institutions are often hoodwinked by strategies of impersonation, espionage, subversion, deception, and manipulation. In effect, the shortfall of behaviourism has paved the way for insecurity since one does not know the actual experience existing within the mind of the other and thus external behaviour cannot be a reliable or conclusive way of discerning that the other person is really or fully human.

It is this possibility of error that paves the way for insecurity, especially man-made. Also, our limitations or our finitude as humans can be linked to cultural, historical and biological shortfalls. These constraints pave the way for errors of judgment with respect to externally induced insecurity. This is called fallibility. This behaviourist challenge can be used as an explanation of terrorism and the problem of human nature as it relates to security. The challenge of behaviourism is itself an emphasis on the character of physicalism. For the physicalist, the things that we do and the things that are in this world are inevitably connected to the material or physical form of things. The only real things are physical things and the only influential things are material categories of consciousness and understanding. One of the strongest material causes of human action is the economic foundation of life. There is also the operation of the (normal or pervert) psychological framework of the human mind. Security can be threatened by greater ethno-cultural intolerance, religious irredentism, ideological demagogy, political manipulation, economic deprivation and social anomie - all of which operate on the mentalist and physicalist planes.

Supernaturalism, the Thin Crust of Civilisation and Causal Security

The shortfalls in the theory and practice of security cannot be separated from the reality of human nature and the contexts of the linkages between metaphysics and physicalism. This point is significant in an increasingly complex and modern world where there is a struggle between tentativeness and permanence, good and evil, civility and savagery. The question, then, is; where do our ideas and institutions stand or lead us in the quest for security and civilisation? What roles do our conceptions of ethics, epistemology and metaphysics play in the quest for security? It must be stated that the struggle between good and evil has been fundamental to the history of human beings. This struggle has been viewed in some ways as the competition between security and insecurity.

The reason for good and evil, security and insecurity, can be traced both to the world of the physical and to the supernatural. Let us quickly recognise that most Africans have a cosmological belief that entertains the possibility of the visible and invisible worlds having ontological contacts. And these affect their lives. Some fundamental causes and expressions of the crisis of security in indigenous and modern Africa remain the problems of ethnic and political inequalities and social disorder arising from systematic and dominant trends of institutionalised onto-logical closure and an inter-generational traditionalistic anachronism. As Davidson observes, 'the ancient inequalities of African societies were severe' (Davidson 1978: 54). This is a significant point in the conceptualisation of the axiological operations of a hierarchical, inward-looking community that exemplified full-blooded authoritarianism and gerontocracy. Therefore, it must be emphasised that 'within this tightly knit corporate society where personal relationships are so intense and so wide, one finds paradoxically the heart of security and insecurity, of building and destroying the individual and community' (Mbiti 1969: 209). Security, distribution and other constructive tasks are inextricably tied to matters of the dual realms of 'this-worldly' and the 'other-worldly' involvement. In Africa, this dual connection in security is tilted in favour of the supernatural, which exerts greater control over the physical realm. There has been a great struggle for the control of the explanation of the ontological and cosmological planes. The ideas of physicalism and supernaturalism have been at the heart of this dispute. The supernaturalistic account of reality as seen in Africa insists that there is a connection between the physical world and the supernatural or non-physical world and that this connection is tilted in favour of the supernatural, which exerts greater control over the physical realm. It draws upon the strengths of ontologism, which defines and sustains a hierarchy of beings and postulates a stratified and hegemonic relation between the beings above and the beings below. It is instructive that man is placed somewhere in the middle of the hierarchy of beings. Supernaturalism is thus an irrevocable belief in the causal powers of unobservable or non-physical categories over the physical plane of life.

In the clarification of the scope and bounds of security there has been an argument that humans suffer a problem of security due to certain contradictions descending from the supernatural. In one view, security problems arise from metaphysical evil or that metaphysical imperfection seen in human nature which has a transcendent origin and which man has no control over. The philosopher, Leibnitz, was of this inclination. Metaphysical evil is the source of many human failings, and of the dire consequences of these for security either of the individual or collective. The idea, then, has been to identify the visible and tangible shortfalls of humanity with a set of supernaturally defined imperfections or transcendentally imposed predicaments.

These predicaments or imperfections are temporally associated with the historical, biological and cultural contingent traits or situation of humanity. These contingent features deny human beings the full capacity to articulate and sustain the security imperatives. The problems of security are therefore things that derive from the supernatural delimitations of a physically constrained human endeavour. In a sense, virtually anything can be defeated by the nature of man, which yields on a consistent basis a privation of the good and the fact that with humanity there can be no guarantee of the effectiveness or success of a programme, however ingenious or laudable.

From the above account, which ties the security dilemma to the struggle between transcendentalism and temporalism, we are necessarily faced with the reality that man is himself as fragile as the very institutions and structures that he has installed to sustain, protect and uphold him. We are faced with our physically and non-physically induced finitude and limitations as humans. Our imperfections that limit the capability to conceive and assure security are intrinsic to us as humans. We share the view that a large part of this fragility and corruptibility or 'thinness' dwells within us. We all know how easy it is to relinquish our sense of kindness, justice and confidence. It must however not be forgotten that humans come into the world with capabilities, beginning with small capital and having the propensity to improve. We are thus bound to the struggle to acquire a genuinely humane and progressive society where 'all participate more or less in the pleasures, the advantages, and the resources of civilized society' (Bentham 1978: 53).

How does security connect to civilisation? What are the gains of civilisation? Civilisation is the systematic use, improvement and combination of those characteristics that comprise humans. Samuels (1991) offers a normative definition of civilisation as a constantly evolving amalgamation of parts that together provide an 'interpretative vision about man and society' (Samuels 1991: 23). For Newman (1979: 475), civilisation is a 'state of mental cultivation and discipline'. This is important when we realise that civilisations may have been defined by scholars in terms of a tripartite conception. The three dominant features of civilisation are obedience to the rules of civil intercourse, the scientific and intelligent exploitation of nature, and the pursuit of peaceful relations with members of other communities. Also, the idea of civilisation implies three distinctive features; the power of conceptual thought, the substitution of moral and civil laws, considerable scope for initiative and the acquisition of a conscience (Murphy 1942: 251). Civilisation implies law and acts of justice. Three features are crucial to civilization, 'freedom from barbarity, politeness, and rule of decency' (McKeon 1981: 422).

Other values that are conducive to civilisation include 'honesty, modesty, intellectual integrity, self-criticism and self-control' (Kolnai 1971: 204). All of these values of civilisation are crucial for peace, well-being and security at the human, personal and social levels. The power of civilisation highlights the main aim of human society as 'a positive one of providing a social environment, a set of institutions, in which and through which men and women can grow to their full stature' (Wilson 1977: 318). The human person and the powers that derive from his or her ideas and actions are central to the phenomenology of liberation and transformation. We are in need of a conception of the human person 'with a conscious mind that perceives, remembers, imagines, and then reflects, chooses and acts' (Samuel 1956: 207).

In our view, this is where security and civilisation, as well as the linkages between them, come to bear on the challenge of our humanity. Societies are confronted by new challenges on all levels. We are in need of upgrading our quality of perception and living as central to the rectification of the human situation. The character of our world today is seen in the extremely tentative character of things. There are major shifts in power and influence. There are demands for the redefinition of priorities; there are major convulsions of thought and identity. The reality of turbulence and contradictions in the world today suggests that the threats facing humanity are daunting. There have been insinuations that these threats are not merely operative in the physical world.

From Transcendentalism to Temporalism, From Possible Causes to Possible Effects

The challenge of security as deriving from a supernaturalistic origin can be further reconstructed through an analysis of the exclusive struggle for security in the celestial or transcendental worlds. The film titled *Megiddo* (directed by Brian Trenchard-Smith) is a captivating account of this trans-world nexus in the security dilemma. In the same way, Augustine's masterpiece, *The City of God*, is an appealing and unassailable account of the transcendent and immanent struggle for values and the consequences for security. In any case, following *Megiddo* and *The City of God*, the ordinance and ordering of the celestial planes were configured under the auspices of the virtues of obedience and humility, but contained by strict hegemonic or hierarchic stratification.

The security of the transcendent and its constituents were premised on the juridical concepts of obedience, perpetual order, faithfulness and love for the Divine Creator. This transcendent order would be vitiated and eventually fragmented into two large groups that would wage perpetual war, not just upon one another, but also on humanity in the context of the struggle for the control of the souls of men (individually and collectively). Indeed, the spirit and the body of man had become a battleground. If the supernatural account of security is endorsed, then the reality of the resulting wars, genocide, racism, cruelty and inhumanity among humans cannot be overlooked. The world of men as it exists in an abandoned form is left the worse, due to the internal contradictions that were ushered in by the quest to entrench the alternative visions and values of unhealthy destabilising competition, disobedience, factionalism, hate, acrimony and wars in the celestial places.

Thus the challenge posed by Lucifer's ordinance or Luciferism was essentially a conceptual challenge and struggle for the core ideas, visions and values that would guide the individual and collective operations of the heavenly places. The attending struggle for control of physical and non-physical spaces would demonstrate the concern for power, influence and follower-ship that were needed for the entrenchment of visions and actions. The acquisition and retention of power could then be seen as central to the quest for security. But then power would itself be ephemeral when employed for dubious motives and inclinations. The multiple impacts of antinomies, anomie and perversion remain obstructive to the proper realisation of the benefits of power. The value of power would be seen as positive if it was devoted to the promotion of peace, goodness and order.

But the relativistic problem of the perception of power and the goods that it can provide can be seen in the fact of divergent visions and ideas. By this means we see that values (those desirable, important or interesting things) are crucial to the quest for security. In the process, security problems would ultimately be narrowed down to the effects of phenomena such as hate, lack of peace, division, wars and acrimony, even among humans in the world. We shall see that the major vectors of the security dilemma would be realities such as religion, politics and ethnicity among others, especially if negatively used or appropriated - a very prevalent trend.

From Insecurity to Inhumanity: Of Terrorism and Civilisation

Even the more conciliatory of theoreticians have admitted the need to review the attitude of humanity and states to threats and affronts, especially terrorist ones. For instance, Dewey (1972: 293), the American philosopher and a certified optimist, makes the strong point that 'the fundamental beliefs and practices of democracy are now challenged as they never have been before. In some nations they are more than challenged. Everywhere there are waves of criticisms and doubt as to whether democracy can meet pressing problems of order and security'. This statement implies that something should be done about it. According to Teichman (1989: 513), terrorism is typified by violent acts that have social and or political undertones and which are perpetrated against innocent or randomly selected peoples using atrocious means such as killings, mutilations and torture. In the view of Wellman (1979: 253), every act of terrorism must be a threat that some great harm will be inflicted if the coercion is resisted. 'Every act of terrorism is by its very nature an act of communication. Only in this way can it sow the terror created as a means of intimidation' (Wellman 1979: 253). Wellman insists also that we must repudiate the phenomenon, and affirm the wrongness of terrorism because 'one reason that terrorism is prima facie wrong is that the terrifying act is almost inevitably harmful. The right to liberty reminds us that there are other human rights typically infringed or denied by terrorism. Worse still, terrorism necessarily violates the most fundamental of all human rights, the right to be treated as a human being' (Wellman 1979: 254, 257).

Related to the foregoing, Hughes states that 'the aim of policy for a government faced with terrorism should then be to consider plans for victory. There is surely a moral obligation to reconsider these immutable security needs' (Hughes 1982: 22-23). Sandlers (1997: 5) holds that terrorism has become more dangerous in its transnational form, in which 'a terrorist attack in one country involves victims, targets, institutions, governments or citizens of another country'. Former US president Clinton argued in the USIA document (1997: 12) that 'as long as there are human beings struggling for power and resources there will be conflict. Ideas, information, technology and people across borders of open societies make us more vulnerable to the forces of destruction [such as] an increasingly tangled and dangerous web of international terrorism. These threats are struggles between the forces of order and disorder, freedom and tyranny, tolerance and repression, hope and fear. They threaten not just peoples and nations but values and ideas'. This is a very important and sensitive issue for the survival of humanity and human institutions. In fact it is the question of whether we are in need of a redefinition of civilisation, security and its associated values.

Security is a form of power, and the quest for security is the quest for power. If humanity refuses to take security theory and practice to higher levels or if humanity is situated out of context with the realities of the security challenge, then it will eventually lose out in the struggle for survival and control when challenged by terrorist forces which employ conventional, chemical and biological weapons. Even the more conciliatory and pacifist theoreticians have admitted the need to review the attitude of peace-loving regimes and societies to such threats as terrorist action. Given the failure of existing notions of morality and security as strategies for confronting terrorism, we must move on to examine the issue of modality and its concerns with the possibilities and actualities as a strategy for the redefinition of the problematic of terrorism. The phenomenon of terrorism compels us to review some of the cardinal problems of philosophy such as the problem of other minds, freedom and determinism, punishment, the 'is-ought' distinction, technology and the value of human life, violence and social change, the fact-fiction dichotomy, possible worlds analysis, the issue of causality, the problem of the person and personal identity, and the crisis of values. Our point is to show that the challenge of terrorism brings to light and refreshes some of our traditional problems of philosophy, and seems to lead some of these problems and their solutions in other directions. Terrorism is more than anything else an attack on our sense of trust and feeling of confidence as humans in our selves and in the institutions that we have built to protect us and ensure our safety. It is a challenge to our values and the idea of being human. It is an attempt to place a different price on our individual and collective humanity. It is a demand that the idea of security be redefined without fear or favour.

Prolegomenon to the National Security Problem in Post-colonial Nigeria

Nigeria's national security is threatened by the problem of inefficiency, collusion and despondency of its major institutions and structures as instruments of social action and rectification. This has ensured that the various governments and the state agencies have been unable consistently and institutionally to guarantee the adequate protection, peace and well-being of their citizens. This lapse has occasioned serious conflicts, situations of uncertainty, helplessness and instability that have compromised the very territorial and national integrity of this nation and exposed the bulk of the citizens to unnecessary fear, deprivation and chaos. Thus in setting up a framework for the critical and discursive analysis of the national security problem in Nigeria, we are in need of a new idea or vision of security that can effectively ensure the redemption and rectification of the Nigerian situation. At the heart of the study of national security in Nigeria is the urgent and persistent search for the rules and patterns of action that will guarantee human survival and national integration in the Nigerian nation. This reconstructive task is the more significant owing to the failure of existing approaches to national security employed within the country. The failures of these approaches have led to insecurity. The real context of the spectral insecurity that has continually plagued the Nigerian state is an indication of the urgent need for a conceptual and theoretical examination of the core visions and values embedded in the idea of national security in Nigeria. As an example, there is a need to determine the unique approaches to security such as are relevant to the needs of a particular country.

The greater threat to Nigeria's security arises from the inefficiency of its institutions and structures as instruments of social action at the individual and collective levels. It has bred a cadre of individuals in almost every sensitive sector of national life who share the same general quality of engaging in negligent and insensitive conduct as it affects their fellows. The inability to guarantee trust and obedience to laws has made human life most unmanageable. The problem of national security in Nigeria is seen in the serious conflicts arising from situations of uncertainty, helplessness, hopelessness, violence and instability in the society. Most African countries suffer a similar fate.

Central to the crisis of security confronting the nation has been the general trend towards the misconception of the foundations of security. This has led to difficulties. The most pronounced is the deterioration of the quality of human, personal and social life in Nigeria. The view of Peters (1983: 115) is illustrative of the nation's security policy. According to Peters, the ultimate aim of Nigeria's national security effort is to protect it from attack, whether direct or indirect. But to get to the stage where it is possible to adequately determine the structure of the armed forces, there must be, one, a policy that reflects stated national objectives, and two, a national security management capacity that can cope. It is not enough to provide the armed forces with long-range military capability, without a clear-cut strategy as to how these forces are to be deployed and used. Such a restrictive militaristic conception of security cannot lead to the desired form or level of social and economic advancement required by a country confronted by diverse socio-cultural challenges. This policy is not only limited in its scope and method, but is also prone to perversion.

At the heart of the problem of security in the Nigerian nation-state is the fact that the idea of security was reduced to the personal security of the ruler and that of his immediate supporters. Thus, the country's rulers failed in their attempts to maintain stability in the Nigerian society due to their ill-conceived notions of security. The security calculus of the Nigerian state failed because it did not include vital aspects of social and national development such as the provision of basic social amenities. Thus, the Nigerian state could not meet the social, economic, as well as even the military conditions of national security. The failure of the state and security organs to maintain national security in the country can be seen in the inefficiency of the police force. Its abysmal failure to maintain law and order and provide security for the citizens continues to create a vacuum that is being filled by auxiliary ethnic militia, vigilante groups and militant civil society vanguards. The state has employed its repressive instruments, especially the army and the police, in order to regulate and regiment the political, social and economic freedoms and space of the other subordinate groups in the society, and not to promote the general well-being.

Alienated Consciousness, Post-coloniality and Marginality

The reality of alienated consciousness and the threats to national security arising from it indicate that Nigeria, as it exists, may not have fully articulated the conditions for establishing a truly humane and progressive society. The reality of a system lacking in enduring principles of social justice and moral action, which can promote genuine social reconciliation, suggests that Nigeria remains a terrain of conflicting identities after decades of independence. The state is a battleground where individuals fight for whatever resources or power they can capture. This situation is worrying because the long period of co-existence among various groupings has not yielded genuine mutual respect, understanding and common purpose. This is a significant pointer to the potential continuation of insecurity in the country.

The Nigerian state is post-colonial in its form. Post-coloniality is tied to marginality. In turn, marginality can be said to be central to experiences in a post-colonial life-world or discourse. Over the years, different governments, individuals and institutions in Nigeria have systematically entrenched a culture of marginalisation within the social order. The modern social system has produced widespread violence, arbitrary hierarchies and avoidable deprivation. The central feature of marginalisation is the capacity to render regions structurally irrelevant. Evidence shows that structural irrelevance is fuelled by the realities and consequences of the notions of difference and dichotomies. What are the immanent consequences of this marginality? One repercussion is that ethnic and other minorities are under-represented and oppressed by those with power in the social, political, economic and education system. At the heart of marginalisation are the real consequences of differences in language, values and beliefs, and the tensions arising from them when we merge with the different interests and aspirations of the groups. Groups attempt to ensure their dominance over others by controlling the key institutions, while the minority groups struggle for recognition and a fair deal in the distribution of resources. Political life is organised around the desire by the various ethnic groups to further and protect their own interests. These interests are culturally defined and have to do with what groups possess as distinct communities and what they can get from others in a competitive situation. Instability, over-centralisation of power, intense ethnic and elite competition for resources and power, and the diverse forms of repression will affect security at all levels of life. We should note that certain levels of marginality are now beyond the merely ethnic factor. These include the travails of the destitute, the unemployed, the rank-and-file of the different social institutions, the rural peoples, the handicapped, the aged, the abused youth and children, and so forth.

In Nigeria, the military, which appeared most constitutionally and professionally suited to fulfil the task of providing security, has played a particularly negative role in the maintenance of national security. Thus, this large body of security personnel cannot guarantee Nigeria's quest for national security since much of the insecurity, conflicts and crisis that happened in the country from 1960s were in fact due to the actions and omissions of these same security forces (Ujomu 2000: 38). Those who have controlled the state have used the brutality of the security forces and the silent violence of the law in order to browbeat and coerce the oppressed and subordinate classes into psychological insecurity, political submission and material deprivation. The national security problem can be construed as a situation of threat faced by all marginal peoples who have been unable to protect themselves from the violence unleashed on them by the state and other forces within society. The insecurity of the ordinary people is seen in their marginality, which makes them highly vulnerable to various forms of insecurity. The marginal peoples include the aged and neglected pensioners, the handicapped persons and poor people who have no hope of justice, the unemployed educated and uneducated youth, some of the ethnic minority groups, especially of the southern Niger Delta, and even in the north of the country. The fact is that these peoples are usually disadvantaged, exploited and oppressed and their lives are associated with hardship. Our point is simply that even the military approach to security that the government clearly cherishes lacks viable ethical and structural foundations so that its defeat is ensured.

Consequently, the dangerous trend has emerged whereby violent, and ill-trained militia and militants have cashed in on these institutional flaws. Furthermore, the general lack of commitment to the common good has ensured that most military personnel seek only to satisfy their avarice and narcissism. Such people lack the intellectual and moral basis for the proper utilisation of knowledge and power for the good of all (Ujomu 2000: 39). Thus, they ultimately create conditions of insecurity, deprivation and instability in the polity. Conscious manipulations (of a negative kind) can lead to the loss of unity and cohesion. To understand fully the consequences of alienation for national consciousness we need to conceptualise the deplorable state of our national experience as typified by institutional and moral problems. According to Temlong (2003: 13), 'the parlous state of the economy has also reduced the majority of the citizenry to abject poverty and increased unemployment'. We add that the objectionable state of our infrastructure, the moral decay in our society, the pervasive corruption, social discontent, lawlessness, selfishness and cynicism that have taken over all areas of national life are irrefutable manifestations of the security crisis in the land. The security problem is bigger than any group or institution and is a matter of a challenged national consciousness. These are evidence that national consciousness is on the decline. National consciousness has implications for national security, which itself is an important concern in the life of a person, group or society. The central feature in the quest for national security is the concern for national survival, which cannot come about unless there is some degree of joint action and purpose for the common good.

Evidence of the defeat of national consciousness is seen in the increasing attacks on national leaders and citizens by violent mobs, armed robbers, assassins and kidnappers, ethnic militia groups, as well as the invading rebel forces from neighbouring countries to the north of Nigeria. It is ironic that the Nigerian state and its military system have not been able to perfect the art and craft of upholding institutional and regime security. We may recall the various national security problems that have led to the death of top government officials at the hands of assassins and other criminals. We also recall the problems that have led to the predation of infrastructure (civil and military) in which the negligence, laxity and incompetence within certain institutions have been revealed. All of these have had negative effects on the development of national consciousness, both for men and for women.

The Niger Delta Crisis and Some Implications for Nigeria's National Security

The Niger Delta problem, as we construe it, is profoundly a conceptual problem bordering on the tripartite hermeneutics of cosmology, genealogy and geopolitics of the territory in question. Conceptually, the crisis in the Niger Delta is a problem of the definition of the meanings of security, trust, power, recognition, fairness, value of life, justice and human dignity of the indigenous peoples, against the backdrop of the real repercussions of localised insecurity, trans-nationalised conflict, internationalised exploitation, genocidal violence and state-centric marginalisation. This conceptual muddle has compelled a convoluted social disruption of most of the vital economic activities associated with this oil-producing region. The obstreperous processes of marginalisation, discontent, resentment and the vitiation of the dignity of the Niger Delta communities have been linked to many debilitating factors. The Niger Delta variant of the general trend of national insecurity, social injustice and existential discontentment seems a visible index of the state of (in)security in Nigeria. The ensuing spectral conflicts have compelled the continual destruction of oil pipelines and installations, killing or abducting of local and expatriate oil workers and security personnel, hijacking of helicopters, ships, etc. The crisis vividly illustrates the inability of the Nigerian state to properly manage fundamental ethnic and nationality questions and to meet the challenges of development and nation building. The problems of environmental degradation, pauperisation of the people and resource control remain central to the problems confronting the Niger Delta. The demands of the different ethnic groups and communities in the Niger Delta region are essentially for those socio-political conditions which will make their lives more meaningful. Hence, it has become clear that the Niger Delta situation raises irrefutable conceptual and empirical issues and questions about the character and context of political morality in Nigeria and the search for a viable social philosophy in a post-colonial framework.

Stockpiling as a Strategy for National Security: The Nigerian Situation

Furthermore, when we talk about national security we can also examine the impact of the stockpiling of critical goods such as fuel, food, drugs, etc. The point needs to be made that stockpiling is the favoured security strategy of the USA, and it has worked well for them. The United States is far less dependent on imports and devotes a great deal of time, energy, and money to stockpiling and to developing alternative sources of supply. According to Rensburg and Anaejionu (1986: 70-73), there are crucial distinctions between economic and defence stockpiles as well as critical and strategic economic materials. All this evidence shows that the USA has a well-developed theory of stockpiling as a security concept. The point, then, is what security strategy or principle can we say that Nigeria has fully articulated and applied? This question is relevant and is a justification for this essay, given the multifarious crisis of national security that confronts Nigeria.

However, the idea of stockpiling has been criticised as economically unviable insofar as it ties down scarce and valuable financial resources by way of purchasing materials that may not be useful in the immediate term. This raises the question of whether a country that is relatively poor in the areas of human, social, institutional and technological capital can, and should, apply the principle of stockpiling. Granted this critique, the more important issue is: what is the attitude of Nigerian society to the stockpiling of essential goods? This is an important question because the capacity of the Nigerian state or agencies for stockpiling is very limited owing to poor technology or technical ability, financial mismanagement, corruption, lack of proper planning, sabotage, conflicts and other ethno-cultural manipulations. Is it not possible that Nigerian rulers and saboteur citizens will ensure that this strategy does not work through theft, importing fake or expired goods, refusing to deliver the goods, importing and re-selling the goods at outrageous costs, destroying, undermining or sabotaging the installations during industrial disputes or ethno-religious conflicts, and so on? The point that we are making is that there is a need for the country to be industrialised and disciplined before the principle of stockpiling can work effectively. Nigeria may not be effective in using this strategy of security.

The University and National Security in Nigeria

The university as a key social institution has often played a prominent role in national security by serving as a symbol of national pride and by providing high-level personnel to serve the vital needs of government and society. However, the modern role of the Nigerian university is best situated against the backdrop of the problem of national security. The reason for this point is the continual ethnic, political, religious and socioeconomic crises besetting the universities and the country. These struggles centre on the distribution and the management of wealth and resources. The problem of national security in Nigeria has been aggravated by the situation of intolerance existing among the various ethno-cultural and religious groups in the universities and the country due to manipulation, relative deprivation and frustration. Unfortunately, the roles of some intellectuals in the development of the nation have not been very positive. Some scholars have contributed negatively to the issue of social responsibility in the quest for knowledge. This situation, as we clearly see, has adverse effects on the sustenance of national security in the country and it raises questions about the effectiveness of scholars in the determination of social conduct. The university in Nigeria has been inextricably woven into the crisis-ridden character of the society.

The university is affected by the problem of national insecurity and also generates its own problem of insecurity. The universities often breed and harbour criminals, armed robbers, necrophiliacs, cultists, prostitutes and other perpetrators of insecurity, who may have brought these traits from the larger society or have seized opportunistic control of the civil nature of the institution. The crisis of university involvement in national security problems is not unconnected to the pervasive social context of the problem. The university in Nigeria has faced problems of chronic under-funding, bad leadership and administration, a loss of autonomy and the denial of the academic freedom of intellectuals. Let us examine the financial context of the crisis of security facing the education sector and especially the universities. For instance, data so far available on the issue of educational funding show that the Nigerian government has consistently spent less than 13 per cent of the annual budget on education between 1994 and 2001. In 1994, the vote was 7.83 per cent of N 110.5 billion Naira. In 1995, it was 12.96 per cent of N 98.2 billion Naira. In 1996, it was 12.32 per cent of N 124.2 billion Naira. In 1997, it was 11.59 per cent of N 188.0 billion Naira. In 1998, it was 10.27 per cent of N 260 billion Naira. In 1999, it was 11.12 per cent of N 2490 billion Naira. In 2000, it was 8.36 per cent of N 677.51 billion Naira. In 2001, it was 7 per cent of N 894.2 billion Naira (See *The Punch*, 2 April 2001: 46). Furthermore, the statistical account of the Federal Budgetary allocation to education in the years after 2001 showed a continued drop in percentage relative to the year 2000 figure of 8.36 per cent. The education budget seen as a percentage of the total annual budget was 5 per cent in 2002, 4.7 per cent in 2003 and 5.6 per cent in 2004 (Fashina 2005: 11). It can be seen that there has been a progressive decline in the percentage of funds allocated to education generally.

The dwindling funding and diminishing recognition of the role of the Nigerian university in society have adversely affected the inputs of the university to national security, human security and nation building. Thus, there is clear evidence that all is not well in the nation's higher education system. There have been national industrial actions by the Academic Staff Union of Universities in order to negotiate better funding, facilities and conditions of work for the universities and their staff. There have also been demands for significant and increased autonomy and greater academic freedom for the universities and their academics. These are all indispensable conditions for the guarantee of university inputs to the national security and development of the country as things stand.

The crisis in the university vis-à-vis government or university administrations has led to the situation where students spend more than half of an academic year at home due to disruptions in the university system. This situation cannot enhance nation-building and national security. Rather, it has led to moral decadence, an increase in criminality, delinquency, armed robbery and prostitution, human trafficking, and a tendency to desperation as seen in protracted examination malpractices. All of these taken together suggest depreciation in the quantity and quality of manpower development in the country. These are clearly issues that border on the security of the country and its universities. Thus the university in Nigeria needs to be empowered to make its contribution in the urgent and pressing areas. It must seek to create strategies for national reconciliation among the various ethnic groups. It must also seek to apply its resources to the struggle for national development, and the amelioration of poverty and ignorance in the country. It must aim at the deployment of its human and material resources to the achievement of Nigeria's quest for national security and the maintenance of infrastructure.

But there are positive dimensions of the contribution of the university to national security. In the last few years, the University of Lagos in the south-western part of Nigeria has attempted to make significant inputs into the task of nation building and also to national security. It has aggressively sought to diversify its income-generating base and to provide employment for a wide group of citizens under its various employment programmes. The university has established labour schemes such as part-time jobs for students, jobs for people in the informal sector of the economy, service-oriented industries, and a wide range of consultancy projects. It has also involved itself in a variety of distant learning programmes and other capacity building projects in skills, knowledge and motivation. All these have contributed to the mitigation of illiteracy, unemployment and criminality.

More recently, the concept of the university, especially in Nigeria, has undergone some evolution and it has gained greater significance not only as a centre of freedom and truth, but also as a place of refuge and protection. To this effect, the university in Nigeria has widened its concern for the peace, security and well-being of the citizens by redefining itself as a crucial centre of refuge for the protection and safety of distressed and endangered individuals and groups in the society. In one of the most instructive cases, the incidence of ethnic conflict between the Ife and Modakeke communities in the south-western Osun-State transformed our regular understanding of the university. The conflict compelled one of the first-rate federal universities in the country - the Obafemi Awolowo University at Ile-Ife - to offer protection to thousands of people displaced by the fierce communal fighting going on in the area.

This communal conflict between the Ife and Modakeke tribes has been mentioned as a prominent watershed in ethno-cultural conflict (See CDHR, *1999 Annual Report on The Human Rights Situation in Nigeria.* 2000: 210; CDHR, *2000 Annual Report on The Human Rights Situation in Nigeria*, 2001: 261). But we are more concerned with its implications for the nature of the university. The war arose due to largely unconfirmed historical claims to the ownership of land (native-settler crisis), resources (farmlands, gold deposits) and privileges (status and location of local governments, chiefdoms, etc.) in the area. Hitherto, the two warring groups had been long-standing neighbours, living together in peace, and even engaging in intermarriage for centuries. During this crisis the university provided accommodation, water, electricity, medical care as well as psychological and spiritual comfort to many distressed persons. The university made extensive use of its own resources and of assistance from the government and other humanitarian agencies in assisting the displaced people of the area. Fortunately, the federal government sent its military forces to protect the university and to restore some order in the area. However, this situation did not deter some well-armed assailants who realised that individuals were taking refuge in the university community. The attackers decided to launch an attack on the university and were eventually repelled by the security forces detailed to guard the institution. Whatever may have been the reasons for this situation, the experiences of the university at Ile-Ife have set the pace for the redefinition of the role of the university as a crucial factor in the quest for national security and human protection in the context of a federal Nigeria.

In other parts of the country, the role of the university has compelled the expansion and revision of the definition of national and social security interventions. The university provides a fairly constant source of water, wood fuel, formal and informal employment and other materials necessary for human preservation for the people existing in their immediate environs. Again, the roles of the University of Lagos and University of Ibadan are instructive here. These experiences show that the university has the task of making a contribution to the security, peace, stability and progress of the society. For the university to be capable of this task it must itself be capable of nurturing and sustaining humane, just and progressive values among its members. The request by the universities in Nigeria for more funding and better infrastructure must be complemented by a display of individual and institutional probity, accountability and expertise.

Sectoral Political and Economic Concerns in Nigeria's Problem of National Security

This crisis of national security in the nation can be seen in the political and economic difficulties arising from both the struggle for state power among the national elite, as well as in the distribution and management of the society's wealth and resources. It has been noted that the problem of national security in Nigeria has been aggravated by the intolerance among the various ethno-cultural and religious groups. This situation has led to the engendering of mistrust and divisive tendencies in the society. Consequently, there have been communal and inter-tribal clashes and violence. Politics and the economy have a part to play in the quest for security. However, evidence shows that political action may not often lead to social and economic transformation. The social and economic development and hence the security of the various interests and segments of the Nigerian society are hindered by social ills like corruption, poor planning, nepotism, tyranny and selfishness in the society. National security is threatened by the absence of proper principles and values that determine harmonious and productive human personal and social behaviour.

The problem of national security in Nigeria construed in a historical perspective has always centred on the crisis arising from the nature of the relations existing among the various ethnic and interest groups. The problem of security in Nigeria and the consequential conflict situation centres on tension, injustice and marginalisation. The bone of contention is partly that while some segments of the country are carrying the burden that sustains the entire nation, other segments are enjoying the paradise that has resulted from this inequality. This problem has been linked to the character of the state and the actions of the dominant interests of the ruling class.

One important realm of the manifestation of the problem of national security has been the generally overlooked, but extremely important, aspect of values. It is interesting to note that insecurity in Nigeria manifests itself in the form of competing values, beliefs and attitudes.

Thus, central to the problem of national security in Nigeria has been that situation in which there existed a fundamental conflict of personal and social values among various interests and groups with regard to the proper meaning and approach to national security, national integration, peace and stability within the polity. This conflict of values and the various abuses and injustices arising from it ensured that there were no clearly defined and established rules for harmonising the diverse interests, needs and values of the different groups and sectors in the society in view of achieving the urgent task of national development. In short, the lack of shared beliefs, attitudes and values among the rulers and the ruled, as well as between the various segments of Nigerian society, ensured that conflict remained endemic in the nation.

At another level, religion is a powerful tool for fostering peace and corporate existence among the members of the society. But with reference to most parts of Africa, the influx of different religions has created fertile ground for conflict and instability. The abuse of religion in order to serve ethnic or political purposes has often led to severe consequences for the society and its members. This point is the more significant in a multi-religious society such as Nigeria. The perversion and exploitation of the religious sentiments of the people can eventually lead to malice, disarray and violence. The reality on the ground is that the problems of religious and social tolerance facing the society have been worsened by the elite-motivated, often violent struggles for benefits, power and influence within the society. This situation has led to the vitiation of the Nigerian state in the social, political and economic realms of life. The mistrust and hatred emanating among groups, and the heightened intolerance, have led to the proliferation of religiously conscious militia groupings that ostensibly claim to be social liberators. In actual fact, these militia committed to religious violence have opened the opportunity for individuals to foment tension in the society and to violate the vital laws necessary for the sustenance of order, peace and stability.

Thus, to put it bluntly, the lack of trust between the rulers and the ruled in Nigeria ensured that there was an obstruction of national development at all levels of social existence. Furthermore, we can say that the absence or lack of operation of some core social values such as trust, cooperation, compassion, justice, and tolerance among the different interests and segments in the society contributed to the lack of sustainable development. The absence of a sense of responsibility has assumed the form of an institutionalised and sinister abdication of responsibility.

There has been a pattern that things are not always the way they seem to be in the country. This is what Ake (2001: 14) means when he says that 'the state in Africa has been a maze of antinomies of form and content: the person who holds office may not exercise its powers, the person who exercises the powers of a given office may not be its holder'. Ake's point is better understood in the light of the tragedy and crisis of our national consciousness and infrastructure. The physical and social infrastructure that has been put in place to serve the people and make their lives comfortable can now turn against them, becoming sources of insecurity and life threatening danger. This situation has created fear and apathy within the society. This point is relevant to the issue of national consciousness and the phenomenon of infrastructural predation. This situation has emerged out of decades of mismanagement of strategic national infrastructure such as the roads, bridges, oil universities, refineries, telecommunications, railways, airports and seaports in the nation. It is characterised by the neglect, under-utilisation and disregard for infrastructure and its roles in national development. Most of these structures have moved from decay to dereliction. Criminals and hoodlums; the human products of decades of social injustice, neglect, institutional deficiencies in law and education, have now found it easy to capitalise on any social instability however minor.

Apathy to government and the belief that public property ought to be destroyed is regularly seen in the destructive action of even the supposedly more educated people in society such as rampaging university students and mobs. In the case of those involved in the failure of the electricity supply on a national scale, the actors did not consider the effects on national security. They did not consider the chance (however remote?) that the country's enemies could seize the opportunity created by that action. More often, the Nigerian nation has experienced attacks by armed rebel groups and bands of soldiers from neighbouring countries to the north of Nigeria. In all of these actions, the different groups of citizens show a deep-rooted hatred and lack of understanding for a society that has ignored and maltreated them. In the case of the sabotage of the crude oil processing facilities, the country is still importing fuel because of the singular act of sabotage that occurred in the 1990s.

The Mismanagement of National Emergencies: The FGSI Project of 1994 as an Example of Conceptual and Institutional Limitations in Security Planning

The institutional laxity and ineffectiveness of government and its institutions can be seen more vividly with regard to emergencies. In 1994, the government was unable to confront the security threat posed by the oil workers' disruption of a regular supply of petroleum products across the country. And even when the Federal Government Strategic Intervention, or FGSI Project, took off, involving the use of oil ferrying articulated lorries (tankers) provided directly by the federal government, it could not effectively fill the gap left by the actions of the oil workers. The FGSI project was quantitatively and qualitatively defective. Though the nomenclature was good, the design and implementation were defective. The vehicles were in short supply, and the buyers and military escorts diverted their products. There were other technical and human problems.

Worst of all, the programme was just a reaction to the grave situation of the collapse of all semblance of national life. Thus it did not have the smack of creativity and purpose, such as was needed to rectify a national security threat of that magnitude. This was one of the clearest indications of the failure of that government, of preceding governments, and of the FGSI as an example of institutional intervention in national emergencies. It was evident that government had never been prepared for any serious national security crisis. The failures of the national institutions demonstrated the helplessness of a society that had refused to 'make hay while the sun shines'. This problem was seen in the fact that all the highways were turned into football pitches where youth expended their dejection and frustration with an incompetent society ruled by visionless, unimaginative and incapable individuals.

As a further critique of the FGSI project we may point out that if the railway system had been in good shape, it would have been easier to acquire, transport and distribute the different grades of fuel needed. A simple logical and mathematical analysis demonstrates this fact. If it is the case that the biggest tanker that can travel on the type of road available in the country will contain 33,000 litres of fuel, let us assume for the sake of argument that there were 1000 FGSI vehicles (which is most likely to be unattainable given the character of national planning and leadership), then by multiplication, the total payload of fuel (assuming that it is only one type of fuel that will be transported) will be 33,000,000 litres for a country of this size. Of course there are at least three kinds of fuel widely needed by the citizens - petrol, cooking kerosene and diesel - which automatically diminishes the quantity of each fuel that can be lifted at any one time to serve the needs of the teeming population.

Then when we consider that the distance between some parts of the nation can amount to two or three days' journey by road in a heavily loaded and highly inflammable tanker, then the ineffectiveness of an FGSI principle modelled on the use of road transport becomes glaringly obvious. These questions then arise: How long will it take for the fuel to be off-loaded from the seaport in the first place? How many ports in the country are capable of offloading these ships? How many FGSI road tankers will load in a day? How many loading stations exist? How many of these tankers can each station load in twelve or twenty-four hours? The truth is that if there is a transport system predicated on the dual or single railway system as a key machinery for the institutional movement of strategic and industrial goods, one or two good 21 Class trains can move up to twenty-five or more tankers. This would have been a better platform for the FGSI project. The practical implication of this is that one single train can convey up to 825,000 litres or more of fuel. This means that about forty trains can move the amount of fuel that 1000 tankers will move. The train or rail freight option is obviously a better strategy for confronting such threats to national security.

Security and the Evolving Aesthetics of Social Control

The aesthetics of control are tied to the tripartite analysis of values, social order and morality. The clarification of these ingredients of society is the more valuable 'in times of insecurity, and uncertainty, when personal survival is threatened' (Willie 1975: 10). We need a more solid conception of axiological and aesthetic inputs in social order for human and national security. This requires us to pursue a tripartite process of the 'reconsideration of the role of values and individual responsibility' (Duesterberg 1998: 44) in the search for alternative principles of aesthetic control and societal security. It cannot be overstated that the diverse institutions created by man simply aim, in one way or another, at society's efficient operation and continuation. A good society aims at its own notion of the common good through the provision of greater opportunities for participation and responsibility among citizens. Underlying this feeling of mutual responsibility is presumably the attitude of trust or faith in a unique pattern of political administration and social conduct that seeks the inclusion of as many as possible in the management of its affairs. The question is then how we can establish and sustain rules and values that can propel human actions for positive ends. This issue is the more significant in the context of organisations that undertake cultural, educational and expressive functions.

The concept of social order here becomes particularly instructive for evolving the systems and rules for security and social control in society. Social order simply refers to the social systems and schemes of social relations that define the political, economic and social roles, rights and duties of people in a society. Social order is therefore a set of arrangements put in place by man in order to attain certain important ends of all in a social system (Ujomu 2001: 247; Ujomu 2004: 12). Central to the operation of social order is the idea of social roles allocated to each member and group of the society. Social roles delineate the political, economic, religious and administrative functions of people in a society. The idea of social roles as identifiable and allocated political, economic, religious and administrative functions in fact depend upon some ethical and institutional foundations. Within the social order, roles are demarcated by established rules and conventions that guide human conduct and association within social practices and institutions. Hence, the mechanisms of social control are operative in sectors of society (Cohen and Short 1971: 94) such as the criminal justice system, clubs, universities, trade unions, and so on. Social control is a key feature of aesthetic social order. There are fundamental questions about the conditions for entrenching actions directed at the collective good in society in order to achieve 'an especially high level of welfare and security' (Kaufmann 2000: 309). This point is most significant in relation to the leaders and followers who must now be guided by the dual dictates of morality and law for the good of all in society.

Conclusion: The Way Forward in Security and Attitude Change

The need for security demands an interrogation of the core idea of the value of life as it operates on at least other central principles and practices. We place a value on human life when we define a set of operative principles that determine our estimation of the human being as constitutive of certain features that earn him a particular treatment or consideration. The value of life is also related to our axiological premises for considering the human person to be deserving of certain goods. Security is aimed at affirming and upholding the value of life. The quest for security may in fact be the essential quest to place a positive value on human life. In seeking a conception of fuller human social participation in security there is a presupposition of the rights that individuals retain to effect the rational pursuit of their well-being and happiness in a constructive and non-hostile manner. The attainment of security implies the creation of a social arena imbued with greater public trust and collective adherence to the rule of law for the assurance of peace and progress. Above all, the idea of security presupposes the establishment of a nation of people oriented to the common good on the premises of fraternity, equality and liberty. Security can be most effectively established and sustained through an idea of society which upholds the values of increased human participation, responsibility and wider input to social well-being. This view of society promotes security by recognising that values such as cooperation, consolidation and continuity are themselves usually uppermost in the minds of people when they form or participate in commonwealths.

The promotion of national and human security through cooperation, consolidation and continuity is possible only through the conceptualisation of the idea of excellence as a directing principle of social and institutional life in Africa. The ideology of excellence requires the theoretical and practical confrontation between our current human and social attitudes, values and cultural institutions in relation to how things ought to be. On the one hand, this is an ideological task, and on the other hand, it is an axiological commitment. Ideologically, we are in the quest for social order or social systems whose values are expressed mainly in a set of closely related beliefs, preferences, ideas, values or even attitudes (Macridis 1989: 2, 3; Toyo 2001: 23) and characteristic of a group or community. What, if at all, will be the content and context of ideology vis-à-vis the search for excellence?

The search for a multifaceted personal, social and institutional excellence is equally an ethical, aesthetical and phenomenological task. For Hogendorn (1996: 66) it is the demand that we overcome difficulties emanating from unsustainable practices. Indeed, Becker (1974: 111, 112) has informed us that excellence is suggestive of moral character. For its part, moral character can be discerned from human behaviour, especially when we move from behaviour to form conclusions about character on the basis of what is acceptable or ideal. The idea of human excellence suggests an emphasis on a combination of concepts that include virtue, good person, good society, ideals, and values. The critical justification for pressing home the argument from excellence in human conduct is that 'our attitude can change' (Schultz 1982: 108). Kiesler, Collins and Miller (1969: 82) are right to hold that behaviour is modified as a result of experience that can guide or influence later behaviour. As individuals go through life, they strive to attain certain goals and avoid some situations. They develop positive attitudes to objects that serve their purpose, while showing negative attitudes to objects that thwart their needs. (Kielser et al., 1969: 305, 316). This question of the possibilities of attitude change for excellence can be designed and installed as a 'distinct new area of policy intervention' (Reddock 2004: 25).

Therefore, we can agree with Burns (1928) that 'social life is amenable to human control. Human character, emotion and intelligence can be made by human acts different from what they now are. The indications by which we steer our course in such a control over institutions and personalities are called values' (Burns 1928: 483). If the above is true, then we must understand the quest for excellence as the reconstruction of 'a new self-image, conferring a sense of worth' (Goulet 1983: 617) on a people that have been plagued by historical, cultural, moral and spiritual weaknesses. These peoples have seen themselves and their institutions as unable to perform efficiently and effectively, their youth have been unable to achieve higher goods through the exercise of vigour and genius, and the rulers and elites have been unable to live according to decency, civility, fairness and humane principles that can serve as role models to others. It is such shortfalls that the quest for excellence seeks to overcome.

The challenge of excellence is indubitably a call for the engendering of social values such as diligence, civility, sincerity, discipline and industry, as well as the fruits of these so that the body politic can achieve progress. However, this calls for trust, a feeling of accommodation and other social capital for development. According to Fairbanks (2000: 270), social capital involves a combination of human and institutional capital. Together, these factors ensure the operation of legally sound, efficient and optimally performing organisations and firms and knowledge resources, including universities. Simply put the demand for excellence calls for 'better social arrangements and better conduct on all our parts' (Hartshorne 1974: 147).

One important social arrangement is the economic approach to security, which emphasises the appropriation of the capabilities, talents and strengths of every sector of the society with a view to income and wealth generation and distribution for national development. Indeed, 'economic security and wealth have a vital bearing on the larger problems of individual and social well-being, which are the concern of ethics' (Tsanoff 1951: 11). This approach emphasises the proper and careful management of scarce national resources meant for enduring social and economic development. Adopting the economic approach to security requires that Africans and African countries must tackle problems of corruption, lack of vision and mismanagement of resources by politicians, soldiers and bureaucrats. Proper resource management is therefore a central means to the maintenance of economic security. Economic strength can be squandered by reckless financial speculation and material profligacy. The degree of material well-being (security, peace and progress) generated by any economy depends not only on its ability to fully employ the productive resources (labour, capital, materials, energy), available to it, but also on its ability to employ them in ways that contribute to the heightening of the societal standard of living.

The dividends or advantages in cost and investment which the economic approach to security yields are to be measured not only in terms of increase in monetary or financial revenue, but also in terms of the production of economically and socially useful goods and services. It is also to be seen in terms of the psychological and material enhancements of human productivity given the nation's labour, capital and natural resources. The economic security and development of a nation can be measured using core indices. Such indices include its economic growth, the quality or standard of life of the citizens, the availability of basic infrastructure, efficiency of social amenities and productivity of industrial manufacturing systems, capacity for wealth generation and consolidation, an enabling financial environment and a viable system of human resources development.

Beyond the economy, there is the chance to utilise general and specialised education and formal and informal education as principles of guaranteeing security. But then the question of education and security takes us back to the realm of values, things that are desirable, important or interesting. The clarification of the issue of values is important in the question of security. It is our view that the reconsideration of key ethical values guiding the entire gamut of personal, social national life can make some of the much-desired difference in the area of security theorising. Education is a cardinal way of instilling these desired ethical values. Education as a basic means of social progress and reform contributes to the establishment of human and national security in various ways. It provides opportunities for individual and social growth, it gives culture to the individual and society, and it develops human abilities and trains useful citizens. Education contributes to the establishment and sustenance of human and national security by enhancing the people's understanding of themselves, their society and environment. It improves living skills, fosters creative capacity, imposes core visions, values and character, and increases productivity and social mobility.

Access to relevant knowledge, that is, to scientific and technological knowledge, is an imperative and the cornerstone of any security development strategy. However, knowledge without values or virtues cannot yield any enduring fruits. One must be certain to ensure that one seeks or produces the knowledge that one needs, and that this knowledge is capable of yielding result-oriented action and promotes human survival both in the short and in the long term. It is painful but true that security is tied to a scientific culture. A scientific culture is tied to a strong, practical and effective system of education. To find out the truth of this claim, one must picture one's own society as facing a similar crisis that other more scientifically developed societies have faced. Imagine that Nigeria, for example, is beset by a tragedy of the magnitude of the September 11 terrorist attacks or an earthquake that destroys a whole city and kills thousands and displaces tens of thousands. There is no doubt that the story will be different for Nigeria because at present not only is the society largely unprepared, but also it does not have the requisite scientific and technological capacity to overcome such challenges. Thus, there can be no security without the development and dividends of a scientific culture. From all that has been said above, our aim has been to search for those core values that can make human life more secure, stable and harmonious. We face the challenge of reconciling our values with the demands of modern change. Moore (1973: 409) makes a valuable point that 'national security decisions must consider a range of component issues. Legal considerations like political, military and economic considerations are relevant to each of these issues'. We are in need of a more 'vigorous and imaginative implementation' (Moore 1973: 411) of the principles of security to the fundamental areas of human life. We must return to our visions and values which guide actions. Many of the attitudes of the individual reflect his values or his conception of what is desirable. As members of a human community, we must preserve the values essential to the security and redemption of life. These are ideas that raise the level of human dignity. Human dignity begins in the minds of human beings. There is a need to reconsider the moral basis of social existence, and enhance the more qualitative aspects of development such as humaneness, justice, etc. The point about the connections between values and security has been fully made. In any case, we can agree with Munkner (1998: 87) on some of the values that he mentions: 'self-help, self responsibility, solidarity, social responsibility'. O'Keefe (1985: 56, 58) agrees on the fact that security must emanate from 'an individual sense of responsibility among citizens' that can guarantee 'taking preventative actions'. Human beings can survive only because there are shared or public values and interests, which ultimately foster the good of all. We are in need of specific behaviour for security; joint action for the common good. According to Jeter (2003: 8), 'if we are deceived into concentrating on our differences and not common interests then enmity and rivalry will trespass where hope and cooperation should prevail'.

This essay has attempted a theoretical and conceptual interrogation of the idea of national security using the typological, philosophical and prolegomenon approaches. It situated the problem in the context of a post-colonial setting and has tried to engage the core ideas and values required for a proper methodological conceptualisation of security.

References

Ackermann, Werner, 1981, 'Cultural Values and Social Choice of Technology', *International Social Science Journal*, Vol. XXXIII, No. 3, pp. 447-465.

Ake, Claude, 2001, *Democracy and Development in Africa*, Ibadan: Spectrum Books.

Alaya, Flavia, 1977, 'Victorian Science and the "Genius" of Woman', *Journal of the History of Ideas*, Vol. XXXVIII, No. 2, April-June.

Appadurai, Arjun, 2002, 'Tactical Humanism: The Crisis of Names', *Polis, R.C.S.P, C.P.S.R.* Vol. 9, Numero Special, pp. 97-101.

Augustine, Saint, 1990, *The City of God*, Translated Dodds, M., *Great Books of the Western World*, Alder, M. J., ed., Chicago: Encyclopaedia Britannica Inc.

Ayer, Alfred J., 1973, 'One's Knowledge of Other Minds', in Gustafson, Donald F., ed., *Essays in Philosophical Psychology*, London: Macmillan, pp. 346-364.

Ayoob, Mohammed, 1984, 'Security in the Third World: The Worm about to Turn', *International Affairs*, pp. 41-51.

Bacon, Francis, 1972, 'The Four Idols', in John Herman Randall Jr, Justus Buchler, and Evelyn Shirk, eds., *Readings in Philosophy*, New York: Barnes and Noble, pp. 91-101.

Becker, Lawrence C., 1975, 'The Neglect of Virtue', *ETHICS.*, Vol. 85, pp. 110-122.

Bell, Wendell, 1994, 'The World as a Moral Community', *Society*, July/August, pp. 17-22.

Bellamy, Alex J. and McDonald, Matt, 2002, 'The Utility of Human Security: Which Humans? What Security? A Reply to Thomas and Tow', *Security Dialogue*, Vol. 33, No. 3, pp. 373-377.

Bentham, Jeremy, 1971, 'Bentham Jeremy 1748-1832', in Clarence Morris, ed., *The Great Legal Philosophers: Readings in Jurisprudence*, Philadelphia: University of Pennsylvania Press, pp. 261-288.

Bentham, Jeremy, 1972, 'The Direct and Indirect Consequences of Actions', in D. H. Monro, ed., *A Guide to the British Moralists*, London: Fontana/Collins, pp. 204-209.

Bentham, Jeremy, 1978, 'Security and Equality of Property', in C. B. MacPherson, ed., *Property*, Oxford: Blackwell, pp. 39-58.

Berry, Christopher J., 1986, *Human Nature*, London: Macmillan Education Ltd.

Biscop, Sven, 2003, 'Opening up the ESDP to the South: A Comprehensive and Cooperative Approach to Euro-Mediterranean Security', *Security Dialogue*, Vol. 34, no. 2, pp. 183-197.

Brunner. A. and Raemers, S., 1937, *Fundamental Questions of Philosophy*, London: Herder Books.

Burns, C. Delisle, 1928, 'The Philosophy of Social Life', *Journal of Philosophical Studies*, Vol. 111, No. 12, October, pp. 483-494.

Bush, George, W., 1997, *George W. Bush: 43rd President of the United States of America*, Office of International Information Programs, US Department of State.

Caprioli, Mary, 2004, 'Democracy and Human Rights Versus Women's Security: A Contribution', *Security Dialogue*, Special Issue on Gender and Security, vol. 35, no. 4, pp. 411-428.

Citizens' Forum For Constitutional Reform (CFCR), 2001, 'Review of The 1999 Constitution: What are the Issues', *Citizens' Forum For Constitutional Reform*, Lagos Ikeja: CFCR.

Clancy, Tom, 1994, *Debt of Honour*, New York: Berkeley Books.

Clinton, Bill, 1997, *Bill Clinton: 42nd President of the United States of America: A Second Term*, United States Information Agency, USIA.

Cohen, Albert. K. and Short, James. F., 1971, 'Crime and Juvenile Delinquency', in Robert K. Merton and Robert Nisbet, eds., *Contemporary Social Problems*, Third Edition, New York: Harcourt Brace Jovanovich Inc., pp. 89-146.

Committee for the Defence of Human Rights (CDHR), 2000, *1999 Annual Report on the Human Rights Situation in Nigeria*, Lagos: CDHR.

CDHR, 2001, *2000 Annual Report on the Human Rights Situation in Nigeria*, Lagos: CDHR.

Cuffel, Victoria, 1966, 'The Classical Greek Concepts of Slavery', *Journal of the History of Ideas*, Vol. XXVII, No. 3.

Dandeker, Christopher, 2001, 'The Military in Democratic Societies', *Society*, September/October, pp. 16-24.

Davidson, Basil, 1978, *Africa in Modern History. The Search for a New Society*, London: Penguin.

Dewey, John, 1972, 'Democracy', in John Herman Randall Jr, Justin Buchler and Evelyn Shirk, eds., *Readings in Philosophy*, New York: Barnes and Noble, pp. 288-293.

Dewey John, 1974, 'Does Human Nature Change?', in Daniel Bronstein, Yervant Krikorian and Philip Wiener, eds., *Basic Problems of Philosophy*, Third Edition, New Jersey: Prentice. Hall, pp. 116-121.

Dewey, John, 1977, *John Dewey: The Essential Writings*, David Sidorsky, ed., New York: Harper and Row.

Duesterberg, Thomas J., 1998, 'Reforming the Welfare State', *Society*, September/October, pp. 44-53.

Edelman, Murray, 1975, 'Language, Myth and Rhetoric', *Society*, July/August, pp. 41-21.

Eggerman, Richard W., 1975, 'Is Normative Aesthetics a Viable Field for Philosophic Inquiry?', *The Journal of Value Inquiry*, Vol. IX, no. 3, pp. 210-220.

Fairbanks, Michael, 2000, 'Changing the Mind of a Nation: Elements in a Process for Creating Prosperity', in Lawrence E. Harrison and Samuel P. Huntington, eds., *Culture Matters*, New York: Basic Books, pp. 268-281.

Fashina, Oladipo, 2005, 'Reforms in Nigerian University System - What Direction?, Paper presented at the ASUU/CODESRIA Conference on Reforming Higher Education in Nigeria, 21-22 March, Abuja FCT.

French, Peter, 1995, *Corporate Ethics*, Florida: Harcourt Brace.

Goodman, Nelson, 1972, *Problems and Projects*, New York: The Bobbs-Merrill Company.

Goulet, Denis, 1983, 'Obstacles to World Development: An ethical reflection', *World Development*, vol. 11, no. 7, pp. 609-624.

Grayling, A. C., 2003, *The Reason of Things: Living With Philosophy*, London: Phoenix.

Grimm, Robert, 1980, 'Purposive Actions', *Philosophical Studies*, vol. 38, no. 3, pp. 235-259.

Hare, R. M., 1973, *Applications of Moral Philosophy*, Los Angeles: University of California Press.

Hartshorne, Charles, 1974, 'Philosophy after Fifty Years', in Peter A. Bertocci, ed., *Mid-Twentieth Century American Philosophy*, New York: Humanities Press, pp. 140-154.

Hogendorn, Jan, 1996, *Economic Development*, New York: HarperCollins.

Holme, Richard, 1972, *Psychology Today*, Second Edition, California: CRM Books.

Hoogensen, Gunhild and Rotten, Svein Vigeland, 2004, 'Gender Identity and the Subject of Security', *Security Dialogue*, vol. 35, no. 2, pp. 155-171.

Hughes, Martin, 1982, 'Terrorism and National Security', *Philosophy*, vol. 57, no. 219, pp. 5-25.

Jeter, Howard, 2003, *Reaching out to the African Diaspora: The Need for Vision*, Abuja: Embassy of the United States of America.

Joseph, Richard, 2002, 'State Governance and Insecurity in Africa', Keynote Address presented at The CDD Centre for Democracy and Development Launch for Endowment Campaign, pp. 1-10.

Kaufmann, Franz-Xavier, 2000, 'Towards a Theory of the Welfare State', *European Review*, vol. 8, no. 3, pp. 291-312.

Kiesler, C., Collins B. and Miller N., 1969, *Attitude Change: A Critical Analysis of Theoretical Approaches*, New York: John Wiley and Son.

Knudsen, Olav F., 2001, 'Post Copenhagen Security Studies: Desecuritizing Securitization', *Security Dialogue*, vol. 32, no. 3, pp. 355-374.

Kolderie, Ted, 1987, 'What Do We Mean by Privatization?', *Society*, September/October, pp. 46-51.

Kolnai, Aurel, 1971, 'The Concept of Hierarchy', *Philosophy*, vol. XLVI, no. 177, pp. 203-221.

Kupperman, Joel. J., 1972, 'Aesthetic Value', *American Philosophical Quarterly*, vol. 9, No. 3, pp. 259-264.

Lamont, W. D., 1945, 'Politics and Culture', *Philosophy*, vol. XX, no. 75, pp. 39-58.

Liotta, P. H., 2002, 'Boomerang Effect: The Convergence of National and Human Security', *Security Dialogue*, vol. 33, no. 4, pp. 473-488.

Locke, Edwin, 1991, *The Essence of Leadership*, New York: Macmillan.

Mackenzie, J. S., 1963, *Outlines of Social Philosophy*, London: George Allen & Unwin.

Macridis, Roy, 1989, *Contemporary Political Ideologies*, Illinois: Scott, Foresman & Company.

Makinda, Samuel M., 1998, 'Sovereignty and Global Security', *Security Dialogue*, Vol. 29, No. 3, pp. 281-292.

Malcolm, Norman, 1973, 'Knowledge of Other Minds', in Gustafson Donald. F., ed., *Essays in Philosophical Psychology*, London: Macmillan, pp. 365-376.

Mbiti, John S., 1969, *African Religions And Philosophy*, London: Heinemann.

McKeon, Richard, 1981, 'Philosophy as an Agent of Civilization', *Philosophy and Phenomenological Research*, vol. XLI, no. 4, pp. 419-436.

McLean, George. F., 2000, 'Philosophy and Civil Society: its Nature, its Past and its Future', in George F. McLean, *Spiritual Values and Social Progress. Uzbekistan Philosophical studies*, Washington, DC: The Council for Research in Values and Philosophy.

McShea, Robert J., 1979, 'Human Nature and Ethical Theory', *Philosophy and Phenomenological Research*, vol. XXXIX, No. 3, pp. 386-400.

Messari, Nizar, 2002, 'The State and Dilemmas of Security: The Middle East and the Balkans', *Security Dialogue*, vol. 33, no. 4, pp. 415-427.

Mill, J. S., 1974, 'Bentham', in *Utilitarianism*, Mary Warnock, ed., London: William Collins, pp. 78-125.

Mill, J. S., 1975, *Utilitarianism, On Liberty, Essay on Bentham*, Mary Warnock ed., London: William Collins.

Moller, Frank, 2003, 'Capitalizing on Difference: A Security Community or/and a Western project', *Security Dialogue*, vol. 34, no. 4, pp. 315 328.

Moore, John Norton, 1973, 'Law and National Security', *Foreign Affairs*, vol. 51, no. 2, pp. 408-422.

Munkner, Hans. H., 1998, 'Which Values for Africa of the 21st Century?', *Africana Marburgensia*, Special Issue 17, pp. 79-87.

Newman, Jay, 1979, 'Two Theories of Civilization', *Philosophy*, vol.54, pp. 473-483.

Newsweek International Magazine, 2001, Extracts on September 11 terrorist attacks, October.

Nietzsche, F., 1956, 'Live Dangerously', in Walter Kaufmann, ed., *Existentialism from Dostoevsky to Sartre*, New York: Meridian Books, pp. 100-112.

Ochoche, Sunday A., 1998, 'The Military and National Security in Africa', in Hutchful, Eboe and Abdulaiye Bathily, eds., *The Military and Militarism in Africa*, Dakar: CODESRIA, pp. 105-127.

O'Keefe, Garrett, J., 1985, 'Taking a Bite out of Crime', *Society*, March/April, pp. 56-64.

Oladipo, Olusegun, 1996, *Philosophy and the African Experience*, Ibadan: Hope.

Palma, A.B., 1983, 'Imagination, Truth and Rationality', *Journal of Philosophy*, vol. 58, pp. 29-38.

Perlman, James S., 1995, *Science Without Limits*, New York: Prometheus Books.

Perry, R. B., 1968, 'The Definition of Value', *Readings in Introductory Philosophical Analysis*, John Hospers, ed., London: Routledge and Kegan Paul.

Peters, S.B., 1983, 'National Security Management in Nigeria', *Nigerian Journal of International Affairs*, vol. 9, no. 2.

PUNCH, Newspaper, 2001, Extracts on education in Nigeria, 2 April.

Quinton, Anthony, 1993, 'Morals and Politics', in A. P. Griffiths, ed., *Ethics, Supplement to Philosophy*, Cambridge: Cambridge University Press, pp. 95-106.

Rabb, J. Douglas, 1975, 'Prolegomenon to A Phenomenology of Imagination', *Philosophy and Phenomenological Research*, vol. XXXVI, no. 1, pp. 74-81.

Reddock, Rhoda, 2004, *Reflections on Gender and Democracy in the Anglophone Carribbean: Histroical and Contemporary Considerations,* The Netherlands: SEPHIS-CODESRIA.

Rensburg, W. C. J. van, and Paul Anaejionu, 1986, *Strategic Minerals: Major Mineral Consuming Regions of the World, Issues and Strategies*, vol. 11, Englewood Cliffs, New Jersey: Prentice. Hall, Inc.

Roe, Paul, 2001, 'Actors' Responsibility in "Tight", "Regular" or "Loose" Security Dilemmas', *Security Dialogue*, vol. 32, no. 1, pp. 103-116.

Russell, Bertrand, 1995, *History of Western Philosophy*, London: Routledge.

Russow, Lilly-Marlene, 1978, 'Some Recent Work on Imagination', *American Philosophical Quarterly*, vol. 15, no. 1, pp. 57-66.

Ryle, Gilbert, 1973, 'Imagination', in Gustafson Donald. F., ed., *Essays in Philosophical Psychology*, London: Macmillan, pp. 117-153.

Samuels, Warren J., 1991, 'Dynamics of Cultural Change', *Society*, November/December, pp. 23-26.

Sandlers, Todd, 1997, *Global Challenges: An Approach to Environmental, Political and Economic Problems*, Cambridge: Cambridge University Press.

Schultz, Walter, 1982, 'The Philosophy of Inter-personal Relations: I and Others', *UNIVERSITAS*, vol. 24, no. 2, pp. 107-114.

Scott, Charles E., 1972, 'Consciousness and the Conditions of Consciousness', *The Review of Metaphysics*, vol. XXV, No. 4.

Shorter, J. M., 1973, 'Imagination', in Gustafson Donald. F., ed., *Essays in Philosophical Psychology*, London: Macmillan, pp. 154-170.

Singer, Marcus, 1989, 'Value Judgements and Normative Claims', in A. P. Griffiths, ed., *Key Themes in Philosophy*, Cambridge: Cambridge University Press.

Sogolo, Godwin, 1993, *Foundations of African Philosophy*, Ibadan: Ibadan University Press.

Suhrke, Astri, 1999, 'Human Security and the Interests of State', *Security Dialogue*, vol. 30, no. 3, pp. 265-276.

Teichman, J., 1989, 'How to Define Terrorism', *Philosophy*, vol. 64, no. 250, pp. 505-517.

Temlong, J. N., Brig Gen, 2003, 'Security Agencies and Domestic Security Consideration', *Defence Newsletter*, January/March.

Thatcher, Margaret, 1997, 'The Value of American Studies', *Society*, September/October, pp. 48-53.

Thomas, Nicholas and Tow, William T., 2002, 'The Utility of Human Security: Sovereignty and Humanitarian Intervention', *Security Dialogue*, vol. 33, no. 2, pp. 177-192.

Titus, Harold, 1970, *Living Issues in Philosophy*, New York: Van Nostrand Reinhold.

Toyo, Eskor, 2001, 'Ideology and African Development: A Clarification of Issues', in P. I. Ozo-Eson and Ukoha Ukiwo, eds., *Identity and African Development*, Abuja: AFRIGOV & CASS, pp. 23 - 51.

Trenchard-Smith, Brian, 2001, Director *Megiddo. The Omega Code 2*, 8x Entertainment Release, TBN films, Generation Entertainment.

Tsanoff, Radoslav A., 1951, 'Moral principles and National Interests', *Ethics*, no. 1, pp. 11-15.

Ujomu, Philip Ogo, 2000-2001, 'Ethics and National Security in Nigeria: Critical Issues in the Search for Sustainable Development', *Voice Millennial Edition*, no. 39, pp. 38-40.

Ujomu, Philip Ogo, 2001, 'National Security, Social Order and the Quest for Human Dignity in Nigeria: Some Ethical Considerations', *Nordic Journal of African Studies*, vol. 10, No. 2, pp. 245-264.

Ujomu, Philip Ogo, 2004, 'Citizenship and Social Order: Reflections on Plato', *Democracy and Development Journal of West African Affairs*, vol. 4, no. 1, Rain Edition, pp.11-30.

Viscount Samuel., 1956, 'Philosophy and the Life of the Nation', *Philosophy*, vol. XXXI, no. 118, pp. 197-212.

Wellman, Carl, 1979, 'On Terrorism Itself', *Journal of Value Enquiry*, vol. XII, no. 4, pp. 250-258.

Willie, Charles V., 1975, 'Marginality and Social Change', *Society*, vol.12, no. 2, pp. 10-13.

Zehfuss, Maja, 2003, 'Forget September 11', *Third World Quarterly*, vol. 24, no. 3, pp. 513-528.

3

An Aesthetic Theorising of the Challenge of National Security in the Post-colonial Context

Philip Ogo Ujomu and Dapo Adelugba

Introduction and Problematic

Prior engagement with the thematic concerns of aesthetics and security seems generally to have focussed on the restrictive study of improving the components of buildings, protective systems, and so on. But our work engages the theme of aesthetic security from a wider philosophical and ethical viewpoint that is both holistic and sympathetic to the wider socio-political and cosmological processes that underlie aesthetic valuation. The more so, whereas the dominant view of aesthetics come across as essentially discursive interrogations of the domains of natural phenomena and artistic productions, we must now see the aesthetic countenances from the panoramic, spectral approach that makes ideas, institutions and systems susceptible to analysis. While we reaffirm the predominant view of aesthetics as the engagement with the gamut of human action in the ethical, social, technological and economic realms of life, we realise that aesthetic security can be conceptualised in terms of core notions like control, beauty, harmony, satisfaction, imagination, taste and commitment. These are the vital normative, conceptual and prescriptive ordinances that can facilitate the thematic and methodological control of aesthetic themes, valuations and convergences. The crux of this work therefore is to look for the aesthetic and ethical basis of security development in this modern age. In this approach lies the power to elicit novelty and make vital connections within diverse realms of reality.

In engaging the philosophical and aesthetic dimensions of security, our analysis must specifically confront ideologies and cultures and how these try to resist and unseat the diverse centres of dominant influence, power and protection. These convolutions in philosophical and aesthetic security must be tied to the roles of cosmologies, traditions and ways of life in determining the scope and limits of state or social actions. The reasons for these situations are not unconnected to the predisposing factors that constrain change. All of these trends in-sinuate a desire for an aesthetic reconsideration of the trajectory of social vision and social action. Such action for change must be based on the tripartite aesthetical, ethical and logical mindsets that are very much needed today.

The critical mind that generates new ideas and queries old ideas is an impera-tive of alternative forms of conduct that allow us to afford the more rational modes of choice. This pathway inevitably leads either to the re-visitation of the typology of security – a well-worn but valuable pathway – or a regress to the explanations of the primordial principles of human conduct. While these are laudable tracks to follow, we may just engage the illustration of our problems by using the alternative methodological convergence of aesthetic and axiological inquisition. Our work therefore is aimed at finding ways to ensure and enhance the aesthetic manipulation of vision and style through either technological means for control and communication, or through a more economic aesthetic control that focuses on taste and preferences. Direct causal or regulative control if used aesthetically is capable of generating a new way of altering intentions and inner states, while at the same time moderating behaviour. The point then is that a combinative approach that mixes normative, physical and geographical contexts can overcome our multi-faceted security crisis.

Central to overcoming this aesthetic security crisis is the definition and appro-priation of the mechanisms of values and valuation. While value concerns the worth of something and the way we come to attain that worth, valuation is based on the weighted cost-benefits of something as important, desirable or interesting. In either of these ways, the concrete concern is to discover how peo-ple can live in peaceful cooperation, obedience to law, and amenability to social organisation. This is a phenomenological issue that interfaces what we are, what we have become and what we ought to become. In pursuing this track of mov-ing from is to ought, we must pursue the crystallisation of our analysis into the domains of duties, affiliations, representation and conduits of power and infor-mation. This means a regress to the zones of values through cosmologies, tradi-tions and culture, with an express view to eliciting that which can foster the nor-mative and prescriptive re-entry into the tripartite challenge of the social order. The possibility of aesthetic change is thus a fundamental underpinning of our work insofar as it delves into the links between the traditional and modern, the personal and the public in African societies. This track requires an emphasis on the educative mode, law enforcement, moral development, and reward systems. In effect, we are in need of re-establishing the crucial aesthetic basis of key social institutions for national security and social action.

The Need for and the Role of Aesthetic Concepts in the Interrogation of Security

The field of aesthetics is crucial in itself and in relation to security. The context of aesthetics as a vocation of value in itself has been partly elucidated in Adelugba (1990 and 2003). This particular essay is aimed at linking theoretically aesthetics with security concerns. Aesthetics is important because it focuses on the role of human experience and human feelings in the production of art. More so, human aesthetic feelings and experience must be brought to bear on the institutional and social-cultural aspects of human life, especially the prevailing discussions on security and well-being. However, the enduring observation made by Reid (1926: 200) is still instructive in this context. 'The attempt to understand aesthetic problems intellectually is a fact which is quite distinct from the fact of having aesthetic experience, yet the one process may, and in fact does, help the other' (Reid 1926: 200). This means that we can see security as a problem of aesthetics or we can apply aesthetic experience to the definition of security matters. The question then is what are the things or features that are susceptible to the aesthetic investigation.

The objects of aesthetic investigation are what Best (1982: 358) refers to as 'natural phenomena and works of art'. In our case, we are interested in the role of aesthetics because it focuses on the roles of underlying values and practices that determine the quality of artistic characterisations. We believe that aesthetics is vital for security insofar as it seeks to unearth the underlying principles and values that affect the reflection and practices of security in a specific society. To be able to make that contribution to the aesthetic theorising regarding security we must accept that there is a sense in which we require 'some new and self-conscious relationship' (Scruton 1996: 331) that will provide a basis for perceiving our investigation as a quest for redefining the modernity in security that we seek as a core value.

In another important sense, Best (1982: 358) draws our attention to the fact that 'many natural objects seem to have a value that can easily be explained in terms of aesthetic value'. The aesthetic value of natural objects can be said to come from the features or feelings that they elicit in us. The reason, according to Kieran (1997: 383), is that 'aesthetic value is characterized in terms of that which affords us pleasure'. But then, is it only pleasure that we can derive from aesthetic value? If the answer is yes, then how do we account for the fact that we can derive aesthetic value through satisfaction, functionality and effectiveness, even though we may not readily derive any pleasure? In the act of living one's daily life there are a lot of things that have aesthetic value but which do not retain any sustained propensity for pleasure.

To overcome this problem, Kupperman (1972: 259) adds another important dimension to the clarification of the idea of aesthetic value by saying that 'the aesthetic value depends on ethical values, and we become aware of the aesthetic

value by means of awareness of ethical value'. Thus, in a significant sense, there is
a realm of aesthetic value that defines or affects the zones of rectitude and pro-
priety. Put more directly, the task of ethical values to establish order, harmony
and fairness in mutual action can be perceived as being of aesthetic value. This is
so in so far as these ends can be taken as appreciable, desirable and interesting.
From the above analysis, we can see that aesthetics is important to human life, of
which security is a vital aspect. This is so because it brings to the fore the ideas and
ideals that affect and influence the technological, social and economic realms with
a view to facilitating the comprehension of beauty in the experiences of the
reviewers, practitioners and audience.

The aesthetic approach is vital for generating insight into our security theorising because aesthetics is 'a lens through which to penetrate and scrutinize reality.
Others have seen it as a lamp by means of which to explore previously undiscov-
ered dimensions and horizons of human existence' (Gill 1983: 141). Still on the
idea of aesthetics and its capabilities, Lindroos (2003: 235) holds that 'in aesthetic
representation, the difference between the object and subject, which disrupts the
identifying techniques of any representation, is the essential point of departure'.
The point that was made earlier that aesthetics brings to the fore the ideas and
ideals that affect and influence the technological, social and economic realms is
further reinforced by Thayer (1976). The issue is that 'these strictures on aesthetic
production and experience are developed in the wider context of ethical, epistemological and metaphysical theory and criticism' (Thayer 1976: 595). There seems
to be an interconnection between the aesthetic realm and other crucial spheres of
human activity. In other words, the aesthetic analysis of security must focus on
the economic, social and technological ramifications or dimensions of security.
These are definitely vital areas that can determine the outcome of security options and theorising.

It is clear from the above that the aesthetic interrogation of security seeks to
strike at the heart of the human security and national security problem and seeks
to view it from a more holistic perspective. The aesthetic concept is important to
security for a number of reasons. The aesthetic concept can be understood in
terms of aesthetic properties. It is significant to note that in the evaluation of
aesthetic properties, certain epistemological, psychological, logical and metaphysical
issues can and do arise. It is in this sense that the analysis of the historical dimensions of security begins to make sense to us. The spectral issues arising from the
interrogation of attitudes, presuppositions, norms, conduct and systems of
socialisation are all within the province of the aesthetic consideration of security.

To that effect, the following questions can become significant. What is the
whole gamut of our knowledge of security in either thematic or methodological
proportions? What are the trajectories (historical or conceptual) of the theorising
on security? Are there immanent and transcendent, physical and non-physical in-

terfaces between the forms and practices of security? What are the logical and empirical dimensions of the examination of security? In short, what do we mean when we say that a society (understood as any, or a specific, society) is secure? Let us note that the answers to the preceding binary logical question of security need not be the same. It is these kinds of issues that an aesthetic view of security interrogates. Aesthetic properties will inevitably crystallise into the aesthetic concept. It is thus clear that the aesthetic concept is, above all, devoted to the concern for the explanation of things by connecting the physical and psychological aspects that typify our experiences of these realities. The thrust of the aesthetic concept is to merge the subjectivity embedded in the personal assessment of crucial features of the security problematic with the objectivity of the universal responses or convergence on what is central to security.

With special reference to Africa, the challenge of aesthetics represents itself in the effort to revisit the claims regarding certain iconic elements of African 'primitivism'. Such primitivism is certified by the exposition of the doctrine of boisterous buffoonery or by a dark sinister nature. Either option raises that crucial subject of the supervision of the African by a 'superior'. In any case, the reality of the clear and present failure of the Africans in some vital areas of life entails a need to review the contexts of savagery. This is with a view to re-evaluating the content and context of the security imperative that has defined the African reality over the ages. The point, then, is that we are in a need of a review of the African social and cultural realities as they affect the security problematic. The end-result is the quest for a way out of the security quagmire that has plagued the African continent and peoples.

The Scope of Aesthetic Security: The Art of Security or Security as an Art

Is there an art of security or is security an art? The art of security presupposes an entrenched body of knowledge that provides a distinct epistemological and technical style on which basis practitioners can develop their unique evolutionary skills and approaches to the security issue. This view that security is an art suggests that security is open to diverse interventions and that each interrogator may retain a distinct way of dealing with the ensuing issues. Security as an art is a concern for the proper way of doing things or the appealing manner of handling security matters. Security as an art suggests a concern for a cocktail of factors such as the criteria of beauty, the emphasis on the productions of the imagination and the tastes or preferences arising from this. Imagination suggests a concern for visualisation, and the reflective power and extrapolation needed to ensure survival. This is indubitably the province of security. A concern for taste stresses the equally important effort to provide crucial parameters, options and alternatives that can be the foundation of essential choice(s) and committed decision(s) about ways of doing things pertaining to security. In short, security as an art is the stress on core values, norms and contexts that will eventually establish the basis for the rethinking of the visions and values of security and the expansion of the empirical and theoretical frontiers of the enterprise.

Therefore, given that the fundamental question that this essay poses is that of what aesthetics has to do with security, then the preliminary, yet correct, answer is that there are many things that connect both enterprises. Let us continue the analysis by undertaking some vital conceptual navigation. There are fundamental problems that arise in the analysis of aesthetics and some of these problems have significant implications for security. We shall review the ideas of art and imitation. Security may well be an art insofar as it is or can be seen as a production (a finished work) or process (a series of systematic stages leading to a result), similar to the process or production of an artistic work at the musical or visual level. For example, the security afforded by a well-constructed barricaded house is a production. This production can be defined offensively (through the presence of armed guards, guard dogs, and restrictions on movement), or defensively (via high fences, external perimeters, closed circuit television, intricate internal design, and so on).

At another level, security understood as a process can be seen in terms, for example, of the different stages and actions leading to the formation of an efficient road transport system. These will include the formation and sustenance of a national policy on road transport, an effective road safety corps, a well-made and maintained road network and a well-defined and understood set of road safety rules. Also important is the devising of other machinery that can ensure a veritable level of creative modification, positive values and attitude change that can promote the quality of life of a people. As an example, the process of ensuring an effective transport system must guarantee (enforceable and non-enforceable) obedience to the laws set up for the general good of all on the roads. A possible pathway is the designing of a national roads lighting programme, or project for the articulated vehicles on our roads. The ultimate intention of such a project may be to work towards the prevention of road accidents. Such an act of physical security also has its normative elements, a crucial one of which is the reinforcement of the belief in the dignity of the human person and in the sanctity of human life.

Of importance also is the need for the intensive modernisation of our relevant categories of roads. The reconstruction of the national roads networks must take several dominant factors into consideration. Such factors include the interlinking economic needs of communities and geopolitical sub-regions as well as national security and human security issues. The structural integrity of such an infrastructure, which compels that they should be constructed according to internationally acceptable specifications, is also of vital significance In more concrete terms, these standards will entail the provision of effective drainage, well-placed road shoulders, parking lots, room for future expansion, and so on. These features are crucial to security on our roads. This procedural pattern of security is equally effective for the reconstruction of other aspects of society. All of these are the provinces of aesthetic investigation of security matters. These lines of security planning have much to do with the technological, economic and social realms of human existence, especially in a post-colonial society. Inevitably, the interface between aesthetics and security must decisively connect with the need to ensure the maintenance of crucial proportions, standards and preferences that can facilitate the total security of individuals and groups in the society. The crux of the aesthetic vision is the insistence on discipline and on rectitude. Aesthetics is the quest for the rules and parameters that will guarantee the proper integration of hitherto distinct and diverse properties for a more systematic, harmonious and consolidated human development. This means that there is a need to institutionalise joint action at different social and governmental levels for the common good.

Beauty, Harmony and Satisfaction as the Imperatives of Security

There will always be insecurity where there is dissatisfaction. Dissatisfaction is an aesthetic quality that is vital for the comprehension of complex security situations. A good work of art must retain a core potential for, and actuality of, beauty, harmony and the eliciting of satisfaction in the producers, users and observers. To be able to enjoy security in any area of human endeavour, there must be some level of harmony, beauty and total satisfaction. Kieran (1997: 384) states that 'we can use the characterization of aesthetic value to generate general principles of aesthetic evaluation. The core thought is that what we take delight in is in itself delightful, in terms of unity, harmony, coherent structure and complex development'. The theoretical appeal of harmony suggests an integrated security or holistic vision of things that has accounted for the needs and interfaces between all the systems in the society.

For example, in the area of military action for national security, only a joint action for physical security and sharing of intelligence can make the required difference in the quest for security for a less developed society that is critically deficient in capacity utilisation, inspiration and technology for sustainable security arrangements. The power of, and need for, collaboration of agencies with mutual interests is imperative in a less developed society. Such a society suffers from inefficient infrastructure, corruption, scarcity of intellectual and financial resources, its raw materials production, and generally suffers from an endemic moral crisis seen in the pervading lawlessness, laxity, incompetence and anomie that permeates all levels of national life. Nigeria is an incontrovertible illustration of such a society.

The linking of security to satisfaction among the producers, users and observers is most clearly seen in the general state of dissatisfaction that members of the society have expressed about the state of affairs. Such objections have been varied but they underscore the same point that there is insecurity in the land and that the bulk of Nigerians are very uncomfortable with the existing situation. The whole idea of satisfaction at one level is tied to the concept of feelings. According to Kraut (1986: 644), 'feelings are mental states known primarily by their qualitative phenomenological properties. There seems to be an intimate connection between emotions and feelings'. The point must be made that in the case of a feeling such as 'fear', there are clear physiological and social or normative aspects. The physiological aspect connects to the physical changes that the human being undergoes in the state of fear. These changes affect the mind and the body. At the social level, there are certain institutional frameworks that imbue fear or certain symbolic structures that deliver the message of fear. These can include agents and institutions of sanctions, cultural totems or traditions such as rites or cults.

The feeling of security is therefore largely tied to the feeling of satisfaction that things are going well or that one remains in control. Incontrovertible evidence of the dissatisfaction of the people and therefore the reality of security problems in Nigeria can be seen clearly in the following facts. One is the demand for a sovereign national conference that can place its stamp on the essentially corrupt, primordial, unjust, repugnant and uncoordinated character of Nigerian society. The complex and threatening ethno-cultural and militia violence in the Niger Delta underscores the moral and institutional failure of government and people to ensure social order.

In addition, there is the absence of the values of tolerance, dialogue, trust, peace, and well-being as seen in the rise of rabid neo-ethno-nationalism across the different geopolitical zones of the country. There is the emergence and internationalisation of core anti-oppression and anti-injustice movements such as MOSOP, MASSOB, etc, which show clearly that there has been a dearth of distributive justice, social justice and obedience to moral rules and laws. There is also the persistent disruptive industrial action by trade unions such as ASUU, NASU, NMA, NUPENG, PENGASSAN, and NULGE which reveals the denial of the dignity of labour. There is the anti-government posture taken by pro-democracy and civil liberty coalitions which is evidence that social cooperation, mutual respect and joint vision and action for the common good is lacking. There is the crisis of pensioners that implies a government, people or society that fails to plan properly for the future. All of these activities ensure the crystallisation of tension, insecurity, fear, uncertainty, which eventually underwrite the lack of satisfaction with the way things are going. These factors pose a crisis for the construction of aesthetic security. From the above, we can understand the philosopher

Bertrand Russell (1975: 136) when he says that 'those who face life with a feeling of security are much happier than those who face it with a feeling of insecurity'.

The study of aesthetics must require some concerted effort towards attaining the common interest. According to Guyer (1977: 586), 'an empirical interest in beauty, exists only in society. An impulse to society is natural to mankind though this can be established only empirically and psychologically and this impulse leads us to take an interest in whatever can promote society'. Genuine security cannot be installed where there are divergent interests working for divergent goals. Only anarchy, fear and mistrust can emanate from such an arrangement. It seems then that harmony must be conceived in terms of the social principles for living a human, secure and progressive life.

Furthermore, the idea of beauty suggests a non-negotiable level of professional and ethical competence. For example, we may ask whether there is aesthetic beauty in the repugnant and objectionable actions (brigandage, extortion, harassment) of the policemen we see on the streets during our daily rounds of activities. We can ask whether these policemen are following the rules defined for their profession. What manner of aesthetics can emanate from extortion, tattered attitudes and uniforms, derelict equipment, perversion of justice, incompetence in investigations, and a general image of the worst that a society can produce? This same principle of analysis is applicable to other social and national institutions.

The Philosophy of Beauty and the Aesthetic Quest for Security

There is, however, the more important dimension of beauty in aesthetic analysis. How does the idea of beauty connect to the question of aesthetics? Beauty itself is suggestive of an emphasis on appropriateness or fitness to function; it refers to efficacy and efficiency. Beauty is also linked to the beneficial or the pleasurable or desirable. In a way, beauty is linked to value because value is understood in reference to what is appreciated, desired, interesting or important. What then are those features of our national and human security that we can desire or appreciate? The ideas of beauty and desirability further suggest that beautiful things are made with care and respect for symmetry, proportion and an eye for excellence. How can we apply excellence and caution in our quest for security at the practical or theoretical levels? It then becomes clear that there is an interface between security and the demands of an aesthetic notion of beauty.

The whole issue of beauty must transcend that which is merely pleasurable as an object of aesthetic experience. Rather, the aesthetic notion of beauty will re-emphasise the features of an idea or object that moves us deeply. That is, there is an emphasis on the things that guide and determine our lives; the things that we are committed to. The idea of aesthetic beauty also emphasises those things that reorient our perception or vision of reality. Thus to talk about beauty is to talk about aesthetic value or for that matter, the willing and dedicated effort to see alternatives and reassess the phenomena before us.

What are the consequences of connecting beauty to security? The emphasis on appropriateness or fitness to function refers to efficacy and efficiency. More than that, it stresses the sanctity and integrity of the moral and professional elements of an institution, system or security principle. It draws attention to the character of rule following, stability and synchrony. On the issue of the beneficial or the pleasurable, the implication is that there is a need for a more appealing and captivating way of creating security. Innovation, synergism and versatility are taken as aesthetic virtues in the fostering of security. The suggestion that beautiful things are made with care and a respect for symmetry clearly demonstrates the vital nature of discipline, demeanour, form and steadfastness in the management of issues affecting security at the personal and institutional levels. But then in order to escape from the accusation of perfectionist expectations, we can only insist on a set of directing principles, namely, the higher values that are painful to sustain, but significantly beneficial in the long run as the crux of security.

The Crafting of Security or Security as a Craft

Still on aesthetics, the idea of art that retains the potential for, and actuality of beauty, harmony and the eliciting of satisfaction, is known as craft. The idea of craft is suggestive of skill, expertise or competence. It means that security is the task of skilled people. Security can be more effectively produced by skill or expertise. The idea of skill is itself suggestive not merely of physical prowess demonstrated by a police officer or soldier in maintaining order. This sort of physicalism is no doubt valuable for success in some areas of security. More importantly, aesthetic skill presupposes a more fundamental emphasis on the creativity and innovation emanating from a consolidated power of judgment, the imaginative and visionary employment of the mind as the producer of a new and authentic epistemology on an issue. The value of the aesthetic principle is seen in the view of McLean (2000: 183) who says that we need 'a set of categories, namely those of aesthetic judgment integrating the realms of matter and spirit in a harmony which can be appreciated in terms of human creativity working with the many elements of human life to create human life and meaning which can be lived as an expending and enriching reality'. This intensely phenomenological account of aesthetics offered by McLean is supported by Kieran (1997: 387), who maintains that our engagement with aesthetics facilitates the hope that 'we may learn and develop our cognitive understanding of what human possibilities would or could be like'. The evidence available in Africa suggests that this latter conception of aesthetic skill as imaginative ability is difficult to find and apply, thence the grave security problems that abound on the continent and especially in Nigeria. It is quite clear by now, and confirmed by the investigations of the NWG, that central to the problem of security in Nigeria is the inescapable crisis of values, vision and imagination plaguing the post-colonial states of Africa.

The idea of aesthetic craft or skill that is valuable for security theorising can be divided into two parts, the acquisitive and the productive. The productive craft can be further subdivided into two parts, the production of actual objects by human or divine elements, and the production of images or reflection by human or divine elements. The idea of an image is itself divided into two parts; it is assumed that an image imitates its original but cannot fulfill its function. There is the genuine likeness having the quality of sameness with the original model. There is the second view, which refers to apparent likeness, which has to do with semblance; it merely looks like the original. Therefore, there is false imitation which brings about a deceptive semblance of things.

At the human level, the productive aesthetic craft of actual objects is similar to the point that we made earlier about the design, formulation, creation and construction of a secure building. This idea can be applied to other institutions or structures that require security such as refineries, universities, military bases, and so forth. The issue here is that of design and form on the basis of a combination of environmental factors, mainly geographical, cultural, economic and social-political. At the level of the divine, we can draw an analogy using the rules and forms employed in the creation of the heavens or the transcendental worlds. St Augustine's analysis in his work *The City of God*, is instructive here. He defines Heaven as a place guided by its own specific rules that ensure its survival, beauty and harmony. Its visions and values ensure a satisfaction with the rules, conventions and operations of things therein. The eventual aim of all of these ordinances is to maintain the security of that world. Other researchers of the NWG have undertaken this analysis of transcendentalism.

At the level of the aesthetic craft of the production of images or reflection by human or divine elements, the idea of an image is itself divided into two parts; genuine likeness or sameness as opposed to apparent likeness or semblance, that is, deceptive semblance or false imitation. At the human level, the issue of an image brings to the fore once again the question of imagination and conceptualisation. But then there is the issue of whether it is every idea that can be represented by an image. This question is significant given the communicability or otherwise of ideas and the more difficult point of the translatability or conversion of images. In other cases, there is the more practical question of the role of images in security affairs. We readily recall the use of mannequins, decoys and simulations in the reconciliation of security problems. Ingarden (1961: 290) puts it to us that 'the possibility of purely fictitious objects, which are devised by ourselves ... indicates that we may imagine a ... situation to obtain for people although we know that it has never existed, and also that we have never perceived in our intercourse with real persons'. Thus, there is a strong affinity between aesthetics and security at the level of aesthetic imagery or the use of imitation. Security is, no doubt, a product of the higher levels of creative innovation.

Art, Morality and Security

On the aspect of art, morality and security, we once again fall back on the question of roles, social order and social responsibility. Classical aestheticians such as Plato in *The Republic* insist that the supreme craft is the art of the legislator and educator. His argument regarding the role of the guardian class and the value of education for the security of the ideal state is legendary and unassailable. It then seems that there is a value in the quest for some idea of security that cannot be devoid of the inputs of the educational system and the legislative body. In short, security would come from better enlightenment, training and lawmaking.

There seems little doubt, therefore, that aesthetics and the arts have a role to play in the security of a people. Aesthetics focuses on the cultural life of the people and the education of the citizens as they attempt to strike at the heart of the security problem. This is the role of the human agents and the latent and manifest presuppositions embedded in the ways of life of a people. The concern of the arts and aesthetics is to guarantee the indispensable and proper character formation of humans, to make people better and more virtuous. The emphasis on character and virtue inevitably underscore the need for morality, attitudes and ethical notions that define a secure environment. Simpson (1975: 196) makes the point that 'in the case of moral qualities, evaluations are linked to natural qualities and the conditions for their satisfaction. Moral virtues, presumably, enhance the viability of any free, secular social organization, and participation in such a community involves expectations about the behaviour of one's fellows and appreciation of those qualities of behaviour which facilitate that organization'. In a way, aesthetics seeks to build a conception of social responsibility which makes all concerned groups act in ways that are conducive to the common good. Thus, the quest for the common good and total structural integrity and efficiency of things is the irrefutable province of aesthetics.

Imagination, Taste and the Quest for Security

There is a link between aesthetics and security vis-à-vis imagination and taste. The role of imagination in aesthetic production is unquestionable. In relation to security theorising, it seems that poor imagination will inevitably lead to insecurity. The power to imagine, plan, think ahead and generally to be one step ahead of things is the crux of the ability to ensure personal and social security on an enduring basis. The power of imagination is irretrievably tied to the capacity to rearrange ideas and things in the mind and in reality. Ingarden (1961: 291) makes it clear that 'the reality of an object is not thus necessary for the accomplishment of an aesthetic experience'. Imagination makes sense mainly in the context of taste. The problem of taste is captured by the challenge of the moral sense, reflected in the task of our aesthetic impression or preferences of beauty. According to Simpson, it is through aesthetic appraisal that we can come in contact with "aesthetic qualities" and the "exercise of taste" needed for their identification' (1975: 190). Taste, in our view, therefore has to do with aesthetic preferences, which may depend on the type and context of interest, appreciation and prominence.

Aesthetic preferences can be determined according to era, culture and similar factors, which together insinuate the absence of an objective basis of taste. But this mutable feature of the aesthetic preference, if translated into security reflections, inevitably places a stamp of variability and transformation on the security project. This is evidently an advantage because for security to be guaranteed, some level of innovation, alteration and adaptation is essential. This, then, is the value of aesthetic sensitivity which, as McLean (2000: 73) puts it, is what 'enables one to take into account ever greater dimensions of reality and creativity and to imagine responses which are more rich in purpose, more adapted to present circumstances and more creative in promise for the future'. With regard to security, taste has to do with the combination of expectation and judgment of correctness and incorrectness of things and strategies. Thus, aesthetic tastes or preferences in security define the way people (ordinary and experts) assess the total picture of a security strategy or system using parameters such as the need for it, its effectiveness and the innovative appeal of the design, among others. In short, taste is the concern for harmony, effectiveness and quality standards in security production and provision at all levels.

Déjà Vu, Fiction, Cinematography and Possible Worlds: Alternative Visions and the Re-imagination of Security

Indeed, the new quest for security must come to terms with the reality of alternative conceptual and methodological spaces. The world of fictional entities and fictional depictions is not only a problem of philosophy and literature. It is also a key problem of meaning, logic and ontology. The problem of ontology in philosophy is the search for being and the need to examine things that exist in the world or universe. The problem takes on a new dimension when we realise from the sources of knowledge, reason, authority, revelation, intuition, inference and participation and experience that various things or entities are in this universe. There are abstract, metaphysical, physical, fictional, visible and invisible entities, all of which have definite effects on the lives of men. Fictional entities and fictional activities were before now seen as things that arose from the minds of men through imagination and remained there in the realm of conceptualisation. But today, fictional things have been made physically real by the power and innovation of those who seek to pursue certain ends (terrorists). Fiction has moved from the sense of a production of the human mind to a state of physical reality.

The world of films is the most illustrative of this point. And just before some critics erroneously claim that we should not talk about films here, the point must be made that even foremost philosophers have appealed to the world of literature to buttress their points. Recently, a philosopher and enthusiast of the film realities, Peter French, in the book, *Corporate Ethics* (1995: 317), has shown that films are a crucial symbol of a people's cultural identity, and are necessary to illustrate points about their ways of life. The point must be made that the modern film industry in places such as the USA is the testing ground for the latest and most sophisticated scientific and technological inventions such as cars, computers etc. Hence, these films, even though they are works of the imagination, can provide insights into the real world and offer reliable information. These films and other artistic works stress the value and need for viable alternative theorising that acknowledges the role of epistemological spaces and multi-disciplinary viewpoints. The example of the United States is instructive. The imaginative, aesthetic and ethical imperatives and denominators are articulated individually and collectively in modern films such as *The Terrorists* (1975), *The Enforcer* (1976), *Commando* (1986), *Terror Squad* (1987), *Die Hard* (1988), *Die Hard II* (1990), *Under Siege* (1992), *Sudden Death* (1995), *Hard Justice* (1995), *Executive Decision* (1996), *Riot* (1996), *Air Force One* (1997), and more recent films such as *Con Air* (1997). These works of filmic excellence and a host of unmentioned others have defined the presumably underestimated American film industry as a major beacon of hope in a society plagued by insecurity from terrorism. These films, which are works of the imagination, displayed social and psychological processes that were a quantum leap ahead of the social and military processes of the actual world. The American theatrical and filmic ventures have actually become valuable contributors to the theoretical and practical struggles for security in this modern age.

Similarly, insights into security-related issues have unsurprisingly come from the genre of factual and fiction novelists all around the world. Indeed, some of the details of recent operations of global terrorists have been foretold with uncanny accuracy and precision by extraordinary novelists of the day, such as Douglas Terman, *First Strike* (1978), J. C. Pollock, *Pay Back* (1989), and the numerous works of Tom Clancy. More recently, the American government recognised this fact and drafted the Hollywood Film Corporations into the National Security Programme on anti-terrorism in the wake of the September 11, 2001 terrorist attacks. The immense conceptual capabilities and visualising powers of the filmmaker have become an inestimable asset for US national security.

The imaginative, aesthetic and ethical imperatives of security in a post-colonial society are visibly articulated individually and collectively in modern novels such as the Nigerian Pacesetters series. Stories such as these describe the deep anatomical, cosmological and sociological ramifications of the security problematic ravaging most of our African societies. Such stories include Joseph Mangut, *Have Mercy*; Philip Phil-Ebosie, *The Cyclist*; Kalu Okpi, *The Smugglers* and *On the Road*; Sunday Adebomi, *Symphony of Destruction*; Dickson Ighavini, *Death Is a Woman* and *Blood Bath At Lobster Close*, together with a host of others.

An analysis of a few of the above mentioned novels should suffice here to demonstrate the impact of literature on security theorising. In *Have Mercy*, we have a moving tale of the security-related travails of youth in society, as specifically situated against the background of the social difficulties faced by one young man who passes through all manner of life-threatening experiences in order to finally make peace with himself, with society and his true love. Whereas this story putatively ends well, insofar as some people's lives and sanity are salvaged, the same cannot be said for the protagonists in *The Cyclist*. Situated against the backdrop of the dislocations caused by the civil war and the post-war era, *The Cyclist* is a mind-rending account of how a devious combination of uncertainty, fear, tradition and undying love can become such a broiling experience in a humble and serene rural setting. The pathetic struggle of two unfortunate men over a hapless woman, within the wider context of an acrobatic festival, creates a twist of fate that inevitably leads to pistol shootings, machete fights and for the woman, a blissful relapse into the embrace of perpetual insanity. The losses are total and final.

In *Mark of the Cobra*, the metaphor of spectral danger is immanent and imminent as the male and female members of the secret services, acting to protect society, suffer heavy causalities at the hands of a megalomaniac terrorist and martial arts expert, renowned for his demonic killing powers. The empathetic realisation of the unacceptability of a monomaniacal social capture, coupled with a relentless sequence of grievous mortal dangers to people, comes to a zenith when the hero and heroine simultaneously encounter killer snakes - king cobras, in separate do-or-die fights for their lives. Ultimately, the world is saved from one more villain by a dying naval officer who fights for all that is good in a high-stakes mortal combat during the final battles on a ship.

This brief summary of the thematic concerns negotiated in these works clearly illustrates the almost overwhelming concern for security-related issues in the context of developing African societies.

Furthermore, the point must be made that apart from the fact that alternate disciplinary commitments such as the film enterprise can contribute to security issues, it must also be noted that solutions to the security problem may come from areas hitherto underestimated as external to mainstream security activity. The point, then, in our quest for security has been well made by McLean (2000: 174), who says that 'first there must be an imagination which can bring together the flow of disparate sensations. The imagination must have also a productive dimension which enables the multiple empirical intuitions to achieve some unity'. Thus there may be the rise of such areas as philosophy, anthropology, religion, indigenous knowledge systems, psychology, etc.

The Aesthetic Perspective, Aesthetic Attitude and the Quest for Security

The idea of aesthetics is further tied to the fundamental question of what it means to view something from an aesthetic perspective. What do we mean by the aesthetic attitude? Reid (1926: 201) offers an insight in terms of a question: 'Is there any difference, or ought there to be any difference, between our attitude of mind in what we have called ordinary perception, and our attitude in our perception of beautiful things?' This question is significant insofar as we are in need of determining whether the aesthetic attitude is coterminous with the visions and practices of security. According to Best (1982: 359), the aesthetic attitude implies the aesthetic appreciation of natural phenomena through the understanding of art forms as the central cases.

The aesthetic attitude is often juxtaposed with a series of attitudes such as the practical attitude - which is concerned with the utility of the idea or object in question. Ingarden (1961: 295) holds that 'the aesthetic experience is change of attitude from a practical one, assumed in everyday life'. The practical utility of security is not in doubt, since without it humans cannot attain well-being, peace, survival and progress at the personal and social levels. The cognitive attitude or the concern with the knowledge of that thing is also vital for security. The knowledge of the different stages of security evolution and the reconstruction of the diverse yet interconnected thematic concerns and methodological convergence certify the discussant, practitioner or innovator of security matters as competent.

The aesthetic attitude presupposes that we either review the worth of that thing or that idea for its own sake or for the sake of pleasure. In other words, the aesthetic view of security seems to be all-inclusive and all-embracing, taking cognizance of the holistic vision of the reality in question as well as the contextual functionality of the idea. Thus, central to a viable aesthetic attitude is the commitment to the display of foresight, a sense of posterity and public- spiritedness in handling matters of national planning and policy. Aesthetic security is geared at making 'a contribution to the well-being and preservation of the human community' (Ujomu 2001: 256-258). The importance attached to the notion of security makes it a matter worthy of concern and investigation in its own right. There is thus the concern for the intrinsic and instrumental value of something, which, taken together, will pave the way for a more systematic appreciation of the issues at stake. The entire panoramic view of it, the solid aspects, the nuances, sublimities and connotations are very much in need of analysis. It has also been suggested that the aesthetic attitude requires some level of detachment or disinterestedness to the extent that we know the limits of the realities presented before us.

For example, there is a recognisable difference between a stage performance and the real life occurrence of the same phenomenon. A simulated or staged armed robbery is different from a real armed robbery. For one thing, the emotions displayed and the sequence of events have a closeness or immanence that can have very consequential effects on people both far and near. The simulated scene appears to be an imitation of the real scene, but it is without the dangers and uncertainties that define the human factor or the unknown quality attached to human actions. Thus the aesthetic factor will be novel given the indeterminacy attached to real life events as opposed to that of make-believe. It may well be that the province of the real life events must be the domain of the genuinely aesthetic.

Conclusion

Finally, to derive the best from the social realities before us, the aesthetic state requires a close and complete concentration on the issue or subject of investigation. This suggests that the aesthetic perceiver does not miss any feature of the reality under survey. That means that intense perceptual awareness is needed. The point of emphasising the aesthetic state as an imperative of security is to highlight the role of detail, thoroughness and an integrated approach not only to security as a task or vocation but to the analysis of security as an intellectual enterprise. All of the above issues are clearly the salient elements of the attempt to engage national and human security theorising from an aesthetic perspective.

References

Adelugba, Dapo, 2003, 'Theatre Arts Studies: Old and New Challenges', Inaugural Lecture, 1990, University of Ibadan, Nigeria, on behalf of the Faculty of Arts.

Best, David, 1982, 'The Aesthetic and the Artistic', *Philosophy*, vol. 54, pp. 357-372.

Da Sylva, Ademola, 2003, 'Dapo Adelugba on Theatre Practice in Nigeria', Ibadan: Ibadan Cultural Studies Group.

French, Peter, 1995, *Corporate Ethics*, Florida: Harcourt Brace.

Gill, Jerry H., 1983, 'Philosophy as Art', *Metaphilosophy*, Vol. 14, No. 2, pp. 141-150.

Guyer, Paul, 1977, 'Interest, Nature, and Art: A Problem in Kant's Aesthetic', *Review of Metaphysics*, pp. 580-603.

Ingarden, Roman, 1961, 'Aesthetic Experience and Aesthetic Object', *Philosophy and Phenomenological Research*, vol. XXI, No. 3, pp. 289-313.

Kieran, Matthew, 1997, 'Aesthetic Value: Beauty, Ugliness and Incoherence', *Philosophy*, vol. 72, pp. 383-399.

Kraut, Robert, 1986, 'Feelings in Context', *The Journal of Philosophy*, pp. 642-654.

Kupperman, Joel. J., 1972, 'Aesthetic Value', *American Philosophical Quarterly*, vol. 9, no. 3, pp. 259-264.

Lindroos, Kia, 2003, 'Aesthetic Political Thought: Benjamin and Marker Revisited', *Alternatives*, vol. 28, pp. 233-252.

McLean, George. F., 2000, 'Philosophy and Civil Society: Its Nature, its Past and its Future', in George F. McLean, *Spiritual Values and Social Progress. Uzbekistan Philosophical studies*, Washington, DC, The Council for the Research in Values and Philosophy.

Reddock, Rhoda, 2004, *Reflections on Gender and Democracy in the Anglophone Carribbean: Historical and Contemporary Considerations*, The Netherlands: SEPHIS-CODESRIA.

Reid, Louis Arnaud, 1976, 'Intellectual Analysis and Aesthetic Appreciation', *Journal of Philosophical Studies*, pp. 199-210.

Russell, Bertrand, 1975, *The Conquest of Happiness*, London: George Allen & Unwin.

Russow, Lilly-Marlene, 1978, 'Some Recent Work on Imagination', *American Philosophical Quarterly*, vol. 15, no. 1, pp. 57-66.

Simpson, Evan, 1975, 'Aesthetic Appraisal', *Philosophy*, vol. 50, pp. 189-204.

Scruton, Roger, 1996, 'The Aesthetic Endeavour Today', *Philosophy*, vol. 71, pp. 331-350.

Thayer, H. S., 1976. 'Plato on the Morality of Imagination', *Review of Metaphysics*, vol. 30, pp. 595-618.

Ujomu, P. O., 2001, 'The Transience of Epistemology and the Transcendence of Method: Descartes and the Quest for a Moral High Ground in the History of Philosophy', *Nsukka Journal of the Humanities*, no. 11, pp. 246-263.

4

Rethinking Traditional Security in Africa: The Reconstruction of the Cosmological Foundations of Security

Dapo Adelugba, Philip Ogo Ujomu
and Felix Amanor-Boadu

Beyond Traditionalism and Mysticism: Recreating an Idea of Security from an African Past

The problems of national security in this modern era can be seen mainly in the inability of the various governments and the state agencies consistently and institutionally to guarantee the adequate protection, peace and well-being of their citizens. The weaknesses of existing strategies for overcoming this problem may have limited the potential of the post-colonial state for institutional efficiency. This situation necessitates an interrogation of the traditional and historical trajectories of the security problematic as viable epistemological conditions for national integration and human reconciliation. A survey of the history of the discourse will show the perennial tracks of security activities and designs. We can agree with Latham who says that 'security is an object of every group organization if security is understood only in its elemental sense of the survival of the group itself in order to carry forward its mission' (Latham 1956: 236). But what then happens when security is construed in a wider sense that embraces cosmology, progress and so on? The need to broaden the interpretative capacity of thematic concerns and methodological convergence in security theorising is also appreciated by Nielsen who has rightly put it that we must be interested not in mere survival but also the quality or character of that survival (Nielsen 1973: 24). This study, which is a part of the wider research on the humanities as a contributor to national security, is necessary in view of the hitherto restrictive analysis of the nature of national security and the unexplored character of the critical, conceptual and empirical interface between the ethical and aesthetic dimensions as key contributors to national survival and integration. The idea of security in Africa can be reviewed in terms of the ontology, cosmogony and especially, the cosmology of the people.

In Africa, the interest in security and development arises out of the reality of crisis due to the pervasive presence and influence of a historic culture affected by a foreign and dominating tradition or culture. To start with, tradition is the matter that is handed down and transmitted from one generation to the next generation. According to Goulet (1987: 167), 'the term tradition suggests teaching and habits dating back to a distant past. But in order to survive traditions must prove themselves useful to each new generation'. Through a tradition, I can retain an identity in the life and actions of my space and community and thus adopt a life plan at the personal and social levels. Practices have histories. Any structure or institution that bears tradition is constituted by a continuous argument as to what that thing is as opposed to what it ought to be.

The abandonment of a tradition can arise from two factors: internal criticism or external inducement. What aspect of African tradition constructed as knowledge is suitable for survival and security? In Africa, the interest in security and its development arises out of the reality of crisis in the social and cultural environment. Nwala (1985: 27-30) holds that 'in traditional society the universe is basically structured into two main inter-related parts, there are two realms of existence the spiritual world or supernatural order, the human world or visible order'. This implies that the African conception of security is operational at two levels, the temporal and the transcendental realms.

On the nexus between the transcendent and the temporal in the African idea of the cosmos, Ejizu (1987: 6) holds that 'traditional cosmology postulates a fundamental moral vision as it charts the place of man in the universe. Man depends on the spiritual beings for his life, his welfare. Man's moral behaviour and cordial relationship with the spirits and fellow humans are crucial in the maintenance of order in the universe'. To maintain the cosmic order and harmony of forces in the universe and thence the security of the categories of existence, the African man must keep and abide by the culture of his people. Thus, there is an interface between culture and security. According to Ezekwugo (1991: 4-5) 'culture is defined as a type of civilisation which a people have practised over time. *Omenana* refers to the culture of a people. Thus *omenana* is an instrument for attaining a balance of the spiritual and material forces'.

The Principles of Offensive and Defensive Security

African security has been a matter of both offensive and defensive security. War was the chief means of guaranteeing security and indeed procuring vast human and material goods on a rapid and cheap basis. The internecine and devastating nature of these inter-communal wars in Africa also paved the way for entire societies to devise defensive strategies where offensive action had failed. Consequently, many peoples or communities resorted to using either alliances or the natural forces of nature for self-preservation. Thus many tribes employed indigenous security strategies such as living in valleys, on mountains, on islands and other inaccessible geo-territories or regions. Also tribes sought to place formidable fortifications or obstacles such as gorges, waterfalls, canyons, mountains, rocks, rivers, etc., between themselves and their aggressors.

Physicalism in African Traditional Security of the Northern and Southern Kingdoms

Reports on the past of Africa and the idea of security show that security was seen mainly as the effectiveness, perseverance and projection of the power and wealth of the emperor or monarch, his chiefs and his society. Large cities were annexed or constructed. Leaders developed large institutional armies by themselves or went into military alliances for mutual defence. The reality of the northern kingdoms that cherished the visions and values of the warrior kingship and monarchical sovereignty ensured that security would be construed in essentially physical terms, in order to tally with their geo-location on large expanses of land – desert and savanna. According to Osae and Nwabara (1968: 14), 'in the general state of defencelessness created largely by the open nature of the land, kingdoms rose and fell, often quite quickly'. Thus in the northern kingdoms, wealth, food, protection and comfort depended on the principles of mutual pacification and the annihilation of the warring tribes. With special reference to ancient Egypt, Davidson (1991: 157) writes that 'in Pharaonic history, mighty rulers over the Egyptian empire made themselves into gods'. This style was designed to consolidate spiritual and temporal authority. According to Greaves, Zaller, Cannistraro and Murphey (1997: 24), 'a strong pharaoh was both the symbol of and the principal reason for national unity; some of Egypt's earliest pharaohs had pyramids constructed to serve as their tombs and as sites of worship and devotion'. The character and operations of the fundamental principle of security as embodied in the northern kingdoms has been effectively captured by Fagan (1998: 406) who states that 'at the centre of the state lay the concept of a great king, a terrestrial ruler, who symbolized the triumph of order over universal chaos'. This image is representative of an almost omniscient being retaining the powers to make literally all things possible, the power of life and death, the Leviathan.

On the other hand, in the case of the southern kingdoms their aura of self-sufficiency occasioned by their relative geo-cultural isolation and existence in the economically productive hinterlands of the coast ensured reasonable and relative internal security, internal stability and comfort. These kingdoms existed in 'a belt of tropical rain forest. The principal example was Benin. By about 1700 the *oba* (king) was no longer a warrior-king but a spiritual leader who typically remained secluded in his palace and left government to the chiefs. When the Portuguese first saw Benin in 1485, the capital Benin city was a walled town 25 miles in circumference' (Greaves, Zaller, Cannistraro and Murphey 1997a: 554). The clear commitment of the southern kingdoms to the principle of ceremonial kingship, their relative wealth at least in natural and mineral resources, came together to define an alternative vision for the southern societies. Also, their isolation ensured some level of difficulty in terms of access to these city-states of sub-Saharan Africa. The overall effect was to diminish the threats to these societies. But it is not clear whether they were therefore less vulnerable. The fact is that the immanent reality of dense jungles, diseases, and dangerous creatures all served to provide security for the peoples of the southern kingdoms of Africa and to make them vulnerable to these dangers.

Security in the traditional African sense was therefore defined according to the principles of internal social actions using the rules of religion, divination, cults and age grades and so on. The special connection between African religion and African security can be seen more clearly in the view of some scholars. For example, according to Davidson (1977: 297-298), religion 'was far more than a mere comfort in these traditional structures, based as they were on ancestral charters fashioned by the imperatives of daily life, and fastened by a corresponding moral order. When the priest interpreted the message he gave to the king, however picturesque and peculiar his methods may be, the effective task of this priest was to safeguard community welfare and survival. Seen in this way, "religion" stands for an apprehension of reality across the whole field of life. Out of it there emerged what may reasonably be called a science of social control'.

In some other cases, there were cultural organs of security such as the cult of warriors, the youth and age grade formations, joint community action, the cult of masquerades, etc. Let us note that in the past the cult of masquerades was an instrument of both temporal and supernatural justice. It was capable of enforcing sanctions. We recall the operations of the masquerades that destroyed Okonkwo's kindred and banished him to exile in that eternally memorable work of literature, *Things Fall Apart* by Chinua Achebe. The power of the masquerade depended on the cult of secrecy, unyielding militancy and the generation of fear. According to Aremu (1995: 7-9), the '*egungun* cult was very important in the life of the Yoruba people. The coming of the *egungun* masquerade is capable of removing any evil that lingers around the various communities. The spiritual powers inherent in *egungun* and other deities are approached according to the needs of an individual. *Egungun* is usually used for social control'. In that period, the ability of a society to enjoy security depended on the degree to which it was able to execute the incapacitation and annexation of potential threats or enemies.

The Dualism of Magical Realism and Mysticism in African Traditional Security

At another important level, security in the traditional African context was highly dependent on magical and supernatural support. The heavy dependence on mysticism and metaphysicalism was seen in the strong belief in magical powers and forces. These supernaturalistic beliefs are still held by many Africans in the modern day.

Many reports have been given about outlandish forms of life and action in the quest for security in traditional Africa. There have been claims of individuals and even entire families or tribes possessing powers that made them immune to a wide range of entities or forces in nature. Some people are said to have powers or capabilities that protect them from the activities of dangerous creatures - snakes, lions, spiders, wasps, bees, scorpions, mosquitoes, etc. Others are said to have powers that allow them to use these dangerous animals as vectors to protect themselves or harm their aggressors. There are reports in some places that certain herbs, ingredients and incantations are capable of incapacitating this class of entities. There are reports in other places that some individuals are immune to knife cuts, gunshots, and other forms of physical attack from men or animals. Some reports talk about the capacity of humans to evade capture or harm by disappearing from sight and confounding their assailants. There have been reports of native hunters possessing an extraordinary capacity to use incantations to attain greater human strength or speed, project harmful substances, stem blood flow, unlock fetters or traps, expel foreign bodies such as bullets and mend broken limbs. In relation to the task of security, Olaoba (1997: 26) adds that supernatural means that are beyond human comprehension can be employed in disputes and defence. These are 'the magical display of power, inflicting harm through charms, death resulting from witchcraft and sorcery, sending thunder to kill people, and putting bad medicine in public places which might result in the wide spread of plagues and epidemic in society'. Mbiti (1969: 197-198) reinforces this idea by insisting that 'there is mystical power which causes people to walk on fire, lie on thorns or nails, send curses or harm, to spit on snakes and cause them to die'. Also covenants were another means of guaranteeing security in the African traditional society. According to Abogunrin (1996: 3), a 'covenant is a solemn agreement made binding by rituals and oaths. Covenant is known as *imule*. Covenants are major means of maintaining cohesion, peace and political stability, not only within the societies, but also with their neighbours'.

There were of course other processes and powers that could be used to assure personal and social security in traditional Africa. According to Olomola (1991: 50-51), '*alile* is a common terminology for the traditional security system consisting of semiotic tags and charms used for the protection of places or things by owners or other vested interests. These charms are believed to possess certain magical powers capable of causing misfortune and disaster to intruders'. However, not all the powers or charms were used for harming or deterring physical or supernatural evil. Some of the magical powers could be put to positive use. As Olomola (1991: 50-51) writes, we have '*awure*, an amulet or a potion credited with power to bring good fortune. *Awure* is self applied for personal good luck in business and other transactions'. Thus security in the African traditional sense could be seen from a positive view and a negative view. The powers harnessed and unleashed by agencies of proactive security were instruments for further enhancing one's chances for personal and social preservation and well-being. In essence, it was a means of fortifying the potential prospects and actual gains attained in human life. The powers embedded in the instrument of negative security were significantly prohibitive and obstructive. They were meant to reclaim security and justice where these had been vitiated or to prevent their loss in the first instance.

Prophetic Powers in African Traditional Security

In the African life worlds, people employed certain futuristic or spiritual extrapolation as means of attaining security. Hence, there was a strong tendency towards consulting oracles, soothsayers, diviners, etc. One major security strategy of the African worlds was the idea of preemptive security through the use of extraordinary powers of divination to see and alter the future, to repel attacks, human or spiritual, from affecting the two levels of the operations of the African consciousness - physical and supernatural. According to Mbiti (1969: 198), 'there is power that enables experts to see into secrets, hidden information or the future, or to detect thieves and other culprits'. On the role of prophecy as a security device, Olaoba (1997: 27) informs us that 'consultation with *ifa* oracle is considered one of the significant means of reaching the unknown realm. *Ifa* is the god of wisdom who has the ability of discernment and fortune-telling'. Also, in the African life worlds, people employed the services of gods and deities to ensure their personal and social security. The appeal to supernatural forces was one of the key ways of achieving security. According to Olaoba (1997: 30), the action of *Yemowo*, a deity against evildoers or wicked people, is akin to that of the goddess of *Aiyelala*. The victims of the goddess were wicked people who usually concealed their acts of wickedness from human beings.

Critique of the Strategies of Traditional Security

According to theoreticians on the African traditional worlds and experiences, there are certain distinctive features of African life. We need to know what these are, before going on to clarify their effects on the security problematic. Oladipo (1996: 47) in his analysis of a foremost African philosopher - Kwasi Wiredu - points out that 'a limitation of traditional culture which Wiredu is unsparing in pointing out is its authoritarian orientation manifested in the unquestioning obedience by people to the authorities of elders. Because traditional society was essentially communitarian not much room could be made for deviant ideas or social practices. Little premium was placed on intellectual qualities such as curiosity or independence of thought'. This is how the issues of authoritarianism and anachronism arise. Moreover, the idea of supernaturalism is tied to what Sogolo (1993: 57) refers to as 'the recognition on the part of man of some higher unseen power as having control over his destiny'. Such a disposition to life reinforces the critical belief that the security of the person and society emanates from both the transcendental and the temporal realms of life.

It is therefore clear that the concept and context of cultural particularities and the possibility of insecurity arising out of them, are important issues for national and human security construed as individual or collective survival or well-being and progress (Ujomu 2001: 176). More specifically, African traditionalism in relation to security is defeated by supernaturalism or the belief in non-physical causes of physical things, which paves the way for primary and secondary causality to subsist. The problem is that supernaturalism ensured a kind of transcendentalism that in turn occasioned an esotericism. Taken together, these features ensured the dangerous closure of the epistemic and moral spaces to free enquiry and the dissemination of knowledge. Knowledge seemed to be a hidden affair, to be dispensed as a favour or to be used as an instrument of oppression of opponents and rivals. Let us recall the magical and political processes used for identifying witches and wizards as put to us in the popular adventure novel *King Solomon's Mines*. Some of the activities enumerated in that story were also significantly true of other African societies.

Supernaturalism, esotericism and the closure and lack of control that went with them were significantly tied to the issue of a monopoly of knowledge. The outcome of the monopoly of certain knowledge on security inadvertently paved the way for authoritarianism or the high-handedness associated with unregulated power and exclusivist control of knowledge. As Dewey (1977: 153) has rightly noted, 'absence of arts of regulation diverted the search for security into irrelevant modes of practices'. Specifically, authoritarianism in the context of cultural security had other far-reaching repercussions. Mainly, it paved the way for the loss of human and moral support in relation to the quest for security. It also paved the way for the closure of outlets of information and the eventual consequence of betrayal and alienation of the retainer of knowledge. With authoritarianism in place, it was difficult to seek alternatives or to purify existing options in knowledge, life and security. The authoritarian entrenchment of dogmatism, patrimonialism and hegemony paved the way for the demise of creativity, ability, vision and wider participation of persons in the security strategy of African traditionalism.

Thus the efficacy of traditionalist security seemed to rely on the covert character of the specific capability. Another reason for this secrecy could have been the need to avoid the neutralisation of a potent power or its duplication. Magical instruments of security were seen as things to be protected, given the truism that whatever has a defined principle of operation can be effectively nullified. Thus security strategies in traditional Africa were designed to work in combination to ensure better potency and effectiveness. Or the security strategy would be designed alongside its neutraliser or antidote. The use of antidotes was common in African traditional security: to maintain continual control over the power or instrument; to be able to abolish the power when necessary; or secretly to counteract any hostile powers that may have been unleashed with or without one's knowledge. This esotericism in the metaphysical control of security could lead to a lack of public comprehension and control as well as the reality of the loss of knowledge in the event of the demise of the sole bearer of knowledge. This situation is not unconnected with the fact of oral traditions which made sure that crucial *episteme* or knowledge was passed on from generation to generation by word of mouth. The essentially unwritten character of these traditionalist accounts of life and security culminated in a gradual loss of core capabilities.

The vertical movement of power and knowledge brings about a restriction in the social framework of ideas and methods. Authoritarianism did not permit a horizontal or spectral dispersal of ideas and power. This combination of authoritarianism and supernaturalism led to anachronism and the lack of openness to new and better ways of doing things. Anachronism made sure that the wrong things were done almost persistently. The same old customary methods were considered as divine, and a cult of followers arose who were expected to render unquestioning obedience. For now, let us note that the context of the failure of the traditional and modern approaches to security have compelled this analysis. It has brought to the fore the chance of a unique intellectual contribution to security theorising as a way out of the crisis of human development and security in African worlds.

The Methodological Transience and Thematic Proclivities in the Stages of Security in Human Evolution

Naturalism in Security Theorising

From early times, humans have been interested in security matters simply because 'human beings, obviously, cannot exist without having certain of their needs met' (Bell 1994: 19). The failure of institutionalised security strategies has paved the way for an alternative theorising on the security problematic. This work is a quest for a traditional and ethical view of security understood as the need for a new basis of human social life and a new set of strategies that can ensure emancipation and transformation. Thus, it is true that there can be no security in traditions that have failed us intellectually, culturally or historically. There can be no security if there is a closure of spaces - conceptual or theoretical.

From the earliest ages, the challenge of security was highlighted via the 'survival interaction between human beings and their surroundings, when they began to develop techniques to cope with the harsh realities of nature' (Perlman 1995: 25). Early humans were interested in security to the extent that they needed to migrate and navigate in search of food, shelter and protection. At this stage man sought protection from the vagaries of nature. Mackenzie (1963: 35) observes that 'the dangers that have to be guarded against are sometimes heat, sometimes cold, sometimes drought, sometimes flood, sometimes wild beasts or other men'. The interest in security and development arises out of the reality of crisis in these areas. Thus many communities resorted to using the natural forces of nature for self-preservation. Later on with the increase in human population, man sought protection from his fellow men as individuals. At a later time, people would seek protection within the context of human organisation. Thus at the heart of the human struggle for security is the attempt to confront nature or the natural environment, human nature and human action and human social organisations.

The vision of naturalism in security arose out of human self-consciousness, and the needs and the obstacles to the realisation of a secure existence. The evasion of the natural forces, the association with other humans were all an attempt to live out the primordial instincts of security. The point must be made that security, as an adaptation to the natural environment, was not altogether sustainable. Security faced the problems of the gross uncertainty, lack of control and predictability that attended the availability, suitability and conduciveness of natural security features. There was also the problem of human adaptation, efficacy and systematisation of the use of the natural phenomena. These factors taken together meant that humans were not in control of certain natural defensive strategies. The protection of one's interests and the guarantee of well-being essentially implied that threats to the survival and sustenance of a person or group would be mitigated only if one took deliberate steps to safeguard cherished materials. The name for this is self-preservation.

There comes a point at which the historical analysis of security can snowball into the quest for aesthetic foundations derived from intervening imperatives. It is clear that the aesthetic dimensions of human security in the early stages of human life were inevitably tied to the challenge of thinking in a systematic and holistic manner. This style implied a sense of taste or preference that could make the choice of natural features valuable either for survival or comfort. This seems the inevitable beginning of the interconnection between the aesthetic and security in human life.

Humanism in Security Theorising

Even though it is true that 'some human needs such as those for love, and communication can only be satisfied fully by interaction with other humans' (Bell
1994: 19), the mere fact of the increase in human population, and the competition arising from it, caused men to become a source of insecurity to one another.
Thus man sought protection from his fellow men, who in turn had become
threats owing to the difficulties of living together in an environment where resources were scarce, civic values were not developed, and laws were not clearly
defined and enforced. Under these condition of life, men seen as either individuals or groups were in need of protection from other men. The immediate confrontation between men in their quest for the understanding of the self and
other, as well as their implications for the material and psychological dimensions
of life, directed the attention of men towards the establishment of some sort of
rule-following system. At a later time, human beings sight protection within the
type of human organisation called society. At the heart of societal security was its
character as a rule-following system or law-based order that depended on the
clarification and allocation of rights, duties and other attributes of human social
life. Society itself would also trigger its own forms of insecurity.

The condition of insecurity arising from the vagaries of human activity was
aggravated by the increasing scarcity of natural resources and the means of har-
nessing them. According to Mackenzie (1963: 36-37), 'we may regard competition and strife as connected with impulses that help to give rise to mutual aid and
rivalry' at this stage of human development. Beyond the question of materialism,
there was also the issue of psychological states and security. Men needed security
from other men as a result of psychological states such as hate, greed, envy, pride,
wickedness and other problems related to the context of morality.

Humans had become creators of tools, systems and ideas related to aesthetically guided security. Much of the challenge of aesthetic security would be defined at the level of the creativity and imagination of men as well as the carry-
over into the realm of technology. This humanistic form of aesthetics and security
operated at two different levels corresponding to the divergent needs of men in
either the state of nature or the state of society. In the state of nature, such
aesthetic security concerns were mainly physical and personal, but in the state of
society the aesthetic security concerns were predominantly institutional and policy-
based. The contexts of human security, therefore, varied according to the differing conditions of human existence.

Humanism in security became dominant given the increase in human population. Such expansions in the physical numbers and potential for innovative acts
(good or bad) compelled a redefinition of human interrelations. The confrontation between men in their quest for the understanding of the self and others, as

well as the implications for the material and psychological dimensions of life directed the attention of men towards the establishment of some sort of rule-following system in society.

Militarism or Realism in Security Theorising

Natural security paved the way for militarism or militaristic security. The increase in human populations and the generally lower levels of awareness of the rules of wider cosmopolitan habitations heightened the spate of wars and conflict. This age ushered in the trajectory of militarism; which depended on the 'active use of military force for political purposes and in defence of national interests' (Blau and Goure 1984: 13). All through human history, it has been shown that mere militaristic powers will never be enough as a long-term guarantee of security. Vulnerabilities, threats or actual attacks to undermine security will never be stopped by the traditionalistic (realist) or wider liberal accounts of security. The reality of the shortfall of the realist or militaristic approach has been glaring for many states all over the world.

No amount of military power, intelligence-gathering ability or even economic strength will be sufficient by themselves to maintain security where basic ideas such as appropriate imagination, the will to action and ethical character are lacking. Militaristic security therefore smacked of a rigid deterministic motion towards an arms race, which could only be overcome by a greater amassing of weapons. The logic of militarism can be seen as a faulty one, with its dependence on force and the illusion of power that has consistently heralded the defeat of great civilisations. Realism as a theory of security suffered a two-pronged defeat: first, the problem of the ascendancy of a greater military power over another led to spiralling conflict, arms races, genocidal violence and eventually the mutual decline or expiration of the combatants. This is what we mean by a security dilemma, a process by which 'states are permanently arming themselves in order to protect their borders. Through this, the unintended consequence of pursuing such a policy is to create a feeling of insecurity among one's neighbours. Thus, one state's effort to ensure its own security becomes a source of insecurity for other states' (Messari 2002: 416-417).

The tracks of aesthetic militarism were seen clearly in the rigidity and haughtiness that heralded that peculiar vision and form or stage of security theorising. The features of militarist aestheticism were defined by the concern for order, efficiency, utility and power. These were the aesthetic preferences that defined this version of aesthetic security. It may well be that aesthetic militarism was the perfection of the institutional or societal form of aesthetic humanism. The resounding defeat of militarism paved the way for the emergence of liberalism as a core position in security theorising.

Liberalism in Security Theorising

The appeal and strength of the liberal approach has been based on two pillars: firstly, widening the scope of issues that can be discussed under the umbrella of security. These issues have been expanded to include gender, environment, social, medical and allied ideas. Secondly and more importantly, liberalism repudiated the military technocratic elitism, methodological isolationism and epistemological ethnocentrism of previous security doctrine. We can clarify the liberal view by noting the statement of Prewitt (1985: 12) that 'the term security requires substantial conceptual expansion. It does mean extending and broadening the term beyond its present base'. Aesthetic liberalism was founded on a belief in the lack of a monopoly of knowledge or control by any one man or group due to both natural (human, physical) and unnatural (providential, supernatural) forces. This belief naturally led to the implication that there were competing spaces of multifarious identities and attention in security matters. The aesthetic concern for preferences would therefore be best played out in liberal aesthetic security.

But there were problems with the liberal approach. Essentially, this liberal approach was not sufficiently articulate in its visions. There were existential, ethical and phenomenological shortfalls leading to the inability theoretically to overcome the finitude problem that affects human investigations. The questions of culture, history and social conventions were vital, rightly so, for the clarification of liberal thinking regarding security. There were also shortfalls in the conceptual realms of liberal security theorising. Some of the domains classified under the security problematic were often in themselves contested areas or ambiguous ideas, which, in turn, depended on another set of concepts for their clarification. Hence, liberalism paved the way for a wider and more autonomous conceptual approach to security theorising. The critical problem of articulating and confronting the diversities in the historical, cultural and social specificities of the security problematic ensured that the problem of security at one time and place would not be the same at others.

Conceptualism in Security Theorising

These problems taken together ensured a general inadequacy of conceptualisation and theoretical and practical applications. In effect, both realism and liberalism failed to place a premium on the specific analysis of the core ideas of imagination, vision, values and action that were central to security. The clear deficits in the earlier approaches paved the way for the emergence of a conceptual and philosophical account of security. Incidentally, this conceptual approach to security is undoubtedly the province of the philosopher, who has the double advantage of a long and clear line of historical thought as well as the unique tool of conceptual and phenomenological analysis.

The History of Security and the Security of History

The idea of security is better understood by an analysis of the history of core theoretical and philosophical thinking on this idea. Valuable insights on security can be discerned from the core contributions of a few classical theorists, notably certain leading philosophers.

Plato: An Ancient Theoretician on Security

The ancient classical view of security is aptly portrayed in the ideas of Plato. This thinker approached the idea of security by insisting on the vital roles of justice, harmonisation, division of labour and education as critical drivers. According to Plato, 'justice is doing one's own business. Justice is having and doing what is one's own or what belongs to one' (Plato 1963: 18). The state is organised on the basis of justice 'when the trader, the auxiliary and the guardians each do their own business' (Plato 1963: 19). A state is seen as just when 'the three classes (namely, the guardians, auxiliaries and artisans) in the state perform their specific functions' (Plato 1963: 20).

For Plato, central to security were the ideas of efficiency and effectiveness. There is security when the principle of justice is understood, upheld and made operational. For Plato, the idea of justice is an imperative of security since it is vital that each man should do his own job or fulfil his own function properly. By this means, Plato felt that the security of individuals and society could be guaranteed via the effective and efficient practice of specified social roles, obligations and expectations. Thus, he divided the society into the guardians or rulers, the auxiliaries or soldiers, and the artisans or workers. Furthermore, he insisted on the power and development of security through education. The education of the rulers, soldiers and technicians was crucial if security was to be sustained. With education, the people could live the virtuous life capable of ensuring peace and protection of lives and property. By this emphasis on education, Plato drew attention to the problems of human, social and national security that could arise from a shortfall in education, leadership and the vitiation of rules.

What can we learn from the ideas of Plato? Plato, in giving emphasis to the idea of justice as a kind of efficiency or division of labour clearly suggests that each individual or group ought to do that thing which has been assigned to him or her properly or which is best suited for her to do. He therefore suggested that one can be effective either by dint of natural talent or hard work or by the proper assignment of roles and responsibilities. This point is more relevant in the light of Plato's insistence that people and structures fulfil their set objectives.

The ability to fulfil role expectations depends on the character of individuals. It suggests the idea of representation and responsibility. The social order takes on the form of a collection of people with responsibilities for work within various organisational hierarchies. In this way there is an emphasis on greater participation of more competent personalities. Thus we see the value of Platonic analysis. The need for the kind of integrated action suggested by Plato arises, firstly because it has been shown that no man has a monopoly of knowledge. This point demonstrates that the smooth functioning of any system depends on the division of labour, the sharing of knowledge or ideas, as well as the integration of social roles. Although Plato implies a rigidity in the structure of the society in which each individual or group is fixed in a social class, we must now move beyond his position to recommend the possibility of social status enhancement or mobility so that each man or group can attain the fullest development.

Plato's idea of security did not create the opportunity for vertical growth and social mobility among the segments of the society. Plato had insisted on a totalitarian and rigidly configured society that would operate almost in a mechanical manner, with immutable configurations of social classes. This idea was contrary to the human ability to exercise choice as characteristic features of human nature and human endeavour. The class conscious and deterministic nature of Platonic society could not be sustained on any enduring basis because it created internal and external conflict, both psychological and social. This society would not be fully secure, because of its inclination to undermine the natural human tendency to increase in stature. The society would not be secure because it brought about the alienation of women, children and other marginal groups. The failure of Platonic theorising on security compelled the emergence of other theoreticians on security.

Aristotle: An Ancient Theoretician on Security

The failure of Platonic theorising on security led to the emergence of Aristotle who insisted that security emanates from defining a conception of the good. For Aristotle, the community is the highest form of the good, because it is the height of human political affiliation. As he argued, every state is a community of some kind and every community is established with a view to some good, because man always concludes that 'if all communities aim at some good, then the state or political community as the highest form of community aims at the good in a greater degree than any other' (Aristotle 1963: 59).

Aristotle traces the formation of the state from the family to the village and finally the state. For the state to come about, there should exist a union of male and female as beings that could not exist without each other. From the union of male and female, the family emerges. Where there are many families, we have a village as a colony of families. And when we have many villages that are united into a single complete community large enough to be self-sufficient, then the state comes into being. Aristotle further claimed that the state emerges out of efforts to satisfy the basic needs of life and it grows with a view to assuring the good life. Given the fact that the earlier forms of society are natural, Aristotle says that 'the state is also natural because it is the end or goal of these earlier forms. The state is therefore a creation of nature' (Aristotle 1963: 62). For Aristotle, 'man is by nature a political animal and he is able to separate good from evil, just acts from unjust acts' (Aristotle 1963: 62). This ability is seen in human beings that live in the family and state. And so we note that it is within the ambits of life in the family and state that questions about justice and morality arise.

The society is the highest good comprising the aggregation of the gifts and abilities of a totality of people who seek the goal of self-sufficiency. Security is to be seen in the ability of individuals or groups to be self-sufficient. For Aristotle, security would come only from an idea of justice that depended on the establishment of a legal order. This security required the clarification of the idea of citizenship and the role of the citizen in the promotion of security and social life. Aristotle was clear about the constituents of security and he insisted on the need for basic social goods such as opportunities, work, law and order, an army, religion, leadership, self-sufficiency through the retention of material goods, careful application of reason, all of which would pave the way for happiness as the highest good. In effect, the ideas of Aristotle were a systematic and more carefully thought-out advance on the views of Plato.

St Augustine: A Christian Theoretician on Security

The totalitarianism associated with the views of the classical writers on security did not accord well with early Christian philosophers. Their outlook was an otherworldly philosophy of life and took the view that human problems could never be resolved without a grasp of the order of things in the supernatural world. According to Saint Augustine, the security dilemma can be understood by linking the visions and values of the supernatural world with those of the physical world. To this effect, Augustine postulated the distinction between the city of God and the city of man. These two cities are ruled by differing principles and visions. Augustine insisted that humans could only enjoy security if the city of man was willing to affirm and abide by the rule of love existing in the city of God. The rule of security as given by divine ordinance is peace. Only the quest for peace can bring about security. According to Augustine (1990: 9), 'the basic difference between the two cities is what they are committed to. The two cities have two distinct commitments'. Augustine argues that in the city of man or 'the city of evil, men live according to the flesh, while in the city of God men live according to the spirit. To live according to the flesh means to live according to human nature, to sin. The works of the flesh or the human nature in man are immorality, idolatry, enmities, contentions, jealousies, anger, quarrels, factions' (Augustine 1990: 294-296). In the city of God, Augustine (1990: 328, 451) says that 'there is eternal, supreme and untroubled peace. The city of God represents the vision of peace'.

Thus, the quest for peace naturally compels a repudiation of the negative and lower values that had ruled the city of men. For Augustine, security can only be attained through morality, justice, kindness, truth and humility. He noted that the city of men suffers insecurity due to the prevalence of hate, pride, falsity and wickedness. The city of men is the city of evil and darkness, ruled by envy, perversion, deceit and vanity. Its inhabitants remain insecure because they live according to the flesh. The way of the flesh, according to Augustine, is the celebration of condemnation, hate, corruption, immorality, idolatry, enmities, contention, and factionalism. The flesh repudiates, and is alienated from security because it suffers from imperfection and refuses to abide by truth and the divine light.

Hobbes: A Modern Theoretician on Security

Supernaturalism and the interfacing of metaphysicalism and temporalism in the quest for security were alien to thinkers at the dawn of the modern era. Modernity led to the emergence of theoreticians such as Thomas Hobbes, for whom the security factor was of paramount concern. So much so that 'in Hobbes's view, the main object of any form of political association was to obtain security' (Ayer 1969: 250). Hobbes postulated the idea of the Leviathan or the Artificial Man. The Leviathan retains immense and illimitable powers over men and materials and is thus capable of guaranteeing security. Hobbes made it clear that the security offered by the Leviathan became imperative due to the danger and insecurity of life and possessions in the state of nature.

Hobbes argued that the state of nature is a state of war. It is the state of violence and anarchy of every one against the other. This condition of life is typified by the inability to guarantee survival and peace for any reasonable length of time. Tired of the anarchy of the state of nature, people would agree to the formation of a society, or commonwealth, as Hobbes termed it. Each person would surrender their autonomy and agree to obey the great Leviathan, the sovereign state, created to protect and defend the natural man. Obedience to a mutually acceptable sovereign, argued Hobbes, was the only way to overcome the nasty, brutish and short life encountered in the state of nature. Hence people accept the sovereignty of the Leviathan, the 'artificial soul which gives life and animation to the whole body' (Hobbes 1963: 139). The Leviathan is the sovereign who has the power to punish or reward.

Hobbes traces the emergence of the Leviathan to the nature of man and the conditions of the state of nature. Despite the fact that there are differences in the way men are endowed, no one could be certain that a faculty such as physical strength was sufficient to ensure the individual's security. Others, more cunning, posed an ever-present danger. In the state of nature, each man pursues his own self-interest without the restraint of a constituted authority, giving rise to constant disputes and conflict. Hobbes contended that the state of nature is a condition of mutual destruction in which no man can be sure of emerging victorious or sub-sisting for a reasonable length of time (Hobbes 1963: 142). Furthermore, in the state of nature, as really a state of war, where every man is every man's enemy and the security and protection of life and property is not assured, there is no industry or fruitful labour. Worst of all, there is a continual fear and danger of violent death. In short, the life of man 'is solitary, poor, nasty, brutish and short' (Hobbes 1963: 143). Against the background of the absence of a common power, there can be no law, notions of justice and of right and wrong. Hobbes argues the passions and the reason of man lead to a search for peace by willing submis-sion to a common sovereign.

According to Hobbes, the right of nature is the liberty that all men have to use their powers to preserve their lives, while the law of nature is a general rule derived from reason, which forbids a man to destroy his life or the means of preserving his life. For Hobbes, the first and basic law of nature is to seek peace, while the second laws of nature enjoins a man readily to give up his right to self-defence if others show a willingness to do likewise. He notes that a man gives up his right to self-preservation either by renouncing or transferring it. A right is renounced when one does not care to whom the benefit goes, while a right is transferred when one intends that the benefits go to some specified persons. Hobbes maintains that the renunciation of rights is brought about through agree-ment - a social contract - binding on all participants. For Hobbes, contract is the name given to the mutual transfer of rights among men. It is the basis of the commonwealth, which exists in order to ensure that order is preserved. The protection of life and property is guaranteed in the commonwealth only when men erect a common power on which they confer all their powers and strengths. Hobbes argues that 'his common power can be one man or an assembly of men'(Hobbes 1963: 148).

The commonwealth, according to Hobbes, is the only source of security both from human nature, natural forces and other material creations of men. The commonwealth is the aggregation of an institutional arrangement of a mul-titude that has covenanted through the social contract to form and live in a soci-ety in order to assure themselves of mutual defence, peace, progress and protec-tion from internal and external dangers. The power of the sovereign, conceived as either the ruler or the society, is central to attaining security.

The appealing, systematic and well-articulated security theory of Hobbes suf-fered from certain internal contradictions that paved the way for the emergence of other views. The theory of Hobbes effectively marshalled the principles for the guarantee of security from external danger, artificial or natural. But Hobbes's theory of security did not fully account for the dangers arising from the unlimited powers that were bestowed on the sovereign as ruler. Hobbes underestimated the risk of dictatorship, misappropriation, authoritarianism and the eventual denial of security of lives and property under a tyrannical sovereign. It was this unresolved paradox of security that Locke tried to address by posing his doctrine containing the separation of powers, property rights and popular sovereignty.

Locke: A Modern Theoretician on Security

Writing soon after Hobbes, John Locke propounded a different view of the state of nature and the social contract. According to Locke, the state of nature is not a state of licence; man may do as he wishes with his person and possessions, but he has no liberty to destroy himself or his possessions (Locke 1963: 196-170). As such the state is guided by the law of nature, which is reason. Locke holds that reason teaches everyone that since they are equal and independent, no one ought to harm any other person in his life, health, liberty or possessions. The law of nature guarantees peace and preservation of all.

According to Locke, the earth is the property of all men as a whole. But the property of each man is his own person, the labour of his body and the work of his hands. He asserts that 'something becomes a man's property when he has removed it from the common state it existed in as nature, and then, applies his labour, mental and physical, to it' (Locke 1963: 176-178). For Locke, man ought to acquire property within the limits set by reason, to determine what is enough for his use. Locke suggests that consent is important for the establishment of the social order. He holds that a man gives his consent when 'he agrees with other men to join and unite into a community for their comfortable, safe and peaceful existence' (Locke 1963: 178). This community for Locke assures the security of property and protection from external aggression. When a number of men consent to form a community, 'they become incorporated and thereby constitute a body politic in which the majority have a right to act in the interest of the whole' (Locke 1963: 179).

Locke illustrates two kinds of consent, tacit and express. The express consent of any man entering into a society makes him a full member of that society and a subject of that government. In contrast, a man gives tacit consent when he has any possessions in, or enjoys any part of the dominion of a government. Even as a foreigner or traveller, a man is obliged to obey the laws of a government so long as he enjoys its protection. Locke argues that 'when anybody unites his person and possessions to any commonwealth he becomes a subject of the government and a member of the commonwealth' (Locke 1963: 183).

The existence of private property makes the idea of security a necessity. Human beings search for security by constituting society. The basic intention behind creating society is to preserve property. More so, security is possible because a multitude of people give their consent to join and live in community. But security is possible only if society is guided by the doctrine of the separation of powers so as to keep the power of the sovereign power within bounds.

The criticism of Locke has centred on his emphasis on the protection and legitimacy of existing patterns of private property ownership. His views may be construed as a rationalisation of social inequalities. What is the role of property in the security equation when we are faced with a great scarcity of resources and increased human competition? How do we perceive private property if it occasions heightened injustice, exploitation and oppression?

Conclusion

This analysis of traditional and modern perspectives on security suggests that the quest for security has always been a source of concern for human beings. Although these concerns vary from one society to another, they are underlined by a central existential commitment to pursue the widest possible opportunities for human growth, well-being and survival within a social framework. It is clear that the quest for survival, freedom from danger, and peace, comfort and progress will continue to determine the interest of human beings in enduring security.

References

Abogunrin, S.O., 1996, 'Covenants in the Ethical System of the Yoruba', *Africana Marburgensia*, vol. XXIX, pp. 3-15.

Achebe, Chinua, 1958 , *Things Fall Apart,* African Writers Series, London: Heinemann.

Aremu, P.S.O., 1995, '*Egungun* Masquerades as Socio-Religious Manifestations', *Africana Marburgensia*, vol. XXVII, no. 1 and 2, pp. 3-13.

Aristotle, 1963, *Politics in Social and Political Philosophy*, J. Somerville et al., eds., New York: Anchor Books.

Augustine, St., 1990, *The City of God*, Translated M. Dodds, *Great Books of The Western World*, M. J. Alder, ed., Chicago: Encyclopaedia Britannica Inc.

Ayer, Alfred Jules, 1969, *Metaphysics and Commonsense*, London: Macmillan.

Blau, T. and Goure, D., 1984, 'Military Uses and Implications of Space', *Society*, January/February, pp. 13-17.

Bell, W., 1994, 'The World as a Moral Community', *Society*, July/August, pp. 17-22.

Davidson, B., 1977, 'A Science of Social Control', in Peter Gutkind and Peter Waterman, eds., *African Social Studies: A Radical Reader*, London: Heinemann, pp. 296-305.

Davidson, B., 1991, 'Kingdoms of Africa from the 12th to the 18th Century', in Ralph Uwechue, *Africa Today*, London: Africa Books, pp. 157-168.

Dewey, J., 1977, *John Dewey: The Essential Writings*, David Sidorsky, ed., New York: Harper and Row.

Ejizu, C., 1987, 'Healing as Wholeness: The African Experience', *Africana Marburgensia*, vol. XX, no 1, pp. 3-19.

Ezekwugo, C.M., 1991, 'Omenana and Odinana in the Igbo World: A Philosophical Appraisal', *Africana Marburgensia*, vol. XXIV, no. 2, pp. 3-18.

Fagan, B. M., 1998, *People of the Earth: An Introduction to World Prehistory*, 9th Edition, New

York: Longman Addison Wesley.

Goulet, D., 1987, 'Culture and Traditional Values in Development', in Susan Stratigos and Philip Hughes, eds., *The Ethics of Development*, Port Moresby: University of Papua New Guinea Press.

Greaves, R. L, Zaller, R., Cannistraro, P. V., Murphey, R., 1997a, *Civilization of the World: The Human Adventure, 3rd Edition, Volume One: To the Late 1600s*, New York: Longman.

Greaves, R. L, Zaller, R., Cannistraro, P. V., Murphey R., 1997b, *Civilization of the World: The Human Adventure, Volume Two. From the Middle 1600s*, 3rd Edition, New York: Addison Wesley.

Hobbes, T., 1963, *Leviathan in Social and Political Philosophy*, J. Somerville et al., eds., New York: Anchor Books.

Latham, E., 1956, 'The Group Basis of Politics: Notes for a Theory', in Heinz Eulau, Samuel J. Eldersveld and Morris Janowitz, eds., *Political Behaviour: A Reader in Theory and Research*, Illinois: The Free Press, pp. 232-245.

Locke, J., 1963, *Treatise Concerning Civil Government: Second Essay in Social and Political Philosophy*, J. Somerville et al., eds., New York: Anchor Books.

Mackenzie, J. S., 1963, *Outlines of Social Philosophy*, London: George Allen & Unwin.

Mbiti, J. S., 1969, *African Religions and Philosophy*, London: Heinemann.

Messari, N., 2002, 'The State and Dilemmas of Security: The Middle East and the Balkans', *Security Dialogue*, vol. 33, no. 4, pp. 415-427.

Nielsen, K., 1973, 'Alienation and Self-realization', *Philosophy*, vol. 48, pp. 21-33.

Nwala, U., T., 1985, *Igbo Philosophy*, Lagos: Literamed Publications, pp. 27-30.

Oladipo, O., 1996, *Philosophy and the African Experience*, Ibadan: Hope.

Olaoba, O.B., 1997, 'Between Juju and Justice: An Examination of Extra- Legal Devices in Traditional Yoruba Society', *Africana Marburgensia*, vol. XXX, pp. 24-38.

Olomola, I., 1991, 'Alile - Traditional Security System among the Yoruba', *Africana Marburgensia*, vol. XXIV, no. 2, pp. 50-61.

Osae, T. A. and Nwabara, S. N., 1968, *A Short History of West Africa*, London: Hodder and Stoughton.

Plato, 1963, *The Republic*, in *Social and Political Philosophy*, J. Somerville et al., New York: Anchor Books.

Perlman, J. S., 1995, *Science without Limits*, New York: Prometheus Books.

Prewitt, K., 1985, 'Security, Peace and Social Science', *Society*, November/December.

Sogolo, G., 1993, *Foundations of African Philosophy*, Ibadan: Ibadan University Press.

Ujomu, P.O., 2001, 'Cultural Relations, Human Communication and the Conditions for Intercultural Relations: A Critique of Anta Diop and Kwasi Wiredu', in H. Igboanusi, ed., *Language Attitude and Language Conflict in West Africa*, Ibadan: Enicrownfit, pp. 165-188.

5

Cultural Dimensions
of the National Security Problem

Olusegun Oladiran and Irene Omolola Adadevoh

Introduction

This essay examines the cultural dimensions of the national security problem. A cultural policy as an instrument of social engineering is crucial for national survival insofar as national security is, in a significant sense, defined by culture. A critical clarification of the material, institutional, and philosophical aspects of culture can help provide a more systematic analysis of the dynamic elements of culture(s) vis-à-vis national security. This cultural analysis situates the internal and external dimensions to nation security. No nation can achieve total security at all times, and coping with perceived threats to national security can be actualised through the adaptation of the elements of culture to ensure survival.

Every nation draws up strategies to prevent its potential and actual destabilisation. Such strategies are usually contained in a National Security programme. A cultural policy as an instrument of social engineering demands a notion of culture as a strategic instrument (Uchendu 1988: 18). Mazrui (1973) describes this cultural engineering process as the deliberate political effort to channel behaviour in the direction that will maximize national objectives. The vital linkage between culture and security at any level is better underscored by statements related to the nexus between culture and development. According to Odhiambo (2002: 2), 'the real problem of Africa comes from the inability of those in authority to make the right choice and firm commitment to cultural matters because they underestimate the value of culture in development'. We can infer from the above statement that the capacity of a nation to survive is entrenched in the cultural values prevailing at any point in time.

Conceptualisation of Culture and National Security

Culture and national security are interrelated. They sometimes display conflicting variations, which may arise from inconsistencies which we notice in our set of beliefs. Sometimes the challenge to our beliefs may come from outside (Bodunrin 1991: 93). Anthropologists in their study of culture have found that culture has an immense impact on human beings in any society because it helps man to adapt to his society and hence to increase the chances of survival. There are as many definitions of culture as there are diverse cultures across the globe, although these definitions tend to say the same thing. Castro-Gomez (2002: 26) holds that 'culture constitutes a sphere of moral, religious, political, philosophical and techno-logical values that permit man to "humanize" himself, i.e. escape the tyranny of the state of nature'. Uroh (1996: 11) is clear on the fact that 'culture is a product of a people's experience. It is the knowledge of doing things which people have acquired in their attempts to solve some socio-historical problems'. Also, accord-ing to Tylor, culture is 'that complex whole which includes knowledge, belief, art, morals, law, custom and any other capabilities and habits acquired by man as a member of society' (Tylor 1871: 1). Other scholars in their attempt at defining culture have reduced culture to mentalistic phenomena, to ideas or the like in the minds of men. Downs defines culture as a mental map that guides us in our relations with our surroundings and with other people (1971: 35). Hatch sees culture as 'the way of life of a people' (Hatch 1985: 178). However, having assessed the various definitions offered by scholars on culture, we can say that 'culture is the totality of the way of life evolved by a people in their attempts to meet the challenge of living in their environment, which gives order and meaning to their social, political, economical, aesthetic and religious norms and modes of organisation' (see Aig-Imoukhuede 1992: 171).

A crucial factor in the analysis of culture is social control, which helps to ensure conformity to societal norms for an ordered society. Linton (1936) ob-serves that every culture embodies three separate but related spheres, namely, universal, alternative and specialties. Uchendu (1988: 18) clarifies the idea of cul-tural universals, alternatives and specialties in the following way: cultural universals refer to those elements of a culture open to all and shared by every culture bearer. To be competent in a culture implies sharing in its cultural universals. Cultural alternatives are various institutions provided by a culture to satisfy a given cultural end; and cultural specialties are institutions for specialised training and knowledge whose membership may be voluntary or ascribed.

The analysis of the role of culture as the very texture of social contract theo-ries and of viable human organisations is closely tied to the thematic issues of national security affecting both the individual person and the community at large (Gbadegesin 1991: 162). This view tends to imply that the protection and devel-opment of a nation-state is culturally contextual.

However, it is important to note that no nation can achieve total security. According to Omatete (1972: 291), a nation may be considered secure if there is a high probability of the occurrence of its preferred national values. Tukur (1999: 19) defines values as the highest ethical standards and criteria through which individuals, groups and societies order their goals, determine their choice and judge their conduct as these pertain to fundamental aspects of life, be they in the sphere of personal or public affairs. The capacity to make judgments in interaction with the challenges of the human environment and society helps to formulate and institutionalise essential policies on culture.

On many issues, it is widely taken that the critical area for the solution of social and national problem is that of culture since culture contains the ultimate values which motivate human and national action in historical perspective. This view is corroborated further by the fact that, in securing the various compartments of culture, such as language, customs, norms, art, science, metaphysical belief, there is a concomitant security of the human social systems, which in turn creates a sort of individual and community alliance. Hence, the distinctive analysis of culture is historically necessary for any form of security and development. And given the fact that culture and security follow certain autonomous, as well as functionally dependent, dynamic trends regarding social and individual well-being; it is pertinent to analyse their two-tier operational functionalism either as 'culture of security' or as 'security of culture'.

In Search of a Theoretical Framework: The Culture of Security and the Security of Culture

Culture and security are dynamic social realities which involve continuity and change (Gbadegesin 1991: 173). Culture and security cannot be discussed outside of cultural values. Ackermann (1981: 447, 450) states that cultural values are 'ways of ordering and evaluating objects, experiences and behaviours manifesting themselves in all situations of choice. Cultural values are seen as a determining factor in the choice and impact of technology; on the other hand, technology is conceived as potentially transforming cultural values'. From the above, Ackermann (1981: 451) draws the vital conclusion that 'it is important to realize that cultural values and beliefs have a historically acquired force that is to some extent independent of the current social structure. As a result, they will be embodied in the projects of individuals and groups, contribute to the ordering of their priorities, and affect their strategies to achieve whatever goals they have set themselves'.

Regarding the cultural bounds of security, Castro-Gomez maintains that 'if through culture man slowly liberates himself from the chains imposed by nature, then cultural forms acquire ever increasing degrees of perfection to the extent that they permit the unfolding of spirit, that is, the exercise of human freedom' (2002: 26-27). In our struggle for national and human security in Africa at large, we can agree with Nkrumah (1975: 58) that 'we on this African continent can enrich our knowledge and cultural heritage through our cooperative efforts and the pooling of our scientific and technical resources'. The goals of culture and security, which we have set before us, require a world order and peace charter derived from the diverse cultures.

The definitions of culture tend to stipulate a distinction between culture and security, either as a 'culture of security' or as a 'security of culture', which refers to the social and contractual orientation that ensures a people's well-being with a community. The 'security of culture' signifies all modalities by which a people's worldview and way of life are protected. For Castro-Gomez (2002: 26), the culture of security signifies all constitutive spheres of moral, religious, political, philosophical and technological values that permit man to 'humanise' himself. For Uroh (1996: 11), the culture of security in the context of our analysis is a product of a people's experience to enhance their well-being. This means that knowledge about the culture of security is based on the ways people have adopted or acquired it in their attempts to solve socio-historical problems.

To further build a conceptual framework for our essay, Odhiambo (2002) provides a three-tier analysis of culture of security, which is slightly different from that of Uchendu above. The three aspects are ideas, aesthetic forms and values. According to Odhiambo (2002:5), "the culture of security in a society consists of three distinct elements; ideas give rise to habits and beliefs, aesthetic forms reflect the artistic expression of a culture in its visual arts, the values are formed by the interaction between ideas and aesthetics norms of conduct" with a bid to enhance human well being. At this juncture it is imperative to examine how the culture of security is acquired and socialized by human beings in their society. These different aspects of culture can be challenged by internal and external forces. According to Cabral (1998: 261) the culture of security is an essential element of the history of a people, because it allows us to know how to resolve the nature and extent of the imbalances and conflicts (economic, political and social), which characterize the evolution of a society. A culture of security allows us to know the dynamic synthesis, which have been developed and established by social conscience to resolve these conflicts at each stage of its evolution, in the search for survival and progress. The culture of security means literally the protective mechanism, which obtains in the land, a community enterprise, a body of laws and morals along with their metaphysical foundations that guide and ensure peace and order within the community.

In this context, the culture of security can be seen as one of numerous distinct systems in which social theory and action are synthesised. This signifies that the culture of security, as a social system, is dependent on the system of the human personality and positioning. That is, the culture of security is a system abstracted from both protective actions and theories on social existential affairs. In other words, the culture of security is a system of values, meanings or significance and symbols regarding the structure of social life (Halpern 1955: 235). Accordingly, the culture of security can thus be said to provide the perspective necessary to rethink the meaning of life, and the projection of such meanings from the prevalent circumstances of the present. Given this situation, the culture of security gives us the impetus to leap over obstacles that hamper human and social development and chart new pathways for future prospects. Furthermore, the proper clarification of the beneficial purpose of the culture of human and social security gives a clue as to how to bridge the gap between our means and our ends, and how to appropriate these means and ends for man's technological development and for the transformation of the individual and the state in society (M'Bow 1992: 13).

Irele (1991: 52) points out the general principle or ethos governing the security of culture, especially the ones by which culture survives or operates. In this context, the security of culture can be sustained in either a materialised or objectified, as well as an idealised or spiritualised, way. The 'object or material culture' of a people can be those items of culture that can be sustained by empirical verification and justification. This aspect of 'security of culture' is tangible and in fact can be seen, described, and sometimes even touched. And by virtue of its tangibility the characteristics of culture are in fact discernibly protected. Security of the tangible culture thus comprises material, institutional, philosophical and creative aspects, as contained in our cultural policy and practice.

The material security of culture has to do with artefacts in the broadest form (namely: tools, clothing, food, medicine, housing, etc., and institutional monuments such as the political, social, legal and economic structures erected to help to achieve material and spiritual objectives). Indeed, the sociological culture of security measures can be adequately and better substantiated by the nature of object or material culture, that is 'the way in which the society produces its means of existence and the way the individual members and groups within the society relate to each other and organize themselves within the society, as well as the general code and ideas that bind people together' (Irele 1991: 52).

Another perspective on the security of culture is that it can be idealised. This idealisation operates at the level of inner dispositions to reality or a metaphysical projection of such a reality. Although this is where the spirit of the people depicts the subjective aspect of culture, nevertheless it depicts aptly the transcendental reality of the African people. Gbadegesin (1991: 172-174) states that for some social and political theorists security of idealised culture consists mainly of diverse ideas as initiators of action, as if ideas have an independent ontological reality moving in the brains of human beings. This means that the Africans guard jealously the operations of their inner subjective dispositions. This is necessitated by the fact that the operation of an idea in the mind influences the external world and stratifies it in definite and particular referential correspondence and behavioural dispositions.

Against the backdrop of communicating the spiritualised and objectified typologies of culture, the chief global method of the security of culture can be seen as a complex linguistic phenomenon, being constitutive of numerous elements of which the picture of the language of the culture is one. Because of the numerous constitutive elements of a culture, there is a hybrid of cultural overlap, which makes room for cultural interdependence. This consequently makes it also possible for people trying to preserve them to share many aspects of a culture, without a shared language. This is possible if there is lively participation in the activities, goals, aspirations, and the fate of a larger cultural community (Gyekye 1997: 44). The term security of culture is hereby used to refer to the totality of Africa's basic protective orientation in life (Dzobo 1992: 123). Security of culture in this perspective is an open-ended resource of social meanings upon which members of a community draw to mediate the contingencies of their everyday lives. As such the phrase denotes the preservation of the material and spiritual resources of a community's material and moral worlds.

The Juxtaposing of Culture with National Security

In juxtaposing culture with national security, it is understandable that culture as the totality of the way of life of a people has enormous security influence on the nation. This is because national security is the concern for the survival, peace and progress of individuals, groups and the society as a cultural whole. Hence, national security is a concept that cannot be easily comprehended without its application to social and cultural phenomena. McLaurin (1988: 6) corroborates this statement when he maintains that

> Security is a concept devoid of operational meaning in the absence of some identification of threats. Security against what? In all discussions of security from the personal to the international, there is an implicit or explicit determination of threat...

Owolabi (1998: 160) likewise states that the threat to cultural perceptions forms the core of the understanding of national security. Particular threats to cultural perceptions of national security can be assessed by the weakening of states and communities, their erosion and in some cases even their implosion as well as their incapacity to ensure public order and to fulfil other functions (Janusz and Vladimir 1995: 18). Wolfers (1962) observes that, objectively, security is 'an absence of threat to acquired values such as territorial sovereignty and independence, socio-economic interests and political traditions. Subjectively, it is the absence of fear that such values will be attacked' (1962: 279).

The threat to the existence and survival of a nation comes in two broad spheres; the internal and external threats. An external threat is an attempt originating from outside the nation either to destroy the nation or to force on it a line of action contrary to its interests. External threats usually result from conflict between a nation and another nation or even an international organisation. Internal threats are those unfavourable conditions which may result in conflict that threatens public order. These conditions may be due to social, political, economic, ideological, or ethnic reasons. Internal threats may also come about due to influence from outside a country, especially by organisations or groups which promote values antithetical to integration or cohesion in a country. The internalisation of such values may result in actions inimical to national security. For any nation to survive it must be properly positioned to combat any forms of the above-mentioned threats.

On the other hand a nation is considered secured and un-threatened if there is a high occurrence of its preferred values even though no nation has absolute security at all times (Omatete 1972: 291). However, within the context of unavoidable threats, a nation must put in place adequate measures to limit the possible adverse effects. Coping with perceived threats to a nation's security is actualised through the adaptation of the elements of culture to ensure survival. Such elements may be specialised institutions, for example, the military, police, etc., education, cultural institutions, the media, and so on.

Ethnicity, Ethnocentrism and Elitism: Institutional Problems in National and Communal Security

Ethnocentrism and elitism are cultural values that pose problems to visionary cultural leadership and national or communal security. This is because ethnic groups or elites may have internalised conflict and opposition with another group, thus resulting in violence and a threat to public order. In a pluralistic society such as Nigeria, where different cultural groups and values exist, it is imperative to promote values which will minimise tension, allow for tolerance and integration and the overall communal security of all and sundry. Unfortunately in Nigeria, culture has not been utilised as a strategic tool through education for the management of values which may threaten national security. The non-material aspects of our culture such as ideas, values and attitudes can therefore have an appreciable effect on the human body and organisation (Ferraro 1997: 22).

Nigeria's political scene since independence has always degenerated into acrimonious quarrels between factions of the ruling elite and diverse ethnocentric groups. For obvious reasons, the management of the political feuds proved to be a more arduous task than was the case in the pre-independence era. Traditional communities were typically delineated by kinship, and leadership in the society involved a struggle for power, position and people (Goody in Acharya 1981: 109- 111). To reap political advantage, various groups and parties entered into alliances, which depended on the mobilisation of ethnic and elitist loyalties.

Indeed, the Nigerian political legacy has, on this count, been described as tribal, or, to use the more congenial term, ethnic.

The integration of the social, economic and political rights of citizens, listed as democratic imperatives in the *Report of the Political Bureau* (1987), have been increasingly eroded. In Dube's opinion (1988: 507-8), at the root of ethnicity lies the fear of the erosion of cultural identity and group dominance. It can be argued that ethnic and cultural diversity 'has deleterious effects only when it occurs in the context of governments which are undemocratic and as such unaccountable to the broader public' (Collier and Gunning 1999: 9-10). To combat intra- and inter-societal discord, according to Dube (1988: 507), 'a diagnostic understanding of the pervasive phenomenon of ethnicity is essential'. Dube also argued that the salience and persistence of ethnic categories of identification and conflict are not just puzzling but equally disturbing to national integration, the more so because ethnic alliances cut across class-based identities and interests. This signifies that ethnic cleavages have a cultural content, interest- orientation, and political articulation. Cultural symbols - mostly drawn from tradition - are manipulated by ethnic groups for political mobilisation with a view to realising a set of goals and also gaining political power solely for their group.

Against this backdrop of ethnic symbolisation, the Nigerian social, political and economic spheres have been characterised by the following social symbolic indices due to ethnic politics:

(a) The lack of an even distribution of wealth and income due to ethnic bias;

(b) Mono-cultural and enclave economy;

(c) Insecurity of jobs, lives and property;

(d) High and increasing illiteracy rates;

(e) Un-conducive atmosphere for healthy political bargaining and compromise;

(f) Structural imbalances, corruption and increased per capita poverty.

Due to the above situations, which create a high wave of insecurity across the Nigerian state, the polity has become replete with ethno-religious crises and secessionist agitation. Lopsided structuring in the polity has occasioned the Ijaw crisis with Ilaje, Urhobo and Itshekiri and other minorities in the South-south. The rising national insecurity is equally witnessed in the Aguleri-Umuleri, Ife-Modakeke, Hausa-Ibo and Yoruba-Hausa ethnic clashes, where hundreds of thousands of lives have been lost. The perception of marginalisation of the South-south people by the Nigerian state is a factor that has reinvigorated the clamour for self-determination of these people, and where militia groups like Egbesu Boys, Massob, Bakassi Boys, Mosop, etc., have become a great threat to national security in Nigeria.

In another sense, the polarisation along ethnic lines has also affected security institutions like the army, police, etc. This has led to unprofessional attitudes such as the promotion of mediocrity. A case of this form of mediocrity is the promotion of officers and their assignment to strategic duties based on ethnic affiliations. Ethnic stratification and its economically adverse influence on the security agencies constitute another important factor in the inefficiency of these security institutions. The Nigerian economy suffers from the corruption of the political class who administer the nation. Within these leadership echelons, there has been the mismanagement of resources and the looting of the national treasury, which has further helped in entrenching crass materialism and a mass culture of poverty in Nigeria. The resultant effect of this sort of poverty syndrome in the larger populace is the high crime wave the country has been experiencing, particularly armed robbery. It can therefore be said that political and economic perversion and corruption have resulted in the insecurity of the various sectors of the nation, some of which adversely affect the provision of social services, industrialisation, the security sector development, etc. One glaring example is the transfer of public moneys to private accounts in foreign countries by the custodians of our leadership ladder. Such monies are used to fuel the economy of such nations, while our own nation is left to suffer from this gross misconduct.

The very first value of culture in the entrenchment of national security is the development of national personnel and institutions which are essential for true patriotism and national consciousness. The values of national security are thus quite incompatible with paying lip service to the issue of cultural development (Gbadegesin 1991: 184). A major hurdle to cross lies in constraining the unconstrained elite, which has over the years caused a divergence between African leaders and their own populations, the more so because the elites involved in bureaucratic corruption preserve their power, which serves only the interest of a group that comprises a fraction of the population (Ndulu and O' Connell 1999: 42, 53). A salient negative attribute is constituted by the social and cultural value systems, including attitudes towards thrift, profits, risks, education, and even the view of work (Hogendorn 1996: 64). For Goulet (1987: 172), there is great merit in prescribing that sound development ought to be grounded in traditional, indigenous and non-elite values.

We do not hold the view that elitism is an outright evil. This cannot be so, because no 'highly educated and well trained population is poor, but almost all populations with poor education and limited skills suffer from low income. Gross deficiencies in education and training may have the particularly bad result that they prevent workers and managers from absorbing the technologies that could increase growth' (Hogendorn 1996: 311-312). However, care must be taken in extolling the virtues of national integration. Non-indigenous and elitist criteria of leadership in many African nations should be harnessed to prevent hardened autocracy and dictatorship (Collier and Gunning 1999: 3). To do this effectively, there is a need for an enlightenment which must (i) emphasise education; (ii) give greater weight to vocational and technical skills; and (iii) be in reasonable balance with manpower needs (Goody 1971 in Acharya 1981: 138).

The basic argument for the enlightenment imperative is that the intra-elite struggles for power have literally left the nation prostrate and rendered the coop-eration envisaged in the adopted Westminster model of democracy nugatory. The corruption of the political elites has further led to a lack of trust, which results in a lack of obedience to the law and thus the subversion of the system. The corruption of the political class has further entrenched in the citizenry the acceptance of the corrupt practice of having 'a piece of the national cake'. This has normalised corruption as the standard way of life and has equally led to the recent rating of Nigeria as one of the most corrupt nations in the world. Hence, the cultural problem of national security is seen mainly in the failure of cultural institutions to control or change ideas and values which threaten national security. At the political level, it is seen in the idea of policing, military politics, ethnic politics, etc. At the level of belief, religious intolerance is the case due to religious pluralism. At the civil community level it is seen in the idea of non-cooperation or non-participation with the security agencies in communicating information nec-essary for the maintenance of order. At the transnational level, there is the legiti-misation of the culture of violence through the media, especially in films.

The high hopes nursed for development in an independent Nigeria have given way to despair. Rural neglect, the low premium on education, and corruption all combine in inter-locking vicious circles with ethnicity, poor economic manage-ment and undemocratic institutions to promote political instability. Poor political and economic management as fuelled by ethnocentrism and elitism have there-fore in many ways incapacitated visionary leadership. What this means is that ethnic visions, actions, thoughts, arguments, and prescriptions became dominant in national security concerns. And many times securing the nation's well-being in terms of political and economic thought and action may be interrupted if there is a discontinuity in ethnic hegemony. In this context, the significance of the pred-ecessor's originality and viability of ideas may not be appreciated by the succeed-ing leadership group. When Gbadegesin (1991: 174) opined that the historical, political, economic and environmental conditions of a society are the foundation from which cultural leadership and security stem, it can be deduced that the notion of shared lives, and shared purposes and interests is crucial to an adequate conception of communal security (Gyekye 1997: 42). But then the adequate con-ception of indigenous communal or national security faces yet another problem of self-sustenance not only by virtue of internal ethnocentric and elitist rancour, but also from the culture of dominance, fuelled globally by the residue of colo-nialism.

Colonialism, Neo-colonialism and the Problem of Cultural Basis for Security

The early years of colonial rule were characterised by a mixture of the brutal application of force and the founding of the infrastructure of a modern economic state. In their territorial expansion in the quest for commercial opportunities and minerals, the European chartered companies and concessionaires, in collaboration with their mother countries, fought bloody battles of subjugation. After the independence of many African nations, the industrial security concerns of the western nations have brought them back in the form of industrialisation in the quest for economic development of the host nation. In addition, African states were usually the accidents of colonial history, and frequently not congruent with any indigenous cultural and linguistic demarcations (Acharya 1981: 109, 111, 116).

This perspective on the problem of security raises the context of colonial experiences. In other words, security is vitiated by the legacy of mental colonisation, which subjects the African to indigenous cultural alienation. This motivates a negative perception of received traditional cultural knowledge and as such creates the problem of economic dependency on foreign cultural ideas and materials. In Gbadegesin's view (1991: 184), any form of colonialism is culturally rooted and profoundly devalues the culture of the dominated people. This is backed up by the assimilative and associative rationalisation that denies the existence of any distinctive culture to the colony. This rationale poses a problem for national security, especially the sheer equation of colonial domination with the cultural superiority of the coloniser. It is this assumption that suggests to the coloniser the burden of civilising the subjugated territories. According to Munkner (1998: 82), as a result of the western civilising paternalism, 'two or more layers of different value systems developed and were existing side by side, partly overlapping, rarely merging, creating insecurity and the feeling of injustice in the minds of those affected by the norms of a value system which they did not accept as theirs'.

Cabral (1998: 261) informs us that 'the value of culture as an element of resistance to foreign cultural domination lies in the fact that culture is the vigorous manifestation on the ideological or idealist plane of the physical and historical reality of the society that is dominated or to be dominated'. Essentially the effect of the assault of colonialism on culture was a kind of cultural tension and dislocation. These tensions and dislocations, according to Davidson (1991: 16), are manifested in the principles of colonial governance which assumed a form of autocratic limitless power. What this means in effect is that the role of such a dominant cultural development undermines the traditional institutions such as the extended family, patronage ties, ethnic cleavages and loyalties, group linkages, churches, religious sentiment and movement and historic authority. All of which in turn had profound consequences on the foundation and future of black African cultural development and social security (Osia 1983: 37, 39).

All of the above show clearly that the problem of the appraisal of security and development, as conventionally understood, is far from being culturally neutral; it is a product of western ideas and value judgements, without which many of the impulses guiding it would be meaningless. The colonial experience brought about the embrace of western culture and the relegation of our traditional values to the background. This practice has continued in Nigeria even up to the present. Nigeria has been experimenting with Euro-American inspired concepts, ideas and institutions in the regulation and management of its public affairs. This new trend of colonialism entrenches a modality by which there is a failure to maximise all the cultural resources of the home nation. The total acceptance of western values has had other effects on our economy. It has created a culture of economic dependence on western nations. The resultant effect is that it has prevented the development that we so much yearn for. At the institutional security level, it has created a situation where we rely solely on western nations for the procurement of weapons. This is a very dangerous trend, which has far-reaching effects on the security of the nation. It has opened the way for the western nations to manipulate the management of our resources in a way that benefits them and not us. So many other dimensions to this particular problem exist but these few examples will suffice. The above overview explains why the African continent is still in search of a system which will enable it to develop effective integration mechanisms, responsive and efficient institutions, and a style of government which will facilitate the creation of a culturally oriented civil polity.

Fanon (1998: 306) stated that when there is a destruction of cultural values, social, political and even economic security techniques are undermined and mummified. Likewise, Osia (1983: 39) states that by undermining and often eliminating these traditional institutions, without any new ones created, development helped destroy the only agencies in many African nations that might have enabled them to make a genuine transition to modernity. The policies, attitudes, actions, and the efforts of westerners to promote development of their own orientation may have denied black African nations the possibility of real development, while at the same time destroying the indigenous and at one time viable institutions they are now trying, perhaps futilely, to resurrect. M'Bow (1992: 13) maintains that 'while it is true that Africa must rediscover the historical continuity of her cultures and establish the guidelines that inform her collective personality, she must at the same time strive to build a future based on progress and justice, equal to the aspirations of her peoples. Africa from now on, must work towards a form of modernization, which is truly hers. Taking her creative inspiration from the re-interpretation of the traditions of her past, she must seek renovation, freely assuming the responsibility for it and put to good use such rich cultural traditions and social and moral values as will enable her to inspire progress without self-betrayal and achieve change without self-adulteration. What needs to be done is to revive the dynamic elements of her traditional heritage in the light of today's challenge. Our attitude must be both critical and forward-looking'.

A very important reason why uncritically borrowed western ideas have not been very successful is because non-universal values are seldom adequately transplanted from one cultural milieu to another. For any reform to be permanent and enduring, it must be passed on and rooted in the principles of the aboriginal institutions. The failure to recognise this point has vitiated the opportunity to tap into the resources available in our traditional cultural practices. For example, in the area of traditional medicine, a great deal of revenue could be generated for the country through the development of drugs from indigenous health knowledge. Canada claims that it makes US$32 billon per year through the development of drugs acquired from indigenous health knowledge in developing countries. Such developments are capable of generating huge revenues for the country and hence of making our economy, which is in shambles, stronger. This in turn, would create more jobs and reduce the poverty level.

The Social and Cultural Ramifications of Our Problems

The socio-cultural is the most critical dimension of the security problem faced by the country today. Culture represents the fountain spring of all policies employed by the government of a nation, be they political, social, economic, or educational. Strategies for the development of a nation hinge on the understanding of culture as the totality of the way of life of a people. In the case of Nigeria, there has been a widespread adoption of Euro-American models for the managing of the country. Unfortunately, this has not worked very well because the indigenous cultural foundations of the ethnic nations which constitute Nigeria have not been taken into consideration. Our leaders have imbibed the way the colonialists administered Nigeria in the pre-independence era as a national political culture. The motive for colonisation was the exploitation of resources. The political culture used to hold the nation together was coercion. This explains the reason why we have imbibed forceful means of managing our security, which is not working today. The police and the military were set up to repress protests by the people which threatened the stability of the colonial order. It is this culture that has been acquired in the post-independence era which has brought about the exploitative nature of the political class and a failure of social cohesion due to ethnicity, religious intolerance, militarisation of politics, economic deprivation, etc.

The political dimension of the problem is next in importance to the cultural dimension. The evolvement of a new culture dominated by western modes brought about a perverted orientation of the strategy by which a multi-cultural independent Nigeria could be administered. The method used by the colonialists to administer the country was adopted by the nationalists who found themselves at the helm of affairs. Things, however, fell apart due to the exploitation of the resources of the nation, leading to the lack of economic security on the part of the people and a breakdown of law and order.

The economic dimension is the third important dimension of the security problem. The exploitation of the resources of the nation has brought about a breakdown in social service delivery, and entrenched poverty in the land leading to social and ethnic stratification. This has further worsened the security situation, which often manifests itself in disobedience to law and large-scale conflict claiming many lives and properties. An economic poverty perspective can be perceived in the activities of some multi-national industries which engage in exploitative conduct, often resulting in violent national insecurity. For example, after the discovery of crude oil, many multi-national companies came in to assist in the development of the oil sector. The exploration of oil led to the degradation of the environment which the host communities relied on for their livelihood. Also, the basic infrastructure and amenities such as hospitals, roads, schools, were not provided in many of these communities. How then do people survive when their means of existence have been threatened and there are no contingency plans to remedy the situation? One result has been widespread violence which has claimed many lives, including expatriates and security operatives. Since the various ethnic groups in the area are united against the multi-national companies, these companies often employ the strategy of divide-and-rule. This involves the supply of weapons to ethnic groups to fight each other in the quest to position such a group for monetary benefits from these multi-nationals. The wanton destruction of lives and properties in the Niger Delta area has been a major problem for Nigeria's security forces to control. Another dent to national security is the fact that from the Niger Delta area there has been an influx of light weapons into the wider Nigerian community. What this portends is that such weapons can be used for other criminal activities such as armed robbery, political assassination, etc.

Education as cultural transmission has been formatted in the manner it was bequeathed to us by the colonialists. Education has not functioned particularly well as an agent for the transmission of the values cherished by the state. It has failed in the inculcation of viable ethical education for the tolerance of others. Through an ethical education both formally and informally, it becomes possible to see the consequences of involving oneself in any conduct which can destabilise the state. Ethical education is a necessary means of ensuring national security. Questions about national security in Nigeria are the more significant due to the emergence and blossoming of a perverted idea of civil security. This is seen in the proliferation of vigilante groups and ethnic militias that have emerged to fill the gaps and inadequacies in the defence and security functions of the society. There is evidence of a negative civilian input in security matters. The unyielding violence in the country has created a fertile substrate for the expansion of such groups. In some areas of the country, the actions of these groups have been institutionalised and legitimised. The so-called 'area boys' and 'Almajiri' are employed in the amplification of ethno-religious conflicts around the nation. Small bands of political thugs known as 'ecomog' are employed as personal security for political office holders, and are used for political violence. However, the dangerous aspect is that they have received some legitimacy and now form part of the regular entourage of political leaders. There has been a more dangerous trend in the proliferation of ethnic militia and other dubious non-conventional community security and defence outfits, which have been put to the service of wider political, regional and economic interests. The forms of violence produced by these ethnic militia groups surpass even the preceding unstable times. These militia groups retain the capability for violence and mayhem that are unrivalled in intensity. They are often capable of contending with the institutionalised violence of the military.

Police, Culture and the Security Crisis

The case of the military in Nigeria and most of the Third World countries is that of a hangover from colonial tutelage. Conventionally established to defend the cause of the nation internally and externally, the military institution in Nigeria was originally established by the colonialists to subjugate the local people in their quest for territorial expansion. Therefore, from its origin the military institution set itself against the same people they were supposed to protect. This anti-people character of the military institution in these Third World countries, especially Nigeria, is an aberration which subsequently carried over to the post-colonial military establishment. With the all these matters in mind, is it then a surprise to see Nigeria's national security threatened by the following factors under the military?

  (a) Separatist agitations leading to civil war and near ethnic cleansing;
  (b) Institutionalised corrupt practices due to the inequality in social welfare programmes;
  (c) Structural violence;
  (d) Sit-tight syndrome of the rulers;
  (e) High-handedness on the part of military rulers;
  (f) Security racketeering;
  (g) Human rights abuses;
  (h) Poverty.

These factors have bedevilled the Nigerian polity and rendered her national security planning prostrate. A heterogeneous society with over 254 ethnic groups, Nigeria since independence has suffered from one crisis to another, and there appears to be no end to it. The military intervention in the country's body politic enthroned mediocrity, instability, corruption, poor management of the economy and a lack of commitment to national unity. Nigerian national security begs for cohesiveness as the polity is characterised by identity crisis, distribution crisis, penetration crisis, integration crisis and nation-building impasse. The civil war, which ravaged the country for thirty bitter months from 1967 to 1970, was an offshoot of the military's deplorable incursion into politics, as this drew the national security of the nation to the brink of collapse. Apart from the Bakassi debacle with Cameroon, Nigeria since independence has witnessed no external aggression. From the foregoing we can see how the military left their institutional function of combating threats to personal or human lives within the territorial limits of the Nigerian state, and allowed the country's national security to suffer the vicious circle of political violence.

For the military class the concept of national security is better seen and defended from the angle of their personal interest and not the national interest. The situation of national security is so bad in Nigeria that the death-squad type of killings by army undercover units is a popular trend. Some people earn their living form this security racket. For example, Brigadier-General Ibrahim Sabo (Rtd), the boss of the Directorate of Military Intelligence during the Abacha regime, noted in a press interview that during the Babangida and Abacha regimes there was continual intrigue. People would create a problem and then go and report to the system and thereafter ask for a specific amount of money to quell it. Those making money in the name of security would fake situations of insecurity and manufacture imaginary suspects. Similar points have been made by Albert (2005: 49-51). This situation clearly illustrates how the military use the excuse of security to minister to their personal needs and create security problems internally.

Every society has its methods of ensuring that people conform to the accepted norms and values, which ensure peace, security and stability. In countries with urban centres, the police act as the agent of social control. The word 'police' is derived from the Greek word 'Polis', meaning that part of a non-ecclesiastical administration having to do with the safety, health and order of state. According to Nigeria's constitution of 1989, under section 198 subsection 1, the police are supposed to accept the following responsibilities:

(a) The prevention and detection of crime;

(b) The protection of life and property;

(c) The apprehension of offenders;

(d) The preservation of law and order;

(e) The due enforcement of laws and regulations with which they are directly charged;

(f) The performance of such military duties within and outside Nigeria as may be required of them by or under the authority of any act.

In Nigeria the police thus are the first line of defence in the maintenance of the internal security of the nation. However, the police have not lived up expectations as far as their duties to the citizenry are concerned. This is demonstrated by the high crime rate. Police operatives have become very corrupt and extort money from members of the public while discharging their duties. The employment of brutal and excessive force against members of the public has led to many extra-judicial killings, which has caused attitude of non-co-operation among the public with the police. This brutal conduct is a carry-over of the police from colonial times. The Nigerian police were moulded by the colonial powers with the aim of enforcing the laws of the British government and their means of enforcement were brutal and ruthless.

Public participation or co-operation with the police is a very important method of gathering intelligence on the activities of criminals in society. Negligence of this practice has prevented the utilisation of its useful elements for social challenges, for example, in the area of total health care delivery and greater empowerment of the community to complement the policing of the nation. The emergence of vigilante groups and their reliance on traditional cultural practices for their activities are illustrative of the relevance of traditional culture to contemporary security challenges in Nigeria. In fact, this strategy remains one of the cheapest methods of ensuring the safety of lives and property in the community. Cultural norms such as vigilance, diligence, cooperation, integrity, politeness, which characterise and guide group norms must therefore be integrated into any viable security institutions (Hartley 1999: 87). According to North (1989: 1321), security institutions are based on rules, enforcement and characteristics of such rules and norms of behaviour that structure repeated human interaction. In the case of Nigeria, members of the public have not been co-operating with the police in the area of information regarding criminal activities in their neighbourhood. One reason for this is that members of the public do not trust the police with information. This is due to cases of people who have given information and have been exposed by corrupt and undisciplined police officers to such criminals about whom information was provided. This unfortunately has often resulted in the killing of such informants.

At another level, many people do not understand what the concept of policing is about. The maintenance of law and order by security agencies is not just the responsibility of such agencies alone but also that of the members of the public. The mechanisms of social control in any society are a product of culture and imply that it is the responsibility of every citizen to partake in the maintenance of security. Where members of the public refuse to co-operate with law enforcement agencies there are bound to be problems in maintaining law and order. The idea of policing connotes a kind of omnipresence, which cannot be achieved without public co-operation. In Nigeria this has resulted in a situation in which criminality is celebrated, and it has further contributed to lawlessness on the part of some citizens. This is one reason for the militia problem. The result of the prevalence of criminality is a society whose members do not feel secure. After all, the members of the public are always the ones most affected by a high crime wave, hence it is important that this attitude changes for a more effective policing of the nation.

Functions and Values of Creative Culture in the Security of Human and Technological Prospects

For Dzobo (1992: 123-130), the value of creative culture in the security of human and technological prospects subsists in the type of symbolised creative process of life. Thus, in his opinion, the drive to create is the basic and ultimate force behind all human behaviour; because the main aim of human creation is to realise a synthesis of being in all spheres of life. It is in this construct that the conception of creativity and the essence of true human prospects indicate the conception of man not just as a being who ruminates on life's experiences but also as a being who acts to change the world. This implies that man through free action employs basic empirical and innovative criteria in shaping his own history and destiny. Briskman (1980: 83-97) maintains, however, that the notion of creativity is permeated with evaluation. To adjudge a way of life as creative, bestows upon society the necessary standards and values that uplift human life. Existentialists also connect the possibility of human creativity, free and calculated, and not imposed freedom. This stems from the fact that man is creatively free precisely because only he can and must create himself. On the whole, cultural creativity is perceived as something which can be controlled, manipulated, engineered, or predicted. Gotesky and Breithaupt (1978: 23-25) state that the acceptability of a cultural creativity is used to characterise 'a person and the skill he possesses, a process and the new or better way it produces something, an activity and the occupation, vocation, or profession it elicits, a product and the ways it satisfies a long felt need, awakens strong feelings, alters living perspectives, recalls and revivifies the past; offers a total vision; etc., or all of these indiscriminately bundled together'.

The importance of securing human prospects in a cultural technological tradition is thus justified by the view that the value of technology is found in the representation it elicits which can be perceived by a subject as habitually worthy of desire. Some technological values are culturally significant because they signify or give concrete meaning to what is or has been rooted traditionally. Other technological values reflect bodies of knowledge which are normative; and as such they prescribe or direct actions, which ought to be performed. Still other techno-logical values are aesthetically appreciative; they refer to what is worthy of being admired or contemplated with pleasure albeit old or new, past or present (Goulet 1987: 169). As M'Bow (1992: 14) opined, there can be no progress without grafting new knowledge onto the old. It follows then that technological knowl-edge is in itself a product of many inputs, in particular of traditional knowledge, skill and enterprise and their more modern paradigm of diffusion and applica-tion (Landes 1991: 69). It is true to an extent that much of early thinking on technological development did not accord a central place to culture either as a goal or as an instrumentality. However, there should be a re-channelling of cur-rents of thought that can be powerful in the twenty-first century to correct the continuing and obstructive persistence of the view that tradition would block substantial modernisation, as traditional values are incompatible with modernity (Dube 1988: 505). This is because culture cannot be dispensed with to promote technological growth, for it has critical functions, and modern technological de-velopment does not offer an adequate replacement for them (Dube 1988: 507).

Technological change is not an end or value in and of itself, but is rather an evaluation of the appreciation of it as a means to securing human well-being and to preserving human ideas and material innovations. To this end technological change was 'the result of deliberate effort to achieve a mechanical way of life ... The western European conceived of the machine because he wanted regularity, order, certainty, because he wished to reduce the movement of his fellows as well as the behaviour of the environment to a more definite, calculable basis' (Brozen 1952: 251). This means that one set of cultural values for which men strive is to improve the techniques needed to contribute to the attainment of freedom, human dignity, and democracy. This is why some scholars not only fear for the future of freedom and dignity but also fear that technological change is sweeping the world toward more wars and that these wars will be more destruc-tive as a result of the contribution of technology (Brozen 1952: 256-7).

Dube (1988: 508-11) maintains that culture or traditions cannot be treated as vestigial remains of an ancient past because they survive to the extent that they have definite technological functions. They contribute to a community's special sense of creativity and being. They also provide bases of social integration, and offer guidelines to innovative action during periods of uncertainty. Without re-placement by adequate functional analogues, one cannot contemplate disman-tling traditional structures because of their technological relevance as exemplars of bodies of knowledge. Decades have shown that development strategies that are not sensitive and responsive to the cultural fabric run the risk of encountering rough weather. This is all the more reason why cultural creativity is important but the over-mystification of it can result in concocted violation of historical facts.

For Dube, the politicisation of culture has its own inherent dangers, because it can be perverted and utilised to erode the core values and creative purposes of human and social security, such that its vulgarisation can be used to promote discord, conflict and violence. This means that any technological culture used to hamper the normal processes of heterogeneous cultural growth is in want of security. Culture has important aesthetic, psychic, creative and integrative techno-logical functions because most human security situations and goals lean on cul-tural definitions and valuations of the society's technological creation. Hence cul-ture cannot be ruled out from a meaningful consideration of human development (Dube 1988: 508).

For Goulet (1987: 166-176), traditional values play many roles in society; they bring identity, continuity and a sense of meaning to people. But not all traditions have a positive value for genuine development. This is where the humanising potential of technological values must be assessed with sensitivity and balance, especially in the ways that such technological cultures prove themselves useful to each new generation. Even in the context of ancient traditions, technological creativity is not to be received uncritically; rather each new generation should generate its own reasons for ratifying what its ancestors found to be valuable in such knowledge acquisition. And this means that the function and values of cul-ture must be technologically developed to improve the quality of life, such as values of authentic development even if it is in conflict with prevailing dominant traditional values. For Goulet (1987: 176), 'to design or build development on traditions and indigenous values is to espouse a philosophy of change founded on a basic trust in the ability of people, no matter how oppressed or impover-ished, to improve their lives, to understand the social forces that affect them, and eventually to harness these forces to processes of genuine human and societal development'.

Conclusion

A critical examination of the various cultural problems which threaten Nigeria's national security reveals that they are steeped in the cultural-ethical dimension. A lack of understanding of the far-reaching consequences of some of these cul-tural actions remains one important reason why it has been possible to subvert the Nigerian state. As a post-colonial African state and a developing nation for that matter, it is essential to develop a cultural transmission method through for-mal and informal education that will help create a greater awakening to the fun-damental problem of Nigeria, which is basically an ethical one. There is the need to create a vision of a Nigerian dream in which the various groups have roles to play, despite our differences. There is the need to unite the various groups through the stressing of those areas, within our cultures which are similar, as a way of putting an end to the issue of stratification in the society. Very importantly, there is the need for an ethically based leadership. It is therefore necessary to enlighten Nigerians about the dangers of exposing ourselves to foreign cultural ideas, which can destabilise the country. This is necessitated by the fact that culture provides all sorts of nuances in communication and the amalgamation of the ethics of protective differences and communal solidarity necessary for national security.

There is the need to involve educational institutions in the security sector. The formal educational sector needs to be re-invented by incorporating critical ethical education directed at breaking ethnically bound values, religious barriers and so forth. It is necessary to promote and teach social ethics in order to raise the moral consciousness of citizens. The use of electronic media will also prove very useful in this effort because the wider population can be reached in this way. There is a need to involve the various Councils for Arts and Culture in states and at the Federal level. Such cultural administration establishments should be properly staffed with people trained in applied anthropological research methods. These cultural centres can assist in conducting research on the kinds of collective conduct in society which disturb peace and stability.

This work has emphasised the significance of a national cultural policy as an instrument of security and social engineering. This is crucial for national survival, insofar as national security is, in a significant sense, a product of culture. The critical clarification and interconnections of the material, institutional, and philosophical aspects of culture paved the way for a more systematic analysis of the dynamic elements of our culture(s) vis-à-vis national security. This cultural analysis situated the internal and external dimensions to national security.

References

Acharya, Shankar N., 1981, 'Perspectives and Problems of Development in Sub-Saharan Africa', *World Development*, vol. 9, pp. 109-147.

Ackermann, Werner, 1981, 'Cultural Values and Social Choice of Technology', *International Social Science Journal*, vol. XXXIII, no. 3, pp. 447-465.

Aig-Imoukhuede, Frank, 1992, *A Handbook of Nigerian Culture*, Lagos: Jeromelaiho and Associates.

Albert, Isaac Olawale, 2005, 'Terror as a Political Weapon: Reflections on the Bomb Explosions in Abacha's Nigeria', *IFRA Ibadan Special Research*, vol. 1, pp. 37-56.

Bodunrin, P. O., 1991, 'Philosophy and Culture', in Lloyd Thompson, Dapo Adelugba and Egbe Ifie, eds., *Culture and Civilization*, Ibadan/ Lagos: Africa - Links Books, pp. 92-100.

Briskman, Larry, 1980, 'Creative Product and Creative Process in Science and Art', *Inquiry*, vol. 23, pp. 83-106.

Brozen, Yale, 1952, 'The Value of Technological Change', *Journal of Ethics*, vol. LXII, no. 4, pp. 249-265.

Cabral, Amilcar, 1998, 'National Liberation and Culture (Return to the Source)', in Emmanuel Chukwudi Eze, ed., *African Philosophy: An Anthology*, Massachusetts: Blackwell, pp. 260-265.

Castro-Gomez, Santiago, 2002, 'The Cultural and Critical Context of Postcolonialism', *Philosophia Africana*, vol. 5, no. 2, pp. 25-34.

Coetzee, Peter H., 1998, 'Particularity in Morality and its Relation to Community', in P. H. Coetzee et al., eds., *The African Philosophy Reader*, London: Routledge, pp. 275-291.

Collier, Paul, and Gunning, Jan William, 1999, 'Why Has Africa Grown Slowly?', *Journal of Economic Perspectives*, vol. 13, no 3, pp. 3-22.

Davidson, Basil, 1991, 'What Development Model?', *African Forum - A Journal of Leadership and Development*, vol. 1, pp. 13-16.

Downs, J. F., 1971, *Cultures in Crisis*, Beverly Hills, California: Glencoe Press.

Dube, S. C, 1988, 'Cultural Dimensions of Development', *International Social Science Journal*, vol. 118, pp. 505-511.

Dzobo, N. K., 1992, 'The Image of Man in Africa', in Kwasi Wiredu and Kwame Gyekye, eds., *Person and Community: Ghanaian Philosophical Studies 1*, Washington DC: The Council for Research in Africa, pp. 123-132.

Fanon, Frantz, 1998, 'Racism and Culture', in Emmanuel Chukwudi Eze, *African Philosophy: An Anthology*, Massachusetts: Blackwell, pp. 305-311.

Ferraro, Gary, 1997, *Cultural Anthropology: An Applied Perspective*, New York: Wadsworth Publishing.

Gbadegesin, Segun, 1991, 'Contemporary African Realities: The Cultural View', in *African Philosophy, Traditional Yoruba Philosophy and Contemporary African Realities*, New York: Peter Lang.

Gotesky, Aubin and Erwin Breithaupt, 1978, 'Creativity: A Meta-Sociological and Analysis', *Philosophy and Phenomenological Research*, vol. XXXIX, no 1, pp. 23-41.

Goulet, Dennis, 1987, 'Culture and Traditional Values in Development', in Philip J. Hughes, ed., *The Ethics of Development: The Pacific in the 21st Century*, Port Moresby: University of Papua, New Guinea Press, pp. 165-178.

Gyekye, Kwame, 1997, *Tradition and Modernity. Philosophical Reflections on the African Experience*, New York: Oxford University Press.

Halpern, Ben, 1955, 'The Dynamic Elements of Culture', *ETHICS: An International Journal of Social, Political, and Legal Philosophy*, vol. LXV, no. 4, pp. 235-249.

Hartley, Peter, 1999, *Interpersonal Communication*, Second Edition, London: Routledge.

Hatch, E., 1985, 'Culture', in *The Social Sciences Encyclopaedia*, Adam Kuper and Jessica Kuper, eds., London: Routledge.

Hogendorn, Jan. S., 1996, *Economic Development*, New York: Harper Collins Publisher Inc.

Irele, Abiola, 1991, 'Culture and the Arts', in Lloyd Thompson, Dapo Adelugba and Egbe Ifie, eds., *Culture and Civilization*, Ibadan/Lagos: Africa - Links Books, pp. 52-58.

Janusz and Vladimir, 1995, 'Concept and New Dimensions of Security: Introductory Remarks', in *Non-military Aspects of International Security*, France, UNESCO Publishing.

Landes, David, 1991, 'Rethinking Development', *Dialogue*, no 1, pp. 66-71.

Linton, R., 1936, *The Study of Man*, New York.

Mazrui, A., 1973, *Cultural Engineering and Nation Building in East Africa*, Evanston IL: Northwestern Press.

M'Bow, M Amadou-Mahtar,1992, 'Opening Speech', in Irele, Abiola, ed., *African Education and Identity*, London: Hans Zell Publishers, pp. 11-15.

McLaurin, R. O., 1988, 'Managing National Security: The American Experience and Lessons for the Third World', in Edward E. Azar and Chung-in Moon, eds., *The Third World: The Management of Internal and External Threats*, London: Edward Elgar Publishing.

Munkner, Hans. H., 1998, 'Which Values for Africa of the 21st Century?', *Africana Marburgensia*, Special Issue, 17. pp. 79-87.

Ndulu, Benno J. and Stephen A. O'Connell, 1999, 'Governance and Growth in Sub-Saharan Africa', *Journal of Economic Perspectives*, vol. 13, no. 3, pp. 41-66.

Nkrumah, Kwame, 1975, 'The African Personality', Cyrus M. Mutiso and S.W. Rohio, eds., *Readings in African Political Thought*, London: Heinemann, pp. 57-60.

North, Douglas C., 1989, 'Institutions and Economic Growth: An Historical Introduction', *World Development*, vol. 17, no. 9, pp. 1319-1332.

Odhiambo, E. S. Atieno, 2002, 'The Cultural Dimensions of Development in Africa', *African Studies Review*, vol. 45, no. 3, pp. 1-16.

Omatete, 1972, 'The Security of the Nigerian Nation', in Joseph Okpaku, ed., *Nigeria: Dilemma of Nationhood*, New York: Third Press.

Osia, Kunirum, 1983, 'Black Africa and the Dilemma of Development', *Journal of African Studies*, vol. 14, no. 2, pp. 37-45.

Owolabi, A. O., 1998, 'Global Change: Redefining African National Security in the 90s and the Twenty-First Century', in Olusegun Oladipo, ed., *Remaking Africa: Challenges of the Twenty-first Century*, Ibadan: Hope Publications, pp. 159-167.

Tukur, M., 1999, *Leadership and Governance in Nigeria. The Relevance of Values*, London: Hodder and Stoughton.

Tylor, E. B., 1871, *Origins of Culture*, New York: Harper and Row.

Uchendu, V. C., 1988, 'Towards a Strategic Concept of Culture: Implications for Continental Unity in Africa', Ali, Asiwaju and Oloruntimehin, eds., *The Cultural Foundations*, Lagos: Civitelis International.

Uroh, Chris Okechukwu, 1996, 'Africa in The Philosophy of Culture: Demystifying an Ideology of Cultural Imperialism', *Journal of Philosophy and Development*, vol. 2, .pp. 10-18.

Wolfers, A., 1962, *Discord and Collaboration: Essays on International Politics*, John Hopkins University Press.

6

Gender Dimensions of the National Security and Human Security Problematic: Core Theoretical, Conceptual and Historical Issues

Irene Omolola Adadevoh

Introduction and Problem

> All men and women are created equal… yet the history of mankind is a history of repeated injuries and usurpation on the part of man toward woman. (Elizabeth Cady Stanton, July 1848).

This part of the NWG research focuses on the conceptual clarification of the interfaces between gender and national security and the consequences of segregationist policies. It is based on the notion that the discrimination and restriction of women by a male-dominated culture is suggestive of the national insecurity faced by women. In the context of the gender dimensions of security, a theoretician, Alison (2004: 447) has put it succinctly that 'the question of whose security is being discussed is important. Since security has traditionally been conceptualized in masculinized, military terms and women have been excluded', then there is a need for a more intensive investigation of the context of women's security. Alison (2004) does this analysis from an empirical perspective, drawing heavily on the situation in specific countries of interest.

While the above approach is commendable, it requires some intensification and reinforcement, which we have imposed on the discourse on gender and security by seeking to delve into the vital conceptual, methodological and theoretical dimensions of gender security re-conceptualisation. This task is in keeping with our primary vocational philosophical methodology and its fruitful outcomes. Traditional concepts that feature in a putative discussion of women's security include oppression and discrimination. According to Caprioli (2004: 412), 'discrimination is a symptom of both the inequality and the structural violence that undermine women's security'. The fact then is that such a situation can no longer be considered acceptable or even tolerable for the agents, victims and agencies of women's oppression and insecurity.

Women's insecurity is a fact of life that cannot be underestimated. According to Goldstein (1999: 99), we must announce 'repeatedly and in forceful terms that women in Civilization have been severely oppressed and particularly victimized'. This oppression and victimisation have brought about the general insecurity of women. The crisis of national insecurity can be inextricably linked to women's stereotypical traditional roles, which like job descriptions define their member-ship in the community by requiring them to act in certain ways. With special reference to Africa, the situation of women is the more deplorable. To this ex-tent, we cannot but agree with Uko (1996: 4-5), who insists that 'traditionally the woman in Africa functions as a mother, wife and co-wife. Her psyche is affected by the impact of colonial domination as well as male chauvinism, polygamy, dependence and inferiority complex. She is usually contemplated in the sense of dominated, disadvantaged, exploited and excluded'. Given these realities, these roles entrench the expectations that others have of women within many social organisations in a given nation-state.

The problem, as we conceive it, is, firstly, to determine the extent to which discourses on sexual identities and national security take into account the social behaviour of the sexes in the light of the maintenance of the status of masculinised securities. Secondly, and no less important, is to examine the conditions for the affirmation of security, justice and equity for women within a nation-state. The essay tackles these problems through the redefinition of stereotyping myths, and the evaluation of the changing dimensions of national segregationist policies. Thus the impetus for our work, as stated above, is justified again on the basis of the position of Daly (1996: 137) that 'women who have perceived the reality of sexual oppression usually have exhausted themselves in breaking through to dis-covery of their own humanity, with little energy left for constructing their own interpretation of the universe'. We must admit also that although there have been recent expositions on the predicaments of women, as seen in efforts by the Committee for the Defence of Human Rights (CDHR 2001) in the *2000 Annual Report on the Human Rights Situation in Nigeria*, and the Three-day National Work-shop on Gender Violence and Family Poverty for the southwest zone (July 2001) organised by the Special Adviser to the President on Women Affairs. These ef-forts have shown the near intractability of the phenomenon of the abject disempowerment, oppression and subordination of women. As things stand, few, if any, of these works have systematically opened up the discourse on the national security of women in a more conscious and systematic manner, such as is implied by a fuller conceptual account of the problem. There is, therefore, a need for a holistic and careful account of the national security dimensions of women's issues as construed in this essay.

Against the above background, we must agree with Alaya (1977) on the focus of our struggle. Our struggle, as we understand it, is to 'establish a logical basis for the intellectual history of the idea of woman's "emancipation" and "liberation"' (Alaya 1977: 261). Granted the logical justification of our project, we need to clarify the means of attaining the goal. In this context we can accept Attig's statement (1976: 156) that examination of the 'normative questions related to the careful analysis of concepts such as "freedom" and "liberation", "oppression", "rights", "justice" and "equality", "consciousness" and "self-fulfilment"' would be invaluable to the review of gender security in the post-colonial context. The challenge of our work, is therefore, to achieve what Janes (1978: 295) has described as the correction of 'errors hitherto universally embraced, concerning the female character; and to raise woman from a state of degradation and vassalage, to her proper place in the scale of existence, where, in the dignity of independence, she may discharge the duties and enjoy the happiness of a rational being'. Thus, the challenges to women's security are both universal and particular in nature.

In order effectively to confront the task of segregating the universal and particular aspects of women's security, the paper will be divided into distinct parts. The first part conducts a theoretical analysis of gender roles, segregation and allied notions. It analyses the processes of sex-role differentiation in security schema theory. The aim is to appreciate gender studies and to gain an understanding of the effects of the evolution of gender roles on social interpretations of national security. Secondly, we examine the problem of national security for women from a comparative and thematic perspective that takes care to review the traditional and more contemporary dimensions of the problem. Special emphasis is placed on the empirical consequences concerning the shaping of individual and group identity as well as national security. Lastly, our essay highlights the need to capture and transcend these variables, and provides recommendations for social change that may foster secure and positively developed social relationships between the sexes in a nation-state. The import of this emphasis is to underscore the point that individuals have unlimited potentials or capacities and that, when people's roles are defined according to their sex, human and national development is severely limited.

Retracing the Etymology of Marginality in Security Schema Theory

The reality of non-belonging, marginality and inequality of women is closely involved with national security and human security problems. The fact that women are objectified and regarded as property has helped generate the national security dilemma and its ensuing anarchic constitution which cannot itself be (re)solved through the entrenchment of established norms and institutions. The failure of institutional frameworks and the critical security situation compounds the dilemma for women. This is most visibly illustrated by the question of roles. This issue requires philosophical investigation and in fact the view that roles may be related to stereotypes is strikingly analysed in the philosophical works of Plato, Aristotle, Augustine, Hobbes, etc.

However, there are deeper problems arising from the specific works of Plato and Aristotle as they relate to the security of women. In both philosophers' works, women's marginality in the scheme of things does not guarantee the security of their human persons. For Plato and Aristotle, women are an extension of material possessions. In fact, 'women are classified by Plato, as they were by the culture in which he lived, as an important subsection of property' (Okin 1977: 349). In a similar vein, the classical sociological theorists such as Auguste Comte and Emile Durkheim, among others, believed that women were best suited for roles outside of the public sphere (Comte 1975; Durkheim 1964; Elshtain 1981; Kleinbaum 1977). The implication of the above view is that women seem to exist in the bounds of what is, literally speaking, a sort of thraldom or slavery. But as Cuffel (1966: 326) has argued, 'the possibilities of communal and personal slavery raised an ethical and moral problem, a problem in which the notion of the action of fate and the idea of personal inferiority were in opposition'. To repudiate the images of slavery of women we must confront the status quo and seek the establishment of a new set of ideas and values. As such we can agree with Lucas (1973: 161) that in questions of women's security, the 'debate turns on the application of certain concepts of justice, equality and humanity'. These ideas are in need of clarification if the notion of security for women is to be fully articulated.

Most gender and feminist scholars have argued that women were marginalised in the domains designed to guarantee the security of the human person. It is asserted that the inferiority of women and their oppression, exploitation and subjection constitute the basis for the denial of personhood to them and thus also of their insecurity. For instance, Wollstonecraft's works (1759-97) such as 'Thoughts on the Education of Daughters' (1787), 'The Female Reader' (1789), and 'A Historical and Moral View of the Origins and Progress of the French Revolution' (1794), and 'A Vindication of the Rights of Women' (1792), were documents that challenged these parochial perspectives, especially Rousseau's ideas regarding female inferiority.

In a similar vein, Margaret Fuller (1810-50), in exposing the error in the idea of organised classes for 'conversations' among women, made an ardent plea for the emotional, intellectual, and spiritual fulfilment and security of women. Sun Yat-Sen in China in 1923 was one of the first Chinese women to bob her hair in radical and revolutionary protest against women's subjugation (Compton 1995). One immediate point to note is the link between the resistance to myths and representations of women's inferiority and the struggle for the expansion of the conceptual space of security discourses. Thus, there is a fundamental challenge posed to traditional notions of security which demands a re-configuration of the idea of security in more radical and holistic perspectives. Let us now attempt a more detailed analysis of the theoretical discourses surrounding gender and security of women.

Conceptual Security, Ideational Dependency and Segregation: The Problematic of Analytic Juxtaposition

What is needed is a conceptual analysis of the nexus between security, ideology and segregation. The theoretical analysis of sex roles, segregation and security of women is best approached through the critical review of the situation of women as highlighted over the ages. A careful study of security options and the empirical investigations into the manner of interaction between security and gender role activities uncovers evidence of wide-ranging differences of perspective among authors. Grown and Sebstad (1989) attempt a three-tier distinction between what they purport to be stages of women's security. According to these authors (1989: 941), 'for the poorest, survival is the goal; the poorest women strive to generate income to purchase food, shelter and clothing. For those whose basic survival is assured, the individual or household goal may shift to security; additional assets then are acquired by diversifying the livelihoods mix to spread risk and increase flexibility. Finally, for those who have achieved basic security, the goal may change to growth. Women who feel relatively secure may concentrate their investments in higher return but riskier commercial enterprises dependent on the availability of services and purchased inputs'.

However, we are doubtful with regard to the unwarranted optimism implied in this typological analysis of the stages of women's security. In fact, as appealing as this classification appears to be, it still does not strike at the heart of the conceptual challenge to women's security. The real contexts of insecurity in the world of African women may erode this tripartite analysis. In the face of real social, legal, political and cultural denial, domination, and deprivation that women confront, the stages may unfold into one long track of dehumanisation.

For example, the state of gross disadvantage arising from a vicious combination of life-long unpaid and unappreciated women's labour and the inimical widow-hood and inheritance customs as they operate in some African cultures demonstrates that the line is very thin between survival, security and growth. Thus we can agree with Jaquette (1990: 65) that 'women are forced by their poverty to participate in a system that generates and intensifies inequalities and makes use of existing gender hierarchies to place women in subordinate positions at each different level of interaction between class and gender'. The poverty we refer to here must be seen in a more holistic manner that goes beyond mere economic incapacitation to more invidious legal, political and social restriction.

The existence of divergent views on the subject of hypothetical security accurately discloses the gravity of the issues relating to human protection, social development and defence of human dignity. It is for this reason that feminist historians have over the ages fought to preserve and 'concentrate on transforming and enriching mainstream security history, which has traditionally had so little regard for women' (Jackson et al., 1993: 107-8). In pursuing this position, we are committed to breaking the silence and tearing the veil of obscurity and of omission in security history. This orientation prides itself on particularly deconstructing the dominant national ideology that socialises women into subordinate roles and the 'politics of motherhood' (Lewis 1980).

It is in the light of this pattern of security that our task comes down to the demystification of hegemonic constructs and the erection of a new epistemological edifice that can sustain the theoretical and practical expectations of the transformations of traditional security schemas. The implication of the acceptance of the need for transformation is that, as Frenkel (1964: 338) says, 'it is clear that in taking a stand for the dignity of humanity and human society it would be better not to rely on naturalness as a basis'. Such naturalness can be defined in terms of conventional or biologically induced features that can entail the denial and deprivation of essential human values for positive development.

Gender role socialisation with respect to 'conceptual security' has always been problematic. This is because it tends to be seen predominantly in collective military and defence terms, as opposed to the more viable personal developmental connotation. This is possibly why the *Africa Research Bulletin* (2000) construes the traditional concept of national security as the avoidance of conflict and the preservation of the lives of people in society. However, this conception of security is restrictive, not only because it reduces security to the mere absence of conflict, but also because women are not even included in the strategies for the avoidance or management of these conflicts. Thus it fails on these two scores.

To put it more concretely, the conflict theory of security fails because it does not establish a level playing field for the consideration of the security of the afflicted, oppressed and vulnerable. In short, neither the planners nor the executors of these conflicts have the full interest of women's security at heart. The consequence is that women, children and other highly vulnerable segments of a society suffer the most in the event that a conflict (internal or externally motivated) boils over. They are most often pawns in the hands of the perpetrators of violence and conflict. Worse still, this conception of security does not confront the internally induced threats to women's security, and the perpetrators of this insecurity. Thus the militaristic conception of security fails to secure the protection of women, not just because the principle thrives on insecurity and instability, but because it is immersed in the hegemonic ordering of the patriarchal and command structures, with their uniquely magisterial posturing.

The point we make is that the theoretical analysis of national security is itself a harbinger of insecurity insofar as it is alienating and restrictive in nature. To this end, the issue of national security for women has not been given the adequate consideration it deserves. Further attempts to deal with the question of national security for women has led scholars such as O'Brien (1995) to offer an inclusive and sympathetic account of national security, construing it as more than just safety from the violence of rival militaries. To this effect, national security is the absence of inhibition, violence or segregation whether social, political, economic or sexual. The strength of the above view is its intellectual fertility and gender sensitivity, which creates room for the conceptual penetration of security hitherto into erstwhile forbidden spaces. Thus if O'Brien's view is correct, then there is no doubt that the national security of women has not been fully taken care of either theoretically or practically.

The ever-present spectre of violence, threats and hatred against women is clear evidence that new options in the quest for security for women are long overdue. Lodge (1995) agrees that any discourse that tends to view national security in predominantly military or defence terms poses a problem for the proper definition and analysis of the concept of security and segregation. This is especially the case as it affects women's security discourses. The silence regarding the position of women is occasioned by the fact that it is the men who are most engaged in the definition, design, and implementation of security programmes, conceived either in the restricted or broader perspective within the nation state.

Beyond the foregoing conceptual analysis of national security, it is necessary to examine the role of segregation in the initial creation and eventual sustenance of the subordination of women's security demands. Borgia (1978: 27) is of the opinion that sexual activity and role allocation play a large part in human association and the national organisation of life. In this hypothesis, males strive to conquer other females. And by virtue of the peculiar construction of this permissive culture, male domination desensitises the females so that they fail to appreciate their own humanity.

This analogy of social ordering of national security as a contest leaves out the general thrust of co-operative treatment of sexuality within the nation-state. It entrenches national security as a competitive dog-eat-dog attitude. The problem of social segregation on a gender basis takes precedence in national policies. It is worth pointing out that this dominance was opposed in the eighteenth century by early feminists who agitated for a 'Declaration of the Rights of Woman' to protest the French revolutionists' failure to mention women in their 'Declaration of the Rights of Man' (Compton 1995).

The threats emanating from prevailing conceptual security and segregationist policies are consequential in women's attempt to escape the feminine stereotype (Jeffreys 1985). At times, this resistance has led to what has been labelled as 'sexual inversion' (Ellis 1927), or indirectly to an 'accusation of iconoclasm to subvert women's attempt at emancipation from the fetters of insecurity' (Jeffreys 1985: 105-6). The struggle for the emancipation of women is situated against the back-drop of the institutionalisation of patriarchy and its numerous consequences. To this effect, the roles of women in national security matters are defined constitu-tionally by the patriarchal burden of both male domination and female subjuga-tion. Indeed, patriarchy as a major instrument of the subjugation of women creates and celebrates a power structure that bestows more personal, political, social and economic power on men.

The ravaging effects of patriarchal ordering have compelled sexologists in many countries to accede to a tumult of conflicting demands to produce avenues for more rapid development, expanded welfare services and greater gender se-curity. The intellectual shortfalls occasioned by the neglect of this subject by de-velopment analysts have inflicted severe constraints on the planning strategies of the authorities in most nation-states. Patriarchal ordering aggravates the security crisis and security dilemma for women insofar as it defines and perpetuates sexual exploitation. Daly (1996: 136) writes that 'the exploitative sexual caste system could not be perpetuated without the consent of the victims as well as of the dominant sex, and such a consent is obtained through sex role socialization - a conditioning process which begins to operate from when we are born, and which is enforced by most institutions'.

Other scholars argue that there are other vectors of women's insecurity and marginality besides patriarchy. This may well be the case. Wanzala (1996: 85) suggests that 'to take a gender or feminist perspective would unduly de-empha-size forms of power that impinge on the conditions of marginalized women and children which are not explained by patriarchy or male dominance'. This particular point is reinforced by Francis (2002), who observes that 'the concept of "patriarchy" appears unsatisfactory because it cannot account for the multi-plicity and complexity of power relations'. At another level of the analysis, there has been an insistence that the stronger factor in the insecurity of women is that of sexism. According to Warren (1977: 241), 'sexism means unfair discrimination on the basis of sex. Sexism may be due to dislike, distrust, or contempt for women'. Whatever is the case, we must 'see sexual difference as just one among others that contribute to inequality and domination' (Nash 2002: 415). Sexism creates a fertile setting for perversion and hate syndromes that cast women in the image of prey to be attacked and harassed at will.

Most of the cardinal problems confronted by women in the arena of security arise due to the flux and tensions emanating from the construction of sex and allied sex roles in the constitutional framework. As a biological concept, gender refers to a classification used in a distinction between the two sexes and the sexlessness of some human persons. In ancient times, gender roles had been solely about the ways in which people constructed their erotic or sexual relationships, based on discriminatory differences. However, recent conceptions of sexism accommodate the way it governs national attitudes and undermines the uniqueness and realness of the person. Often, the term sex has been used interchangeably with that of gender. In this category the sex-gender identity is depicted in three basic forms, notably, the masculine, the feminine and the neuter. A person's sexuality is extended beyond the biological role and covers a wider range of social relations, political power plays and legal instrumental functions. Accordingly, we can say that gender is used to refer to the non-physiological aspects of being female or male depending on the cultural and national expectations for femininity and masculinity (Lips 1993: 4). The social categories of gender-related security issues integrate a dichotomised ideology of intensive significance in virtually every domain of human experience (Ben 1985: 212). In this way, a number of issues in the national security arena are not treated as sex-neutral, but rather are perceived through the lens of difference and sexual segregation (Sunstein 1995: 5). Central to the analysis of gender therefore is the immediate attention that it draws to the phenomenon of difference as well as to segregation. By virtue of this difference, the idea of gender roles is to be construed as much more than a question of a concept, in that it refers to a social context of stereotypes that go beyond personality traits.

Gender addresses the normative expectations concerning appropriate masculine or feminine behaviour in a particular culture (Appelbaum 1995: 270). These 'normative expectations' stretch across security, justice, independence and the violation of rights, liberty, peace, etc. These norms and rules hinder the upward mobility between the sexes on an equal basis. Along the pattern of the normative micro-politics of national expectations and attitudes, there is a dichotomised empowering of agents and agencies along gender lines.

This dichotomisation is linked to the question of agent-neutral attitudes and agent-relative ones. For example, the eradication of insecurity from the gender-related dichotomy is an agent-neutral attitude, whereas the development of the stereotypical roles to suit one's purpose is at best an agent-relative attitude. By implication, a division of agent-relative values into autonomously distinct forms explains the national ordering that specifies 'protective relationships' between each sex either locally or globally. This dimension of security discourse raises questions about the quality of abstract notions such as freedom, justice and person-hood embedded in the specific relations of national protection existing in the real world. It even poses questions about the specific cultural and national contexts that can nullify or reinforce the ideal ordering of protective relations. The significance for gender and national security lies in the fact that the question of security is an important concern in the life of any person, group or nation. And while Brown (1982) holds that the concern for the security of a nation is undoubtedly as old as the nation-state itself, it is not at all clear how we can measure the extent of its incorporation with regards to the security of women.

Central to our conceptual analysis of national security for women is the rejection of the tendencies to immerse women into the male-configured and segregationist security landscape. It can even be argued that since the nation is composed of individuals, the quest for the security of the human person is a core feature of human personal and social endeavour. However, the question then becomes that of understanding how gender difference affects security propositions in relation to women. The argument of McLennan (1996) here is that the mobilisation of gender disparity in contradistinction to women's security is such that 'the economic, political and spiritual world that we inhabit is ruled by feminine violation' (McLennan 1996: 7-10). The disparity between men and women, which serves as a basis for national insecurity, hinges on the violation of equality in ways that do not favour women. It is for this reason that Appelbaum (1995) says that women have not achieved anything approaching political, economic, legal or social equality with men. Accordingly, many systems of security politics are so 'extensively based on inequalities that any aspect of inequality jeopardizes the entire structure' (Okin 1979: 277).

Another key issue that is central to the tyranny of inequality in national security is the conceptualisation of women in the light of their dependency. Most discussions on gender security are approached through an ideology that modifies the other sex. Thus, given that women remain a group that is dominated, marginalised and subordinated, the central feature in the quest for national security cannot just be concern for the mere survival of individuals. Do we require that individuals survive as mere stooges or acolytes, without developing their own sense of proportion and well-being? Do we require that individuals unquestioningly accept their oppressed existence and thank their detractors and taskmasters for a job well done? The answer must be in the negative.

Rather, genuine national security should focus on the concern for the peace and progress of individuals and groups in society. The idea is to devise a conception of inclusive security that can operate on the principles of justice and dignity for the female sex. In this light, popular attention given to security communities focuses on the supposedly profound 'sense of community' or the 'we feeling', which according to Goldstein (1999: 430) has negative implications for equity for the female sex. Thus a major dimension of the contest for security for women is seen in the tension between the modes of ostracism and integration within the security institutions and the consequences of these for social existence.

It is interesting, yet disturbing, to note that women are portrayed as wilfully security dependent. This dependency is extended to imply the desirability for representation by men in security-oriented spheres of life. Ironically, this is a pervasive and contrary situation, whereby men are perceived as standing-in for women by an implicit but voluntary agreement. Despite the challenge to social and cultural security representation, surveys on national security patterns show that each context legitimises masculine authority and the notion that women who challenge authority deserve to be victimised (Lips 1993: 387). This makes gender prejudice a security struggle that poses an insoluble dilemma for women.

For instance, the facts of the masculine ordering of inheritance and private property, the predominant male role in sexual assault, and the portrayal of girl-woman abuse, and the social context of horrific widowhood rites, and forced marriages are often presented as a service to women. This poses a significant problem for justice, equity and social changes which are a necessary pre-requisite for the enforcement of social security (Lips 1993: 388). The central character of dependency in national life is its capacity to vitiate the security of women through the erection of perverted notions of social ordering. Worse still, this phenomenon raises critical problems about the theoretical underpinnings of human society, especially its so-called modern evolutionary embrace of the social contract principle. The question, then, is how does national insecurity for women undermine the belief in a society founded on mutual respect, tolerance, and consent as the basis of human interpersonal relations for the good of all? This point is the more significant when we review the character of ostracism as a segregationist schema.

Clearly the history of security is replete with suppressive images that ostracise women. Often the depiction of women in the history of security valorises this trend of social ostracism, limitation and subjection by the pervasive helplessness and indirection of silenced accommodation of cultural insecurities (McLennan 1996). Undoubtedly, the disadvantageous hierarchical placement of women on the pedestal of security studies reveals the unequal manifestation of culture, regime and social institutions, embracing classified subject categories such as race, sex, ethnicity, nationality, and indigenous traditions.

Indeed, what has prevailed so far is the propensity to accommodate concrete challenges to the status quo of conscious and egoistic male domination. To this effect, there may in fact be some connection between the absorptive capacity of the hegemonic security culture and the relatively limited protest by women. Feminist gender discourses have therefore revolved round attempts to alter the pseudo-projection of cultural security experiences on the female sex. Despite the confidence mustered by many women in assessing their security posture, it is glaring that they vacillate between the super-women image and a dependence syndrome, both of which are affected by the traditional anti-female bias that grants them only an assimilative mode of interaction because of the influence of tradition on gender stereotypes.

The question then is, can tradition ever be legitimately gender-neutral? It is often implied that the condition of a unified or balanced security operates distinctively outside the domains of domination and repression. Unfortunately, gender security is constructed as a mystified cult of misleading liberation. Besides, female sexuality is used to secure repression. The issue is not whether traditional systems are more secure but rather whether their approaches to security are the measure of security desired by women. This is a very important point that elicits not only the analysis of security, but also its foundational assumptions. Ordinarily the entrenched security disposition towards women has a double dimension. First, it distinguished them by their shared characteristics and social-economic situation and more importantly it co-opts their agreement in counter-balancing the degrees of their insecurities.

Also linked to the theme of security is the correlation of social adjustments and organisation. The advantages of competitive predispositions encountered in certain predetermined norms and values of social life create an exclusivist drift towards divergent roles. The dominant patterns are the material segregation, ingrained learned malevolence, hatred, and other virulent mythical 'falsification of natural and social history' (Reed 1970: 29) concerning the normal development of functional security roles for either sex. Segregation along sexual and security lines is partially congruent and partially opposed in the dilemma between the sexes (Hirsthleifer 1987: 273). This leaves the woman question in a 'security blanket', and a dysfunctional situation that stimulates an inadequate and irrational sense of comfort and protection.

Thus it can be said that the socialisation of sexism and power relations has given strength and vitality to the security dilemma that women endure. The best development and security to which women have been exposed, accrue from the benefit and foresight of professional, educational and economic power. Although even in these spheres, the conferment of 'power' is often misconstrued as the exercise of 'the power of man over the minds and action of other men... and the capacity to impose one's will on others by reliance on effective sanctions in case of non-compliance' (Schwarzenberger 1951: 14). Thus the attempt to broaden the horizon on segregation and insecurity unearths a multiplicity of ways in which women are marginalised. It also underlines the imperative for the enlightenment of the female mind (Wollstonecraft 1792 cited in Compton 1994). Therefore, we can construe the problem in terms of what Loic Wacquant (1996: pp ix-xi) calls the 'silent riot of every day life'. This phenomenon dramatically illustrates the reality of the problem of marginality and insecurity that is often fuelled by the very efforts to gain security. Marginality or insecurity is therefore an imposed condition, the result of the practices of others, or of the action of the state and society on those who become marginal.

On this note, the imputed gender welfare attitudes, as Fox (1975) observed, combine social and genetic relations of security as an inalienable social endorsement of male superiority. This disrupts the welfare propositions in relationships, particularly in ascertaining or ensuring maximum security for the female sex (Kaldor 1939). An evaluation of the scope of theories on gender welfare and development addresses issues that border on differences and inequalities in social ordering. Such inequalities are classified according to types, as we see in the evidence of racism, sexual profiling, ethnicity in the academia and military, etc. Taken together these modes of otherness impact on the social structure and cultural development of the entire global community.

The dominant classical theorising on national security is therefore difficult to apply to gender studies because its central tenet of neutrality does not often weigh national security against welfare losses. However, new foundational security perspectives have a common starting point in their attachment to the collective pursuit of mutually beneficial goals, such as learning processes and technocratic, social, economic and political welfare rights that will enhance the status of all and sundry. Thus, according to Juliet Lodge (1994: xx), women's competitive economic and political participation have great potential in mediating in the process of insecurity. In consequence, women become actively involved and become key players in issues of security.

Pivotal Foundations of National Security and the Segregation Schema Theory: the Ancient Era

A survey of early times shows the negative classification of the role of the 'woman' in the security segregation theory. A history of prejudice as a pivotal foundation for national security thus pervades all spheres of social life. According to Greek myth, Pandora, or the first woman, is a harbinger of pandemonium. In Roman law, she is a child and is thus in need of supervision. St. Jerome, a fourth century father of the Christian church, said: 'Woman is the gate of the devil, the path of wickedness, the sting of the serpent, in a word, a perilous object' (Compton 1995). Forge (2001) puts the historical dimensions of gender in proper perspective with the statement that 'females have not been treated as equal partners and some argue from a biblical perspective that the woman was created out of the ribs of man. Therefore women should be subordinate to men in all respects' (Forge 2001: 49).

The biblical injunction regarding this presumed inferiority states that 'A male shall be valued at 50 silver shekels if it is a female she shall be valued at 30 shekels' (Leviticus 27: 4). The unbroken link of this chain even at the present time, as shown by the US Census Bureau, is evident in the fact that an average full-time woman in the US earns about seventy cents for every dollar earned by a full-time male worker (US Department of Commerce 1991a, 1992b). This devaluation, here expressed in economic terms, goes a long way to pre-determine women's security in social life, such that despite the epochal gap between the Old Testament and contemporary societies, women's depreciation remains quite pervasive (Appelbaum 1995: 270). Elizabeth Cady Stanton's *Woman's Bible* (see Elshtain 1981), published in 1895 and 1898, attacked this derogatory female castigation in the Bible. She believed that male-centred religion would have to be abolished before the true security of women could be achieved. Like many in her class, Stanton worked towards the ordination of women as full members of the clergy.

Some parallels have equally been drawn between women's insecurity and the phenomenon of slavery. Women were seen as slaves, because both were expected to be 'passive, cooperative, and obedient to their master-husbands', such that the preference is always for masculinity and the images of control linked to it. At one time in history, it was not considered respectable for women to speak before mixed audiences of men and women. In one instance, women delegates to the World Anti-Slavery Convention held in London in 1840 were denied participation. The exception to this is what McLennan (1996: 24) described as 'sacramental confession used as the whole first vehicle for the first formalized expression by women in western history' against social injustices and insecurities. The same procedure or method of expressive insecurity was used in the sixteenth century by Marguerite De Navarret (1492-1549).

However, historically an exception has often been made for royalty. This is seen in the recognition given to monarchs such as Queen Elizabeth of England, Catherine the Great of Russia, and Queen Victoria of England (Compton 1995). The attitudinal disposition occasioned by concessions of dignity, power and influence of this sort bequeaths to women vulnerability and anxiety rather than an assured stability and certainty of freedom from danger. The images of security by imposition or security by proxy only offer what is at best the idea of a 'securitan'. This is someone who dwells in fancied security and who can be seized and directed to suit the whims and caprices of 'others'. Hence, there is no true security within the framework of concession security.

Also, in literary historic narrative this syndrome of silence and marginality as illustrations of illusive security extends the dependency theory. De France captures this violation in her twelfth century poem, which reveals a rare and courageous determination to challenge sexism. According to her, 'whosoever has received knowledge and eloquence in speech from God, should not be silent or secretive but demonstrate it willingly'. In demonstrating the insensitivity of the cultural renaissance of her time to women's plight, her poem titled 'Two Lovers' is illustrative of the point of view that the relational self and the personal self were confronted with diverse biases and pitfalls, due to the social learning pattern of submission, parental patriarchal model of authority and uncritical feminine patterns of passivity. In her work, a triangular tragedy occurred between an authoritarian king, her princess and another noble (Marie de France, 1155-1170 in Ferrante 1984). This exposition by Marie De France is highly commendable because the socialising agency of the time is identified with the social structure of secrecy rather than expressiveness on the part of the female sex.

There is no doubt that the insecurity of women is linked to a paradoxical and sinister play of the emotional and psychological nature upon both men and women. Its macabre quality is unleashed by the supposition that insecurity is itself a form of security for which the aggressor must be shown gratitude. The disputation with regard to the egocentric pattern of treatment of the feminine role consists in its inextricable connection with flattery. Elizabeth Hands (1789) in *The Death of Amnon* pointed this out when she maintained that a substantial number of women recall the negative influences experienced as a result of the social and cultural strategies that impose disorder and violence on them. Awareness of the potential problem in the 'securitan' relationship, particularly with respect to gender, sex roles have given impetus to the strange and conspiratorial promotion of assault. One area in which insecurity is mainly propagated is the crucial treatment of sexual assault. In Susanna Haswell Rowson's (1791) *Marian and Lydia*, the generosity of this type of insecurity consists in its treatment as a social favour. The major in his affectation developed a discourse of sexual depression and victimisation of Marian, whose only respite lay in the hope that her already 'sinking fragile frame never would have known pollution more'. Okin (1982: 65) has made the point clearly in respect of the political realm. 'When political theories were built on assumptions of natural hierarchy or of a God-given great chain of being, there was no particular difficulty supporting the idea that women were among the inferior categories of human beings. They could therefore legitimately be excluded from political life, denied legal equality, and relegated to a subordinate position within the family' (Okin 1982: 65). How will this negative historical situation be altered?

The Institutionalisation of Violence: Rethinking Security for the Modern Woman

This survey of women's security in former times enables us better to discuss the modern dimensions of the issue. Violence and violations (domestic or otherwise) against women remain the crux of the challenge to women's security. In any case, the analysis of violence is crucial because 'there are many different forms of violence in our society, some of which are often taken for granted' (Alder 1992: 269). It is true therefore that 'violence follows an ideological continuum, starting from the domestic sphere where it is tolerated, if not positively accepted. It then moves to the public political arena where it is glamourized and even celebrated ... Women and children are the prime victims of this cult of aggression' (Bunch and Carrillo 1990: 71). A good point to revisit is to review women as targets of negative social attitudes, who suffer not just social derogation but also become victims of untimely death.

Central to the insecurity of women in this era is the violence that pervades all spaces, public and private. The endemic problem in this regard is domestic violence, which thrives insofar as women are commoditised, privatised and voiceless in the economic, personal and legal realms. According to the Population Reference Bureau (1998), domestic violence is 'insecurity occurring within the private sphere generally between individuals who are related through intimacy, blood or law'. The effect of it is to devalue the virtue of purity and innocence and thus leave humanity in mourning for the disguised rape of feminism (Adadevoh 1999: 4). Women have become entangled in a yoke of vice which endorses sexual assaults and rape myths, construed not just as a stranger's ploy but also in the seemingly secure domain of good sense or filial piety (Lips 1993: 264). The correlating insecurities further extend their choking tentacles into the oppressive regimen of full-time housewifery and allied battery.

The real context of the insecurity of women under the domestic ordinance has been given a graphic colouration by Moynihan (1975: 159) who argues that 'equally dangerous and equally detestable are the cruelties often exercised in private families under the venerable sanction of parental authority'. This is the machinery for consolidating dominance and for extolling the confrontational and tyrannical regime in the home. It is therefore clear that the insecurity of women arises not merely from the natural hostile features of the external environment, but, more importantly, through the wilful and socially constructed acts of men. The most serious threat to women's security lies in men's fists (Bourke 1994: 62-64). This point is not lost on theoreticians who have seen the paradox in the insecurity of the security of the family space. According to Chesnais (1992: 222), 'the family is a place of paradox. A center affection, a refuge against adversity, it is also the foremost center of violence'.

The Women's International Network claims that despite its hypocritical concealment, family violence is still endemic because adherence to exaggerated sex role behaviour legitimates it. The heightened degree of privacy accorded to domestic violence maintains the culture of victim-hood, simply because a flimsy sentimental approach to the issue, either by the family members or by the police, makes the offender unaccountable to moral or legal sanction. The reason why aggressors elude justice and the victims remain insecure can be traced to an interface of factors. For instance, apart from the emotional, marital or social problems arising from such violence, there are also financial problems, and a 'lack of resources and decision making powers for community groups and statutory bodies to detect and intervene in family violence' which perpetuates the whole cycle (WIN: 1988). It is for this reason that we contend that the spectre of insecurity looms large in the lives of women and it unleashes debilitating effects on their total well-being.

Corroborating this view, the United Nations Human Rights Commission states that 'most domestic violence against a woman affects her mental, physical economic and social well-being. Many women tolerate such abuse because they fear retaliation by their spouse or extended family or both. If they protest, the women's vulnerability to domestic violence is reinforced by their economic dependence, and worse still, upon men's widespread cultural acceptance of domestic violence and a lack of laws and enforcement to combat it' (PRB 1998). Therefore, the reality of violence and the pervasive feelings of fear and anxiety are vitally linked to the sustenance of the regime of insecurity for women. The rights and dignity of women have not been adequately guaranteed because they have consistently been molested and brutalised. They face greater insecurity even from within those spaces where it was thought that their safety and sanctity could emerge. One reason may be that women have been perceived as primarily suited to fulfil special 'female' functions within the home.

Thomas Aquinas, the thirteenth century Christian theologian, said that woman was 'created to be man's helpmeet, but her unique role is in conception since for other purposes men would be better assisted by other men' (Compton 1995). Hence, the biological violation of women's security has been decoratively re-described to appear as normal. One of the most ironic aspects of this situation is that women are faced with the business of guaranteeing other people's security, particularly in terms of the continuity of society as their basic responsibility towards the child and the man. Yet no one is genuinely committed to the task of assuring security for women. The security of the human system is placed on women. What should be their reward in this context? How do women fit into a domestic ideology that envisions conflict of power, and endorses the under-utilisation of the major half of the human resource? Must we tolerate the ideology that affirms the unstable and over-burdened exploitation of female capital resources, constantly made 'negligible "via" productive investment' (Gould 1989: 154)? Can the security of women be assured by the allocation of women to mechanistic job descriptions and redesigns that specify responsibility for simple, fixed and repetitive jobs which require little or no skill development? (Hay, Gray and Smith 1989: 354-355).

Although there were women in significant professions, such as medicine, law, teaching and writing in the twelfth to the nineteenth centuries, these were not regarded as suitable work for women. As the Compton Interactive Encyclopaedia (1995) records:

Indeed, obstetrics was the domain of women. Beginning in the 19th century, the required educational preparation, particularly for the practice of a reputable profession, increased. This tended to prevent many young women, who married early and bore many children, from entering professional careers. Before 1890, women constituted about 5 per cent of the total doctors in the United States. During the 1980s the proportion was about 17 per cent. At the same time, the percentage of women doctors was about 19 per cent in West Germany and 20 per cent in France. In Israel, however, about 32 per cent of the total number of doctors and dentists were women.

In Mitchell's (1987: 178) opinion, social structures generate an attitude of disrespect if status discrepancies in respect of occupation and general social honour remain at variance. Security strategies could therefore not provide much outside formal equality since it has 'no impact upon the structural causes of sex discrimination which lies beyond the workplace' (Mazey 1988: 77), and sets the margin for the feminisation of poverty. In more general and global spheres, nowhere are sexual margins of insecurity more turbulent than those marked out by poverty and race.

The Masculinisaton of Security Institutions as the Basis for a Contemporary Challenge to the Nature–Nurture Distinction

Contemporary challenges to the nature-nurture distinction in security studies are perhaps most evident in the military system of security. According to Clementina (1855-1923), militant unionism fuelled the trend of militarisation (see Compton 1994, 1995). The documented history of the exclusion of women in the history of the military and security activities, according to O'Connor (1993), dates back to 1792 when the Militia Act enacted in the United States of America created a universal obligation demanding that able-bodied males participate in the militia. The edict demonstrated a clear gender bias and has led to the assumption that males fight wars, whereas females are to stay at home. This unwarranted distinction has facilitated the erosion of the establishment of genuine security for women. However, the expansionist and destructive tendencies in male-dominated war games led to the emasculation of the male populations and the bearers of the patriarchal order, thus creating in an ironic way the semblance of the type of space that women envisaged.

In the world wars, the sheer force of the destruction, the need to sustain the military industries and the belligerent national economies, compelled the emergence of women in key labour and industrial processes, albeit at times as peripheral workers. Despite the openings created by the wars, women were still marginal to the industrial and security exercises insofar as they were mere executors of the plans created by others. According to Goldstein (1999: 121), warfare in domestic as well as agrarian and industrial relations is exclusively a male pursuit. The social environment of war retains one specific link to masculinity because of the biological-genetic composition of the male sex with the aggressive deposition of testosterone. In a psychological corroboration of the above view, it can be explained that the propensity of males for aggression acts to counter their inability to procreate. However, because of women's care roles, it is presumed that they are peace loving rather than warlike in order to safeguard their domestic propensity.

As can be expected, the possibility of ensuring peace, safety and dignity of the women in a traditional setting raises important ethically based questions regarding protection. Protectionism is more problematic in war than in peace. The feminist outcry in war situations extended over all spheres of militarism to include both national and international security processes. The corresponding difference for the diversified source of reinterpretations on security covers an extensive range of militarised disempowerment and dependence. The outcome of this divergence is essentially to allocate defence towards the ultimately unprotected persons, on terms that are not necessarily favourable (Deger and West 1987: 10).

To further explicate this point, it would seem that the agent-neutral reason to avert unhealthy competitiveness places men in a far superior position (Sterba 1985: 2). Goldstein (1999) says that up to the present, women cannot serve in combat infantry roles on a basis comparable to men. Worse still, women in non-combatant or civilian roles are confronted by threats of extermination, because they now constitute the cardinal target of belligerents in most of the wars which either begin or end in cities. Historically therefore, the marginal status of women and their vulnerability as a dominated group has ensured that their security has not been adequately guaranteed.

A basic erroneous theme running through this belief is that security in the context of sex roles refers to the military as opposed to other key areas of security (Thomas 1987: 1). The demilitarisation and de-masculinisation of security for women is concerned with the development of schemas that ensure women's security and protection. Feminists have tried to influence the prevailing rules, institutions and power structures which determine their socio-political and economic rights. Unfortunately, some women have traded one form of dependence for another, so that security remains elusive. For example, the increase in economic power for women at the level of financial liquidity has not fully translated into greater education and political influence. In this regard, it is worth citing the comment that 'ultimate security is not the product of the fulfilment of particular military or revolutionary equations simply because the problem of security is political by nature, and as such can be solved only by political means' (Arbatov 1986: 320).

Also, attention must be paid to the concurrent consolidation of the ethics of security balance and of varieties of pacifism. Perhaps following the cue of the Israeli women's combat training, rejections of protectionism have led women's groups in the recent years to use due process mechanisms, such as the courts, to force legislation concerning equality between working men and women (Mazey 1993). There are two advantages that the strategy is intended to achieve. For Brown (1995) such moves aim at avoiding the use of women as cheap and unprotected labour and to secure their competitive advantage.

To specify common conceptions about the life and activity of women in the urban context is often a difficult task. Urban simulations may be based on a structural naiveté that under-estimates security and social mobility. An empirical account of the problem demands an observation of some factors. A look at the major Nigerian markets and their environs shows that women patronise these places far more than men do. However, the problem is that the markets lack basic security infrastructure such as effective pedestrian crossings, parking spaces, toilet facilities, police posts, etc. In the realm of transportation, the fact that traders who are mostly women, have to sit right on top of their goods on over-loaded trucks or lorries, plying roads that are in bad shape, is clear evidence that the security of women as road users is not a major concern for the policy makers in society. Women are the targets of armed criminals, militia groups and the security forces that unleash intimidation, harassment, rape and extortion. Worse still, some women who found themselves holding public office contributed to the insecurity and abuse of women's rights. There have been cases of wives of former Nigerian rulers pulling guns on people, and exhibiting power drunkenness. Indeed, 'some other women suspected to be Abacha's girlfriends were on the instruction of Maryam detained and tortured by Major Hamza Al-Mustapha the chief security officer to the late head of state' (see *Tempo*, 4 February 1999).

In a clear case of the alienation of women from security, a former military governor of one of the southwestern states of Nigeria argued in a masterpiece of male arrogance that his Chief Security Officer, a woman, did not need to know of his purchase of security equipment and arms simply because she was the wife of somebody. This military ruler conveniently forgot that the woman was acting in her capacity as a superior military officer of the state. Worse still, the endemic insecurity faced by women is systematically entrenched in society by the culture of poverty and economic hardship that compels girl-children to be pushed onto the hostile streets as hawkers, prostitutes, and so on. They are exposed to the threat of rape, kidnapping, abduction, harassment etc. The desperation of families to make ends meet has led to the selling of their girl-children as house helps, child-wives and slaves. In this way, these children suffer grievous bodily and health hazards such as genital mutilation, VVF, STDs, torture and other inhumanities of unspeakable proportions.

According to the CDHR (2001: 224-230) *Annual Report on the State of Human Rights in Nigeria* for the year 2000, women are still threatened by acts of violence, hatred and insecurity. The phenomena of forced marriages, domestic violence, intimidation and murder remain prevalent. The rampant cases of maltreatment of women in the house and workplace, rape of children, forced sexual intercourse in marriage, spousal abandonment and neglect of responsibilities are indications that women remain grossly insecure. The incidence of girl-child abandonment, girl-child stealing, and trafficking in young females has been on the increase. There is also the proliferation of spouse battering, child battering, rape, paedophilia, incest, sexual harassment, forced female circumcision, inimical widowhood rites, forced female labour, forced marriage and psychological torture, among other dominant forms of insecurity confronting women of all ages and at all levels. It is on the basis of concrete cases of the violation of women's rights and the threats to women's security that the CDHR document (2001) insists that in the year 2000, the situation regarding women and children had not improved.

Imperatives for Evolving Gender Mutual Supplementation in National Security

Physical, intellectual and other social developments are not the exclusive right of masculinity. The struggle to rise above the current challenges has been aptly put by Grenberg (1999: 731), who states that '[woman] has the power to choose between the assertion of her transcendence and her alienation as object. Such capacity for choice allows woman, despite her situation, to find a path in which her gender does not limit her'. The functional feminist emphasis on security has a direct spillover effect on the preservation and effective assurance of capabilities of human potential. Since part of the reason for insecurity lies in the relationship between prestige, power and position, the prospects for security then become the collaborative arrangement between individuals and 'social-legal" agencies for guaranteeing security. As such, the regulation of sex roles and activities needs to be based on the pragmatic appreciation of the value of the woman. Domesticity is as tasking and labour-intensive as any designated masculine chores. More than this is the fact that 'physiological tests now suggest that women have a greater tolerance for pain, and statistics reveal that women live longer and are more resistant to many diseases' (Compton 1995).

In the light of the numerous problems linked to the quest for the security and dignity of women, there is a need to analyse some of the areas where change for the better is required. We must share the optimism of Daly (1996: 138) that 'despite the vicious circle, change can occur in society, and ideologies can die, though they die hard'. The zones of operation of the change that we seek are manifold but the psychological and the political are two dominant areas of intended impact. We are forced to agree with Schermer (1980: 180) that we need to insist on 'the tenet that women need to be treated fairly, have alternatives, explore opportunities and that prejudices and cruelties which prevent that fairness, those alternatives and opportunities from being actualized must be declared unjust, denied as immoral and beaten out of our society and our psyches'. Even when we push the argument of feminism to its extreme, there is at the heart of it all an undeniable search for positive self-expression and freedom that women require for attaining a meaningful and productive life. According to Achufusi (1996: 46-47), 'the essence of (African) feminism is not hatred for men or blaming men, some of whom after all are also agents of oppression. True feminism is the reaction which leads to the development of greater resourcefulness, for survival and greater self-reliance'. Forge (2001: 56) is equally clear on the fact that 'for society to move away from the strong man rule and inequality to one of deep rooted perception for an interrelated humane society there is a need for valuing freedom with equality, so equality and partnership are the slogans for mapping new futures for gender participation in Africa's socio-economic transformation. Building peace among the sexes is fundamental'.

The whole point of the search for women's security is the affirmation of the integrity of women, which in the view of Mama (2001: 67) 'is actually about popular struggle for material redistribution and justice and related desire for existential integrity and security'. The reason why the imperative of security for women has become non-negotiable is the fact that humanity cannot move forward without the care and consideration of women. According to Zeidenstein (1978: 974), 'women are the principal consumers of the services that nutrition, health and contraception programmes are supposed to deliver. The truth is that women's lives are complex. Their roles in multifarious capacities suggest a more forceful and intensive commitment to the task of ensuring justice and dignity in view of a more sustainable security'.

To this effect, there is a need for a re-visioning of identities, capacities and power, in such a way that will allow for equitable stratification of social hierarchies, in terms of political authority, gendered military consolidation, labour, identities, legitimation, all without recourse to exploitative instrumentalist, elitist and masculine ideologies (Peterson 1992: 32) A crucial security concern for many women is the reconstruction of hierarchy and domination as well as the strengthening of procedures through which they may exert greater control over their own social destinies. To this effect, an obvious area to start is by seeking greater childcare or maternity leave programmes for married women.

There needs to be systematic and pro-women approaches to the reform of abortion laws, and increased and more accurate knowledge of birth control, in order to prevent the several hundred thousands of women who die every year from causes related to pregnancy, child birth and abortion. At the level of statistical analysis, the ratio of maternal deaths to live birth varies enormously through-out the world, ranging from fewer than 8 maternal deaths per 100,000 live births in Europe, to more than 1,400 deaths per 100,000 live births in several countries in sub-Saharan Africa (PRB: 1998). This is a form of crusade for the assurance of medical and bio-ethical security for women. In history, one of the most promi-nent of these crusaders was Margaret Sanger (1910). The point must be made here that genuine security for women cannot but be tied to the question of the definition and sustenance of the rights and duties of all in society. According to Bandman (1978: 215), these rights are 'the right to work, to social security, to just and favourable remuneration, the right to security, to education'. The quest for the security of women must be tied to concrete things. According to Gewirth (1988: 442), 'benefits and burdens are palpable, empirically discriminate states or conditions'. In the case of women's security these features must translate into valuable and positive goods or measures which Gilbert (1994: 30) insists must aim 'to eliminate wage and employment discrimination against women, develop day-care and other public services that reduce the burden of family maintenance, and stimulate greater participation by men in caring and domestic activities'. These actions are intended to accomplish the vital task of maintaining 'freedom and justice among human beings, with the expectation that, ultimately, peace and har-mony can be achieved among peoples' (Olonisakin 1998: 95).

At the educational and political levels the bid to ameliorate the insecurity faced by women has led many women's organisations such as the National Organisa-tion for Women (NOW), Women in Development (WID), SALT (Sisters All Learning Together), WITCH (Women's International Terrorist Conspiracy from Hell), the Women's Liberation Union, pioneered by the author of *The Feminine Mystique* (Friedman 1963) to reiterate that training is essential to women's security. They emphasise the role of education and capacity building as a guarantee of women's security. There is an emphasis on the possible roles of the more edu-cated women in the uplifting of the status of women and in the defence of women's inalienable rights to freedom, expression, self-actualisation, peace and security.

Conclusion

By way of a conclusion we can agree that to guarantee meaningful and enduring security implies, as former US President Bill Clinton (1996: 6) stated, 'giving all men, women and children the tools of opportunity - education, health care, employment, legal rights and political freedoms'. The features itemised by Clinton when taken together will ensure the protection of the dignity of women and their security at the personal and social levels. The question of dignity has been aptly described by Goodin (1981) to mean a combination of features. This im-plies a conclusive repudiation of the 'limits of the patriarchal definition, what we consider as the functional fallacy of the patriarchal culture, indisputably high-lighted by the failure of men especially in Africa to confront the very important age-old question of justice' (Adadevoh 2002: 169). The question of justice must embrace as never before the issues of the common good and dignity of persons and especially of all marginal peoples. According to Goodin (1981: 98-99), 'pro-tecting people's dignity requires more than just prohibiting degrading policy out-comes ... people show each other respect or disrespect through their attitudes and motives whether or not they culminate in action'. This idea of respect is intended to pursue justice and in the view of Owens (1969: 241), 'to endeavour to create those conditions in which men can live their own lives, pursue happiness and fulfil their destiny'. In seeking a way forward, there must be a de-emphasis on creating ambiguities in sex roles in terms of the quest for freedom and com-petence. According to Lodge (1995: 316), the repercussion of these ambiguities addresses 'the question of who has (more competitive) competence for the secu-rity matter'. Therefore our aim is to deconstruct the closure of women, and to prevent the erasure of the perceived less competitive person from the guarantee of social security. Our essay therefore, receives its justification from the prevailing and unacceptable situation of hydra-headed insecurities arising as a result of the fundamental crises in the ethical conduct of the individual and the community. In this case, much would depend, as is often the case, on the cessation of the distinc-tion between nature and nurture.

This work has examined in detail the conceptual and historical issues in the clarification of gender, national security and the segregationist schema theory. The work highlighted the reality of non-belonging, marginality and inequality of women as potential contributors to national insecurity. It insisted that gender role socialisation with respect to 'conceptual security' has always been problematic, because it tended to be seen predominantly in collective military and defence terms, as opposed to the more viable personal developmental connotation. This restrictive conception of security was inherently defective, not only because it reduced security to the mere absence of conflict, but also because women were not fully included in the strategies for the avoidance or management of conflict. Neither the planners nor the executioners had the full interest of women's secu-rity at heart. The consequence was that women, children and other highly vulner-able segments of a society suffered the most in the event that a conflict (internal or externally motivated) boiled over. In repudiating this conception of security, it was shown that it did not sincerely confront the internally induced threats to women's security. Rather, it continued the perpetration of this insecurity, because it remained immersed in the hegemonic ordering of the patriarchal and com-mand structures, with their uniquely magisterial posturing.

References

Achufusi, Ify Grace, 1996, 'Male Domination or Sexual Inequality: An Examination of Pre-colonial African Life', *Africana Marburgensia*, Special Issue 16, pp. 40-47.

Adadevoh, Omolola Irene, 1999, 'The Dominance Duel and the Cultural Emancipation of the African Woman', *International Journal of African Culture and Ideas*, vol. 1, nos. 1 & 2, pp. 1-11.

Adadevoh, Omolola Irene, 2002, 'Functional Fallacy of Patriarchal Culture and Democratic Sustenance of Women's Rights: A comparison of Nigeria and the United States', in S. O. Amali et al., eds., *Consolidation and Sustenance of Democracy*, Ibadan: ASAN & Hope, pp. 32-51.

Akinrinade and Amadu Sesay, eds., *Africa in The Post Cold War International System*, London: Cassell Pinter.

Africa Research Bulletin, 2000, 'Editorial', 1-30 April.

Alaya, Flavia, 1977, 'Victorian Science and the "Genius" of Woman', *Journal of the History of Ideas*, vol. XXXVIII, no. 2.

Alder, Christine, 1992, 'Violence, Gender and Social Change: Women's Liberation', *International Social Science Journal*, vol. 132, pp. 267-275.

Alexander, R. D., 1979, *Darwinism and Human Affairs*, Seattle: University of Washington Press.

Alison, Miranda, 2004, 'Women as Agents of Political Violence: Gendering Security', *Security Dialogue*, Special Issue on Gender and Security, pp. 447-463.

Appelbaum, Richard, et al., 1995, *Sociology*, New York: Harper Collins.

Arnaud, A. J., and Kingdom, E., 1990, *Women's Rights and the Rights of Men*, London: Pergamon.

Attig, Thomas, 1976, 'The Philosopher as a Teacher: Why Are you a Man, Teaching this Course on the Philosophy of Feminism', *Metaphilosophy*, no. 2, pp. 155-166.

Bandman, Bertram, 1978, 'Are There Human Rights?', *The Journal of Value Inquiry*, Vol. XII, no. 3, pp. 215-224.

Ben, S. L., 1985, 'Androgyny and Gender Schema Theory: A Conceptual and Empirical Integration', in T.B Sondereiger, ed., *Nebraska Symposium on Motivation: Psychology of Gender*, Lincoln: University of Nebraska Press.

Borgia, G., 1978, 'Group Selection, Altruism and the Levels of Organization of Life', *Annual Review of Ecology and Systematics*, vol. 9.

Bourke, J., 1994, 'Working Class Cultures in Britain 1890-1960', *Gender Class and Ethnicity*, London: Routledge.

Brown, Lester, 1982, 'An Untraditional View of National Security', in Reichart, ed., *American Defense Policy*, Baltimore: John Hopkins University Press.

Brown, Robin, 1995, 'Globalization and the End of the National Project', in J. Macmillan, ed., *Boundaries in Question*, London: Pinter, pp. 54-68.

Bunch, Charlotte and Roxanna Carrillo, 1990, 'Feminist Perspective on Women in Development', in Irene Tinker, ed., *Persistent Inequalities*, New York: Oxford University Press, pp. 70-82.

Chesnais, Jean-Claude, 1992, 'The History of Violence, Homicide and Suicide through the Ages', *International Social Science Journal*, 132, pp. 217-234.

Caprioli, Mary, 2004, 'Democracy and Human Rights Versus Women's Security: A

Contribution', *Security Dialogue*, Special Issue on Gender and Security.

Clinton, Hilary Rodham, 1996, '61 Ways of Looking at Poverty', *Choices; the Human Development Magazine*, October, pp. 5-10.

Committee for the Defence of Human Rights (CDHR), 2001, *2000 Annual Report on the Human Rights Situation in Nigeria*, Lagos: CDHR.

Compton's Interactive Encyclopaedia, 1994, 1995, Excerpts, Copyright © Compton's New Media, Inc.

Comte, A., 1975, *Auguste Comte and Positivism: The Essential Writing*, Gertrude Lenzer, ed., New York: Torch Books.

Cuffel, Victoria, 1966, 'The Classical Greek Concepts of Slavery', *Journal of the History of Ideas*, vol. XXVII, no. 3.

Daly, Mary, 1996, 'The Feminist Critique of Patriarchal Religion: Beyond God the Father', in Joel Feinberg, ed., *Reason and Responsibility: Readings in Some Basic Problems of Philosophy*, 9th Edition, New York: Wadsworth Publishing Company.

Dawkins, R., 1976, *The Selfish Gene*, New York: Oxford University Press,

Davin, A., 1979, 'Mind that you do as you are told': Reading Books for Bored School Girls, 1870-1902', *Feminist Review*, no. 3.

Deger, Saadet and West, Robert, eds., 1987, *Defence, Security and Development*, London: Pinter.

Durkheim, E., 1964, *The Rules of Sociological Method*, New York: Free Press.

Elshtain, J. B., 1981, *Public Man, Private Woman*, Princeton: University Press.

Ferrante, J. M., 1984, 'Marie De Frances, The French Courtly Poet', in *Medieval Women Writers*, Katherine M. Wilson, ed., Athens: University of Georgia Press.

Forge, John W., 2001, 'Mapping New Futures for Gender Participation towards Sustainable Developments: Lessons from Africa', *Future Research Quarterly*, Spring.

Fox, R., 1975, *Biosocial Anthropology*, New York: Wiley.

Francis, Becky, 2002, 'Relativism, Realism, and Feminism: An Analysis of some Theoretical Tensions in Research on Gender Identity', *Journal of Gender Studies*, vol. 11, no. 1, pp. 37-54.

Frenkel, F. E., 1964, 'Sex-Crime and its Socio-Historical Background', *Journal of the History of Ideas*, vol. XXV, no. 3.

Friedan, Betty, 1983, *The Feminine Mystique*, Twentieth Anniversary Edition, London: W. W. Norton.

Friedan, Betty, 1981, *The Second Stage*, New York: Summit Books.

Gewirth, Alan, 1998, 'Rights and Duties', *Mind*, vol. XCVII, no. 387, pp. 441-445.

Gilbert, Neil, 1994, 'Gender Equality and Social Security', *Society*, May/June, pp. 27-33.

Goldstein, J. S., 1999, *International Relations*, 3rd Edition, New York: Longman.

Goodin, Robert E., 1981, 'The Political Theories of Choice and Dignity', *American Philosophical Quarterly*, vol. 18, no. 2, pp. 91-100.

Gould, J., 1989, *Luapula: Dependence or Development*, Finland.

Grenberg, Jeanine, 1999, 'French Feminist Philosophy', in Richard Popkin, ed., *The Columbia History of Western Philosophy*, New York: Columbia University Press.

Grown, Caren A. and Jennefer Sebstad, 1989, 'Introduction: Towards a Wider Perspective on Women's Employment', *World Development*, vol. 17, no. 7, pp. 937-952.

Hands, Elizabeth, 1996, 'The Death of Ammon, in Karen Jacobson McLennan, ed., *Women's Incest Literature*, Boston: Northeastern University Press, pp29-56.

Havelock Ellis, Henry, 1927, 'Sexual Introversion', *Studies in the Psychology of Sex*, vol. 2.

Hay, Gray and Smith, 1989, *Business and Society: Perspective on Ethics and Social Responsibility*, 3rd Edition, USA: South Western publishing Co.

Hirsthleifer, J., 1987, *Economic Behaviour in Adversity*, Sussex: Wheatsheaf Books.

Hoff, Joan, 1991, *Law, Gender, and Injustice: A Legal History of US Women*, New York: NYU Press.

Jackson, Stevi et al., 1993, *Women's Studies: A Reader*, London: Wheatsheaf.

Janes, R. M., 1978, 'On the Reception of Mary Wollstonecraft's: *A Vindication of the Rights of woman*', *Journal of the History of Ideas*, vol. XXXIV, no. 2.

Jaquette. Jane S., 1990. 'Gender and Justice in Economic Development', in Irene Tinker, ed., *Persistent Inequalities*, New York: Oxford University Press.

Jeffreys, S., 1985, *The Spinster and her Enemies: Feminism and Sexuality 1880-1930*, London: Pandora.

Kaldor, N., 1939, 'Welfare Propositions in Economics and Interpersonal Comparisons of Utility', *Economic Journal*, Vol. 49.

Kleinbaum, A. R., 1977, 'Women in the City of Light', in Renato Bridenthal and Claudia King, eds., *Becoming Visible. Women in European History*, Boston: Houghton Mifflin.

Lewis, J., 1980, *The Politics of Motherhood: Child and Maternal Welfare in England, 1900-1935*, London: Croom Helm.

Lips, H. M., 1993, *Sex and Gender: An Introduction*, 2nd Edition, USA: Mayfield.

Lodge, J., 1994, 'Internal Security and Judicial Cooperation', in Lodge, J., ed., *The European Community and the Challenge of the Future*, 2nd Edition, London: Pinter Publishers, pp. 315-339.

Lucas, J. R., 1973, 'Because you Are a Woman', *Philosophy*, vol. 48, pp. 161-171.

Mama, Amina, 2001, 'Challenging Subjects: Gender and Power in African Contexts', *African Sociological Review*, vol. 5, no. 2, pp. 63-73.

Mazey, S., 1988, 'Women in Europe: The Implementation of the Community: Equality Laws', *Journal of Common Market Studies*, 25, (3).

McLennan, K. J., 1996, *Women's Incest Literature*, Boston: North Eastern University Press.

Mitchell, J. C., 1987, *Cities, Society and Social Perception*, Oxford: Clarendon Press.

Moynihan, Robert D., 1975, 'Clarissa and the Enlightened Woman: A Literacy Heroine', *Journal of the History of Ideas*, vol. XXXVI.

Nash, Kate, 2002, 'Human Rights for Women: On Arguments for "Deconstructive Equality"', *Journal of Economy and Society*, vol. 31, no. 3, pp. 414-433.

Nussbaum, Martha C. & Jonathan Glover, eds., 1995, *Women, Culture and Development*, Oxford: Clarendon Press.

O'Brien, Robert, 1995, 'International Political Economy and International Relations: Apprentice or Teacher?', in John Macmillan, ed., *Boundaries in Question :New Directions in International Relations*, London: Pinter.

O'Connor, Karen & Sabato, Larry, 1993, *American Government*, New York: Harper Collins.

Okin, Susan Moller, 1977, 'Philosopher Queens and Private Wives: Plato on Women and the Family', *Philosophy and Public Affairs*, vol. 6, no. 4, pp. 345-369.

Okin, Susan Moller, 1982, 'Women and the Making of the Sentimental Family', *Philosophy and Public Affairs*, vol. 11, no. 1, pp. 65-88.

Okin,k Susan Moller, 1988, ed., *John Stuart Mill: The Subjection of Women*, Indianapolis: Hackett.

Okin, Susan Moller, 1995, 'Inequalities between the Sexes in Different Cultural Contexts', in Martha Nussbaum et al., eds., *Women, Culture and Development. A study of Human Capabilities*, Oxford: Clarendon Press.

Olonisakin, Funmi, 1998, 'Changing Perspectives on Human Rights in Africa', in Sola

Owens, Merilyn, 1969, 'The Notion of Human Rights; A Reconsideration', *American Philosophical Quarterly*, vol. 6, no. 3.

Peterson, V. S., 1992, ed., *Gendered States: Feminist (Re) Visions of International Relations Theory*, London: Lynne Rienner Publisher.

Reed, E., 1970, 'The Myth of Women's Inferiority', in *Problems of Women's Liberation*, London: Pathfinder Press.

Rowbotham, S., 1973, *Hidden from History: Three Hundred Years of Women's Oppression and the Fight against it*, London: Pluto.

Rowbotham, S., 1992, *Women in Movement: Feminism and Social Action*, New York: Routledge.

Rowson Susanna Haswell, 1996, 'From Marian and Lydia' in Karen Jacobsen McLennan, *Women's Incest Literature*, Boston: Northeastern University Press, pp.58-67

Schermer, Marsha Rockey, 1980, 'Comments on Attig's "Why Are You, A Man, Teaching This course on the Philosophy of Feminism"', *Metaphilosophy*, vol. 11, no. 2.

Schwarzenberger, 1951, *Power Politics*, New York: Frederich A. Praeger.

Simon, R. J., and Danziger, Gloria, 1991, *Women's Movements in America*, USA: Greenwood.

Sterba, J. P., 1985, *The Ethics of War and Nuclear Deterrence*, California: Wadsworth Inc.

Sunstein, C. R., 1995, 'Gender, Caste and law', in M. Nussbaum and J. Glover, eds., *Women, Culture and Development. A study of Human Capabilities*, Oxford: Clarendon Press.

Tempo News Magazine, 1999, 'How Maryam Abacha haunted her rivals', 4 February.

Thomas, Caroline, 1987, *In search of Security: The Third World in International Relations*, Colorado: Rienner.

Tierney, Helen, ed., 1991, *Women's Studies Encyclopaedia*, vol. 1, New York: Peter Bedrick.

Uko, I. I., 1996, 'African Feminism and the Theatres of Zulu Sofola and Tess Onwueme: A Celebration', *Africana Marburgensia*, Special Issue 16.

Wanzala, Winnie L., 1996, 'Emancipating Security and Development Equity and Social Justice', in Ibbo Mandaza, ed., *Peace and Security in Southern Africa*, Harare, SAPES Books.

Warren, Mary Anne, 1977, 'Secondary Sexism and Quota Hiring', *Philosophy and Public Affairs*, vol. 6, no. 3.

Women's International Network News, 1988, 'Women and Violence', vol. 14, no. 1.

Zeidenstein, George, 1978, 'Including Women in Development Efforts', *World Development*, vol. 16, pp .971-978.

7

Rethinking Ethical Security in the Light of European Institutional Security and Integration Strategies: The Quest for Methodological Convergence

**Aduke G. Adebayo, Philip Ogo Ujomu,
Dapo Adelugba and Irene Omolola Adadevoh**

Introduction

This study examines the ethical dimension of the national security problem by using the European paradigm as a framework or model for defining the core principles of national survival and social integration. This work can be defined in terms of the primary challenges of a new global ethical principle. The reality of the security problem in the contemporary era suggests that there is a need for cooperation and integrated efforts to meet the security challenges, especially the transnational and international aspects. As Dower (1998: 109) rightly maintains, 'there are certain global responsibilities in respect of values i.e. there has been an increasing recognition that individuals have responsibilities towards human beings in general, not merely towards members of their own societies'. Such commitment and belief is the motivating factor for examining the linkages between European and African security situations from this ethical viewpoint.

Africa, as it is today, must reckon with the realities taking place in other parts of the world. Indeed, the history of the continent in the last few centuries makes such a consideration inevitable. According to Okigbo (1991: 424), 'it is essential to look at the critical transformation of Europe, its politics, economics and culture and assess how prepared Africa is to come to terms with these changes'. The truth is that Africa cannot afford to ignore the rest of the world since it still depends on Europe and others for major materials needed for the survival of

Africans. Wright (1998: 133) points out that Africa's present condition 'is traceable to problems derived from both internal developments within the continent and from its increasing marginalization in the global political economy'. At a major level, the link between Africa and Europe can be viewed in terms of some cultural dynamics. We may start by agreeing with Huntington (1997: 131) that the European Union is the product of a common European culture. In this sense of the definition, we are still in need of defining the idea of culture used.

This conceptual confusion notwithstanding, Rynning (2003: 481) has more to say on the cultural context of the EU. 'In the analysis of the EU we should treat culture as a context, that if integrated and coordinated, can help actors overcome even serious obstacles to cooperation.' However appealing this idea is, our view is that it raises fundamental questions of cross-cultural ethical relations. The more significant point must be made that the context of the EU is larger than the cultural imperative. For instance, Farrands (1996: 177) tells us that the creation of a European Union is mapped out in terms of three parallel but separate areas of activity; the European Union, the common foreign and security policy, and inter-governmental cooperation in domestic policy and intelligence related activities. This is evidence of the stratification of the European vision of their union or community. Also this is clearly a sign that 'the Europeans are intensifying their cooperation and are doing so precisely through institutions' (Grieco 1993: 329). Why are they using the path of institutionalisation? Why are institutions of great importance, not just to security but also to other areas of life? We shall examine these issues later.

For now, we must define the ethical basis of our work which lies in its irrevocable desire and capability to repudiate existing epistemologies and schemes of comprehension and thus execute a transition from the old to the new in the quest for liberation and transformation. The reason for increased interest in the European systems of life can be understood against the background of some geopolitical events. According to Ross (1998: 166), 'the diffusion of the American model helped reconfigure European national developmental models along with a solidification of democratic institutions, new commitments to social justice and the re-distribution of wealth'. This statement suggests that the Europeans have been at the forefront of the modernisation of the theories of social change and human welfare such as we are interested in here. The quest for the lessons of European security for Africa is valuable and particularly significant because 'in recent years it has been widely acknowledged that a myriad of factors including the European Union have had significant impact on global security and sovereignty' (Makinda 1998: 281). This same point is affirmed by Biscop (2003: 183) with the statement that 'with the development of the European security and defence policy ESDP the EU is gradually emerging as a significant actor in the field of security'. Hence, in our review of the strategies for the acquisition of the proper value orientation for human survival, what capabilities can we develop to enhance the employment of ethical knowledge for human and moral rectification? The quest for security is linked to the identification and sustenance of social ideals such as 'fairness, justice, morality, impartiality and accountability' (Bagilhole 1997: 30). Thus we must tackle the question of how do we establish ethical character as seen in a higher level of duty to self and community? Our concern for highly desired values such as dialogue, fraternity, peace and discipline compel a focus on institutional ethics and organisational roles in a way that accounts for diversity of expectations and interests, and offers a hope for negotiation and compromise.

Theoretical and Conceptual Foundations of Our Study: The Nature of Morality and Institutions

In history, the major goal of any social order, whether national or international, is to promote good conduct within the 'society'. Security and social order are impossible without such qualities. The co-existence of any group or community of people requires some level of friendly feelings shared among them. Such friendly feelings facilitate mutual cooperation, communal rapport and integrated activities. It is also impossible for people to live peacefully, safely, and comfortably together within a community if morality is absent. This point is significant given that 'the European community, as it has developed over the years has probably performed best on the dimension of well-being' (Bertsch, Clark and Wood 1991: 241). Therefore, the quest for a secure human community compels a discussion of morality as an instrument for providing ethical principles that safeguard the right of the individual and points to reciprocal duties and responsibilities.

Wiredu (1992) observes that any society without a modicum of morality must collapse. Thus, 'morality is simply the observance of rules for the harmonious adjustment of the interests of the individual to those of others in society. It involves not merely the "de facto" conformity to the requirements of the harmony of interests, which is inspired by an imaginative and sympathetic identification with the interest of others even at the expense of a possible constraint to one's own interests' (Wiredu 1992: 191-199). Morality is an emanation of man's overriding desire to preserve social harmony by ensuring that moral codes discourage injustice, deceit and anarchy in any system. Morality conceived as a social phenomenon is a crucial and indispensable means of social control, regulation and the prevention of harm among men in society. Morality achieves this social regulation and control not only by ensuring the clarification of rules and laws differentiating good from bad, right from wrong in society, but also by ensuring that specific traits of character or dispositions are instilled in people.

The essence of morality, according to Perry (1974: 373), Bayles and Henley (1989: 10), and Foot (1985: 208), is man's endeavour to harmonise conflicting interests, to play the role of an arbiter, and to secure that greatest possible general good. According to Kupperman (1983: 4-10), the core of morality must be injunctions against harming others. Morality tries to prevent harm to both the individual and the society. This is what Cox (1981: 185-187) refers to as defensive social behaviour adopted against a hazard. Kupperman argues that morality arises out of a need for protection. But this protection is not usually absolute because there are still immoral persons who try to breach moral rules and expectations. However, by ensuring that many people keep within the boundaries limited by morality as much as possible, human personal and social life become more bearable and productive. Frankena (1973: 63-65) holds that morality throughout its history has been concerned with the cultivation of certain traits such as character. By defining the roles and responsibilities of men, morality reveals the character of man as a responsible, free and dignified being capable of self-respect, self-determination and accountability in the things he does.

The question of the need for morality continues to dominate the age-long controversy between the egoists and altruists. Egoism holds that morality should serve the interest of the self and that the goal of a person's action should be his own self-interest. In effect, egoism holds that man should not only seek his own interest in everything he does, but that he should act morally only if he has some benefit to derive from such an arrangement (Hospers 1973: 600; Omoregbe 1993: 79). However, some important questions arise from the attempt to justify morality based on egoism. Can self-interest be a genuine basis for enduring morality? How can the presence of altruism be explained in social life? It seems that a strictly egoistic moral life will not be conducive to personal and social morality. It may in fact be antithetical to the demands conducive to personal and social morality because the promotion of self-interest as the moral rule will ensure that the goal of harmonising conflicting interests is largely defeated. Only confusion can attend any society founded strictly on egoistic principles of morality.

According to Bayles and Henley (1989: 1-10), if moral concepts are used to categorise actions, persons and institutions, and moral judgements concern themselves with the social and interpersonal, then the viewpoint of morality seems to rule out normative egoism. Wiredu (1992: 191) asserts that a certain minimum of altruism is absolutely essential to moral motivation. Altruism is consideration for the interests of others, and only when we consider others can the talk about harmonisation of conflicting interests become meaningful. According to Cox (1981: 185-190), altruism acknowledges correctly that the form of moral behaviour appears generally to be other-regarding. However, altruism fails to acknowledge the individual, social and practical ends served by moral systems. On the other hand, egoism achieves a correct recognition of the function of morality as supportive of human self-realisation but it ignores the social role in self-actualisation. Cox argues that 'both theories express a portion of the truth but neither by itself is sufficient'. Sharing a similar view with Cox, another writer, McMahon

(1991: 250), holds that some connection exists between acting, as morality requires and promoting the interest of others. However, he is quick to point out that affirming a link between morality and altruism does not mean that both cannot diverge. Matters become more serious when we seek the connection between morality and institutions.

The institutions created by man are intended to provide some form of stability, well-being and security for the individual and society. They simply aim at its efficient practice and continuation. The society aims at its own notion of the common good through the provision of greater opportunities for participation and responsibility among citizens. Underlying this feeling of mutual responsibility is, presumably, the attitude of trust or faith in a unique pattern of political administration and social conduct that seeks the inclusion of as many as possible in the management of affairs. This inclusion is premised on certain structural, normative and practical considerations. Parsons (1960: 36) points out that 'the integral problem within an organization most directly concerns the human agents. The central problem concerns the institutionalized norms which can effectively bind the actions of individuals in their commitment to organizations'. The question is then how we can establish and sustain rules and values that can propel human actions for positive ends. This issue is the more significant in the context of pattern maintenance organisations that centre on cultural, educational and expressive functions.

However, it is very possible for us to have a set of institutions that embody key social principles and ideals, but in fact the institutions will not be effective or functional everywhere. Hence, it is clear that the institutions themselves are, at best, a means rather than the end of the human quest. Moreover, the externalised character of these institutions makes them prone to violations. Thus, Hermet (1991: 256-257) rightly observes that the process of institutionalisation does not in any way indicate that the affected institutions have taken root. The reason is that sometimes these institutions serve as a mere facade or smokescreen and actual or far-reaching dealings take place outside of them. Hence, 'there could be aberrations, such that institutions designed to promote accountability could also be used to make it void' (Apter 1991: 470). The excessive emphasis on institutionalisation leads to the loss of the personal dimension that is equally important in successful social life. This is because when there are problems with practice the individuals can act surreptitiously and conceal themselves under the canopy of institutions.

Prevailing Models of European Security: The Classical and the Modern

What is the basis of European security and integration? Why should some of the European values serve as a basis for African security reformations or transformations? These are very important issues especially when we begin to review the values underlying the European models of integration and security. According to

Ross (1998: 177), 'renewed European integration was a complex construction which flowed from multiple motives in response to a variety of pressing problems'. This suggests that the Europeans have had more than their fair share of problems and are now in a position to serve as an inspiration to others on the world scene. In a brief historical account, Baylis, (1992: 385) reminds us that 'the European state system which prevailed from the late 1940s until 1989 emerged following the collapse of the classical European order which had been in place from the end of the Middle Ages'.

This historical challenge facing Europe was the more significant given the security problems in that theatre. According to Mann (1998: 188-189), 'over the previous four centuries most military power had become gradually monopolized by states and this proved the greatest subversion of Europe. Conflicts between European nation states had escalated into hi-tech mass mobilization warfare, using terrible weapons of destruction. In 1945, Europe lay devastated by internecine strife'. The aftermath of that destructive engagement in the European space paved the way for the demise of Europe as a world power and the emergence of the world ruled by two superpowers. Ross (1998: 165) argues that 'in essence the security environment within which European integration began had become a global one dominated by super power rivalry in general, and from the point of view of future EU members, specifically by American power'. This historical situation and the European reading of it eventually led to widespread reforms of the regional geopolitics of Europe with special reference to security matters which have plagued Europe over the centuries. Therefore, Moller (2003: 316) makes it clear that 'a component part of the region building process in Europe's north is the discourse on the prospects for a regional security community'. The quest for a European community can thus be taken as an imperative of history. There are reasons for this. According to Ross (1998: 169), 'European nations returned to integration because changes in their international surroundings oblige them to. The return of energetic European integration was part of a new strategy to de-emphasize the role of national states in economic life and create a regional economic bloc structured around a liberated single European market'.

Under the prevailing state-centric view of security, Ayoob (1984: 41) holds that 'the term security has traditionally been defined to mean immunity (to varying degrees) of a state or nation to threats emanating from outside its boundaries. A nation is secure to the extent to which it is not in danger of having to sacrifice core values. By security we mean the protection and preservation of the minimum core values of any nation: political independence and territorial integrity'. This constituted the classical approach of the European states before the recent efforts at integrating. Hoogensen and Rottem (2004: 158) have offered the clearest possible reason why we must move away from the realist view of security. They observe that 'state security is essential but does not necessarily ensure the safety of individuals and communities'. Simply put, we have to look elsewhere for further inspiration and clarification of the security problematic. This crisis in the state-centric vision of security led to the international security approach or system-oriented perspective to security. According to Ayoob (1984: 41) again, 'this is a broader view or collective interest idea of security that depends on the recognition of the state or better still states as the objects of security. Thus if there is an international society, then there is an order of some kind to be maintained. The security of the parts of the system is inextricably intertwined with that of the whole'.

The international approach to security especially in its more recent contexts created its own problems and led scholars such as Mann (1998: 198-199) to say that 'Europe is obviously not a singular military power. This suggests that our concept of security issues should also become rather softer, more societal, than statist'. Many options arose from the dissatisfaction with the classical models of security. One of these was the human security approach. According to Bellamy and McDonald (2002: 373), 'human security marks a much needed departure from the statist and militarist approach to security that dominated the field of international relations. The approach should prioritize the security of the individual and that security is achieved only when basic material needs are met and meaningful participation in the life of the community and human dignity are realized'. For Hoogensen and Rottem (2004: 157), 'human security embodies a positive image of security'. This idea was placed side by side with the idea of societal security. The idea of societal security is placed in contradistinction to the notion of state security. Hoogensen and Rottem (2004: 162) insist that 'societal security is about identity, the self conception of communities, and those individuals who identify themselves as members of a particular community. Societal security is recognized as a security sector independent of state security but important to the dynamic of state legitimacy'.

But these ideas of security do not retain the capacity to cover the entire gamut of the European vision for their security. Hence, this explains the emergence of other positions below. The comprehensive approach to security is one of such. Comprehensive security, defined by Biscop (2003: 184-185), as 'a broad and integrated approach that will address all dimensions of security: not just military, but also political, socio-economic, demographic, cultural, ecological, etc. Security is the sum of several interrelated factors and therefore requires an approach that encompasses more than just traditional "hard" security'. There was also the idea of cooperative security. The notion of cooperative security is different from the crude state-centric view in other significant ways. According to Knudsen (2001: 357), the concept of cooperative security 'essentially represents the policy, demonstrated in practice, of dealing peacefully with conflicts, not merely by abstention from violence or threats, but by active engagement in negotiation and a search for practical solutions, and by a commitment to preventive measures'. Again there were specific dispositions of particular schools of thought on the security problematic of Europe and other parts of the world. This led to the Copenhagen school and the idea of securitisation. The Copenhagen school uses the idea of securitisation to represent a wider range of visions in relation to security analysis. Central to its concern is what Knudsen (2001: 357) refers to as the stress on the broad security concept. Specifically, 'the concept of securitization was in part a move along the path of the wideners. But its innovative value was to shift attention away from a mere widening of the security concept to spotlighting of the way in which issues do or do not end up on the political agenda. Securitization gave a name to the process of raising security issues above politics and making them something one would never question'.

However, going beyond this theoretical and historical account of European security, there is a need to look at the more recent evolution of the discourse. Castells (1998: 311) has argued that 'European institutions are trying to cope with trends by using new forms and new processes, thereby attempting the construction of a new institutional system'. There seem to be some advantages gained by adopting new approaches to doing things. According to Todd and Bloch (2003: 101), 'intelligence is one area in which the EU may hope to realize its drive for a Common Foreign and Security Policy (CFSP). The avalanche of EU wide security measures brought in after 9/11 has given a new lifeline to agencies'.

It must be observed that some people have a less optimistic view of the European Union. For instance, Mann (1998: 205) says that 'though all societies are composed of multiple overlapping, intersecting networks of interaction, Europe seems especially to lack overall internal cohesion and external closure'. Also Rynning (2003: 480) offers a pessimistic view of the EU's strategic culture. In this sense, 'it would appear that there is neither strategy nor policy because the common security and defence policy is all about internal state building and domestic European affairs rather than external defence'. On the international scene, the EU seems to have some disadvantages. Parker (1996: 172) observes that there are crucial matters regarding the public interest. Are European institutions strong enough to ensure that the public interest in telecommunications embraces the concerns of smaller firms? From the above analysis, we need to find out what African societies can learn from the European systems especially in the areas of values and principles for proper human living. Diggs (1973: 289) has rightly noted that 'if persons are to live together, they must live under common principles and rules'. The question then is, what are the principles and rules that African can borrow or apply in order to ensure national and human security in this modern age?

With specific reference to the European conceptions of security, the following factors have become prominent. The security architecture of Europe is irrevocably predicated on the quest for 'prosperity, security and peace' (Lodge 1993: xiii). To achieve this aim, the principles and policies of the European security architecture are based on the idea of intense or deeper integration that is woven into the character, 'composition, organization and capacity of the institutions themselves' (Lodge 1993: xiv). These institutions are founded on the ideological template of liberal democracy, which eventually is designed to usher in a new conception of the union. This union of Europe is defined by 'processes engaging member governments in a positive form of cooperation designed to maximize their collective interests' (Lodge 1993: xv) in what can be described as a security community. This European security architecture is based on participation and integration, which 'involves a pooling of endeavour, through whatever supranational institutional arrangements are appropriate' (Lodge 1993: xvi). The architecture of European security is also predicated on mutual assistance and the creation of a balance of advantages that will result from cooperation for peace and security.

The whole concern has been on the mitigation of threats to peace, though the machinery for securing that peace remains to be established. Salmon (1993: 256) cautions that 'in some circumstances military measures would not be the most appropriate security action'. Security must be taken more widely as 'relating to the maintenance of values, lifestyles and way of life' (Salmon 1993: 256). In a way, this suggests an expanded conception of security as a basis for articulating the European view of security. Such a conception must include 'concern with fundamental freedoms, human rights, democracy, economic and social stability' (Salmon 1993: 260). The broader concept of security cherished in Europe is founded on the struggle to guarantee ideal of the 'Four Freedoms of Movement (of goods, services, persons and capital)' (Lodge 1993: 315). This means that there is a conscious effort to tie together the economic and political aspects of security. To achieve this wider goal of security some of the European architectural arrangements have focussed on the 'availability and efficient deployment of financial, human, technical and technological resources both within and between states' (Lodge 1993: 323) in respect of police and security, movement of people, transport and movement of goods. More than that, the struggle to calibrate an alternate conception of security must entail the recognition that the differential context of Cold War and post-Cold War security challenges cannot be neglected without dire consequences. The most significant effect of this is that 'security problems can no longer be compartmentalized into national, regional and international categories since national borders have proved to be increasingly inadequate in containing security problems' (Shea 1993: 360). This European view of security with its emphasis on integration, community, institutional and human centred principles can be harnessed to impact on the African situation. What principles and values can best facilitate the crucial sense of belonging and capacity that can enhance security in most African societies?

The Ethical Challenge of Security for Modern Africa: The Need for Civil Security and National Development

By extrapolation, and in the context of modern Africa, the goal of security is nothing less than the cultivation of citizens and rulers with expert knowledge, having the ability to formulate reasoned positions as guides to action. This would imply that the person would be capable of living out internalised roles and be able to meet the expectations of others through his or her occupational roles. The total behaviour of individuals can be meaningfully examined as a pattern of social roles. Social roles represent the particular ways in which persons interact with other actors in terms of their various statuses or positions within social systems. The idea of civil security has been conceived variously. Its earlier conceptual types have ranged from the endorsement of some advanced form of community policing, to larger vigilante structures, and then to civilian volunteer inputs to security as supervised by the regular military (Ujomu 2002: 43-45). Such ideas presuppose some kind of aggregation of capabilities or division of labour. Their foundations can be attributed to the notion of solidarity, which underlies the conditions for cooperation for security within the society. Another established view identifies a link between trust and security and it suggests that the communal method of security is only applicable within the ambit of a small community of men.

Civil security (Lucas 2000: 38) which refers to the systematic and conscious participation of non-military or civilian segments of a society in the provision of national and human security, is distinctive due to its emphasis on the increased role of the citizen in maintaining security. Specifically, it affords citizens, through a national policy, the chance to participate in providing emergency services and certain defence functions, such as providing information about criminals, participating in vigilante activities, as well as other forms of community service. The importance of the civil populace in the provision of security cannot be underestimated. According to Odekunle (1993: 39), the most reliable defence and security that any nation can have is the mobilisation of the citizenry through their involvement. Civil security possesses great potential for enhancing the participatory quality of democratic life. It creates and fosters an atmosphere of trust between the government and other segments of the society. It encourages individuals to be more directly and consciously involved in the construction of a safe and prosperous society.

Two Values Required for Security in a Human Social Context: The Value of Human Life and the Principles of Justice

The need for security requires an interrogation of the core idea of the value of life as it operates on other central principles and practices. We place a value on human life when we define a set of operative principles that determine our estimation of the human being as constitutive of certain features that earn him a particular treatment or consideration. The value of life is also related to our axiological premises for considering the human person to be deserving of certain goods (benefits or burdens). Security is aimed at affirming and upholding the value of life. To this effect, security focuses on survival, as well as the realisation of peace and progress for individuals and groups. Everyone is in need of security whether consciously or unconsciously. In the absence of security not much can be done. Above all, the idea of security presupposes the establishment of a nation of people oriented to the common good on the premises of fraternity, equality and liberty. This implies a quest for a conceptual and practical platform for reinventing the human political community.

Security; construed as the quest for survival, peace and progress, depends significantly upon the establishment of a social order that effectively defines the political, economic and social roles, rights and duties of people in a society. Social order aims at achieving certain important ends, mainly, security, protection and preservation of the lives and properties of people. To ensure individual and collective security, the social order attempts to make sure that every person or group has some stake or interest in, and commitment to, the society. Security can be most effectively established and sustained through an idea of society which upholds the values of increased human participation, responsibility and wider input to social well-being. This view of society promotes security by recognising that values such as cooperation, consolidation and continuity are themselves usually uppermost in the minds of people when they form, or participate in, a commonwealth. The participation of as many citizens as are responsible, committed, or willing to make their input to local or national governance and interpersonal or social affairs ought to be based on shared feelings of mutual responsibility.

Thus security can be assured if certain core principles are in place. The first principle is that of the common good which affirms the state's duty to ensure common justice and fairness in the relationship between individuals. The common good may be understood primarily as the perfection of the members through the existence of the society. What are the means for the improvement of the human security situation? Security can also be assured by an emphasis on justice. The idea of justice under survey is not the warped but currently prevailing idea of 'might is right, 'sovereignty by conquest', hegemony or a dominant metropolitan culture which though it appears appealing to the person gaining the upper hand, in the long run is not sustainable for all parties involved. Indeed the history of failed ideologies, failed politico-economic projects, failed societies and failed dictators all around the world are sufficient evidence of the non-sustainability of any perverse idea of justice.

There is a strong link between rights, justice, security and survival. A genuinely secure society is a just society. A genuinely just society is also a secure society. A just social order cannot allow a society of slaves or marginalised peoples neglected and exploited just because of contexts and facts external to them. Justice is a constant and perpetual will to give every man his due, through rules such as merit, just deserts, entitlement, equality, need, productivity or effort. A just society needs to define and recognise individual rights and to embed these rights in the consti-tutional structure so that the opportunity for abuse is diminished. Therefore, jus-tice emerges here as a set of minimal constraints necessary for achieving social coexistence, co-operation and well-being. Both conceptions of life agree on the need for justice understood among others as the basis of productive human cooperation. The upholding of the legal system and the rule of law are critical factors in the sustenance of a just order. Viewed in this light, security becomes something that is expedient for all men to aspire to, attain and preserve because it is in the interest of all to work for individual and collective security.

Conclusion

This study has attempted to facilitate a better insight into national security by appropriating the creative inputs of ethical and aesthetic analysis. In the quest for a new or alternate theoretical basis for the understanding of the national security problematic, the researchers have shown their capacity to translate the concrete conceptual reconstructive processes into relevant empirical and practical solu-tions to the multi-faceted problems of security. The combination of aesthetic and ethical imagination in fostering positive human values and social reconcilia-tion can be of great importance for national development. The new conceptual and methodological trajectories in national security suggest the imperative of ethical citizenship and the attainment of a just and harmonious society which will restore public confidence in the capacity of the government and society to attain national survival, peace and progress. The commitment has been to intensify the modes of the appreciation of the value of human life, the role of greater public trust in governance, and the necessity of a collective adherence to the rule of law and codes of civility.

Our aim has been to search for those core values that can make human life more secure, stable, harmonious and amenable to the challenges of modern change. We are obviously in need of a more vigorous and imaginative applica-tion of the principles of security to the fundamental areas of human life. We must return to our visions and values which guide situations and actions. Many of the attitudes of the individual reflect his values or his conception of what is important or desirable. As members of a human community, we must preserve the values essential to the security of life that elevate the levels of human dignity and human prosperity. The point about the connections between values and security cannot be overstated. Some of the values of self-help, self-responsibility, solidarity, and social responsibility are now imperatives of security in Africa. Human beings can survive only because there are shared or public values and interests which ultimately foster the good of all. We are in need of specific behaviour for security; joint action for the common good. Behaviour is modified as a result of experiences. Attitude change depends on reviewing the scope of social adjustment, the means of control, the attractiveness of the project, the courage, the reward system and credibility that goes with the new vision.

In situating the problem in the context of a post-colonial setting, the desire has been to obtain the best out of the social realities before us. The aesthetic disposition requires a close and complete concentration on the subject of investigation. This has called for a traditional and historical analysis of the African and inter-cultural perspectives of security. The ethical factor is defined by the need to create a vision of a society in which the various groups have roles to play, despite their differences. The interrogation of culture provides all sorts of nuances to foster the communication and communal solidarity necessary for national security.

The guarantee of enduring security connotes the creation of the tools of opportunity - education, health care, employment, legal rights and political freedoms, so that dignity, security, respect and justice will prevail. The whole issue of security is that of establishing the machinery for sustaining those conditions in which men can live their own lives, pursue happiness and fulfill their destiny. In seeking a way forward, there must be a de-emphasis of those approaches that have created ambiguities of sex roles in terms of the quest for freedom and competence. Therefore, with special reference to marginal groups, we must for instance aim to deconstruct the closure of women, and to prevent the oppression of the perceived less competitive persons (challenged, dependent, vulnerable) from the guarantee of social security.

Finally, this study has examined the ethical and aesthetic dimensions of the security idea as compelled by the hitherto restrictive analysis of the nature of national security and the unexplored character of the critical conceptual and empirical interface between the ethical and aesthetic dimensions as key contributors to human national survival and integration. It insisted on a re-conceptualisation of the visions and values of ethical security and political community in the light of the critical failure of existing approaches to national security. It situated the problematic within the real context of the pervasive insecurity that has continually plagued the different forms of human organisation at various levels, especially the state. It has emphasised the need for a new vision of security theorising and praxis. This study has also examined the ethical dimension of the national security problem by using the European paradigm as a framework for defining the core principles of national survival and social integration. Such a belief in the gains of a cross-cultural view of things is the motivating factor for examining the linkages between the European and African security situation from this ethical viewpoint.

References

Apter, D., 1991, 'Institutionalism Reconsidered', *International Social Science Journal*, 129, pp. 463-481.

Ayoob, Mohammed, 1984, 'Security in the Third World: The Worm about to Turn', *International Affairs*, pp. 41-51.

Bagilhole, Barbara, 1997, *Equality Opportunities and Social Policy*, London: Longman.

Bayles, M. D. and Henley, K., eds, 1989, 'General Introduction: The Importance and Possibility of Ethics', in *Right Conduct*, New York: Random House, pp. 1-10.

Baylis, John., 1992, 'Europe Beyond the Cold War', in John Baylis and N. J. Rengger, *Dilemmas of World Politics. International Issues in a Changing World*, Oxford: Clarendon Press, pp. 384-405.

Bellamy, Alex J, and Matt McDonald, 2002, 'The Utility of Human Security: Which Humans? What Security? A Reply to Thomas and Tow', *Security Dialogue*, vol. 33, no. 3, pp. 373-377.

Bertsch, Gary K, Clark, Robert P., Wood, David M., 1991, *Power and Policy in Three Worlds. Comparing Political Systems*, New York: Macmillan.

Biscop, Sven, 2003, 'Opening up the ESDP to the South: A Comprehensive and Cooperative Approach to Euro-Mediterranean Security', *Security Dialogue*, vol. 34, no. 2, pp. 183-197.

Castells, Manuel, 1998, *The Information Age: Economy: Society and Culture*, Volume III: *End of Millennium*, Massachusetts: Blackwell.

Cox, David F., 1981, 'An Empirical Theory of Ethics: Morality as Defensive Behaviour', *Pacific Philosophical Quarterly*, vol. 62, no. 2, pp. 185-190.

Diggs, B. J., 1973, 'The Common Good as Reason for Political Action', *Ethics*, vol. 83, pp. 283-293.

Dower, Nigel, 1998, 'Human Rights, Global Ethics and Globalization', in Roland Axtmann, *Globalization and Europe*, London: Pinter, pp. 109-125.

Farrands, Chris, 1996, 'The Globalization of Knowledge and the Politics of Intellectual Property: Power, Governance and Technology', in Eleonore Kofmann and Gillian Youngs, eds., *Globalization: Theory and Practice*, London: Pinter, pp. 175-187.

Foot, Philippa, 1985, 'Utilitarianism and Virtue', *Mind*, vol. XCIV, no. 374.

Frankena, William, 1973, *Ethics*, New Jersey: Prentice Hall Inc.

Grieco, Joseph M., 1993, 'Understanding the Problem of International Cooperation: The Limits of Neoliberal Institutionalism and the Future of Realist Theory', in David A. Baldwin, ed., *Neorealism and Neoliberalism: The Contemporary Debate*, New York: Columbia University Press, pp. 301-338.

Hermet, Guy, 1991, 'Introduction: The Age of Democracy', *International Social Science Journal*, 128, May, pp. 249-257.

Hoogensen, Gunhild and Rotten, Svein Vigeland, 2004, 'Gender Identity and the Subject of Security', *Security Dialogue*, vol. 35, no. 2, pp. 155-171.

Hospers, John, 1973, *An Introduction to Philosophical Analysis*, London: Routledge and Kegan Paul.

Huntington, Samuel P., 1997, *The Clash of Civilizations*, New York: Touchstone.

Knudsen, Olav. F., 2001, 'Post Copenhagen Security Studies: Desecuritizing Securitization', *Security Dialogue*, vol. 32, no. 3, pp. 355-374.

Kupperman, Joel, 1983, *The Foundations of Morality*, London: Unwin.

Lodge, Juliet, 1993, 'Preface: The Challenge of the Future', in Juliet Lodge, ed., *The European Community and the Challenge of the Future*, London: Pinter, pp. xiii-xxvi.

Lodge, Juliet, 1993, 'Internal Security and Judicial Cooperation', in Juliet Lodge, ed., *The European Community and the Challenge of the Future*, London: Pinter, pp. 315-339.

Lucas, Raphaelle, 2000, 'Civil Security is Vigilant on every Front', *Label France*, no. 39. April, pp. 38-39.

Makinda, Samuel M., 1998, 'Sovereignty and Global Security', *Security Dialogue*, vol. 29, no. 3, pp. 281-292.

Mann, Michael, 1998, 'Is There a Society Called Euro?', in Roland Axtmann, *Globalization and Europe*, London: Pinter, pp. 184-207.

McMahon, Christopher, 1991, 'Morality and the Invisible Hand', *Philosophy and Public Affairs*, vol. 10, no. 3, 250.

Odekunle, Femi, 1993, 'Security and Development in Africa: Socioeconomic Prerequisites at the Grassroots Level', in Olusegun Obasanjo and Felix G. N. Mosha, eds., *Africa: Rise to Challenge*, Abeokuta: Africa Leadership Forum, pp. 39-47.

Okigbo, Pius, 1991, 'Africa and Europe', in Ralph Uwechue, ed., *Africa Today*, London: Africa Books, pp. 424-436.

Omoregbe, Joseph, 1993, *Ethics: A Systematic and Historical Study*, Lagos: Joja Educational Publishers.

Parker, Geoffrey, 1996, 'Globalisation and Geopolitical World Orders', in Eleonore Kofmann and Gillian Youngs, eds., *Globalization Theory and Practice*, London: Pinter, pp. 72-80.

Parsons, Talcott, 1960, *Structure and Process in Modern Societies*, Illinois: The Free Press.

Perry, R. B., 1974, 'The Meaning of Morality', in W. Frankena, ed., *Introductory Readings in Ethics*, New Jersey: Prentice Hall.

Ross, George, 1998, 'European Integration and Globalization', in Roland Axtmann,. *Globalization and Europe*, London: Pinter, pp. 164-183.

Rynning, Sten, 2003, 'The European Union: Towards a Strategic Culture', *Security Dialogue*. Vol. 34 .no.4. 479-496

Salmon, Trevor C., 1993, 'The Union, CSFP and the European Security Debate', in Juliet Lodge, ed., *The European Community and the Challenge of the Future*, London: Pinter, pp. 252-270.

Shea, Jamie P., 1993, 'Security: The Future', in Juliet Lodge, ed., *The European Community and the Challenge of the Future*, London: Pinter, pp. 360-376.

Todd, Paul and Bloch, Jonathan, 2003, *Global Intelligence: The World's Secret Services Today*, London: Zed Books.

Ujomu, Philip Ogo, 2002, 'National Security, Social Order and the Consolidation of Democracy in Nigeria and the United States of America: New Approaches to Civilian Participation in

Security', in S. O. Amali et al., eds., *Consolidation and Sustenance of Democracy*, Ibadan: ASAN & Hope, pp. 32-51.

Wiredu, Kwasi, 1992, 'The Moral Foundations of an African Culture, Person and Community', in *Ghanaian Philosophical Studies 1*, Kwasi Wiredu and Kwame Gyekye, eds., Washington DC: The Council for Research in Values and Philosophy, pp. 191-199.

Wright, Stephen, 1998, 'Africa and Global Society: Marginality, Conditionality and Conjecture' in Sola Akinrinade and Amadu Sesay, eds., *Africa in the Post Cold War International System*, London: Cassell Pinter, pp. 133-146